John Hunyadi

Defender of Christendom

JOHAN HUNNIAD Gouverneur
van Hongarien etc .

Camil Mureșanu

JOHN HUNYADI

DEFENDER OF CHRISTENDOM

CENTER FOR Romanian STUDIES

The Center for Romanian Studies
Las Vegas ◊ Oxford ◊ Palm Beach

Published in the United States of America by
Histria Books, a division of Histria LLC
7181 N. Hualapai Way
Las Vegas, NV 89166 USA
HistriaBooks.com

The Center for Romanian Studies is an imprint of Histria Books. Titles published under the imprints of Histria Books are exclusively distributed worldwide through the Casemate Group.

Library of Congress Control Number: 2018954789

ISBN 978-1-59211-012-4 (Softbound)
ISBN 978-1-59211-011-7 (Hardcover)

Contents

John Hunyadi

Defender of Christendom

CHAPTER I

JOHN HUNYADI IN HISTORIOGRAPHY

John Hunyadi, who carried on his activities during an historical period marked by resounding successes and dramatic events, captured the attention of both his contemporaries and of generations to come. The result of the continuous research into his life and times is a vast bibliography of materials.

The interest of his contemporaries and immediate posterity in the tumultuous career of John Hunyadi is manifest in documents and studies which belong, from the present point of view, to the category of historical sources. Of these, the internal documentary sources, including official documents referring to John Hunyadi or containing information about him, many of them issued in his name, as well as his extensive correspondence, began to be published much later.

One of these primary sources is the epistolary of John of Zredna (c. 1408-1472), a remarkable scholar, a pioneer of humanistic culture, and friend of John Hunyadi, who occupied successively important positions, namely that of bishop of Oradea (in 1445), chancellor, and, finally, archbishop of Strigoniu. Throughout all this time he carried out numerous and important diplomatic missions. His letters, some of which were written on direct instructions from John Hunyadi, were published by Johannes Georgius Schwandtner[1] in the collection

[1]Austrian historian (1716-1791).

Scriptores Rerum Hungaricarum, in the second volume.[2] A subsequent edition, of better quality, was published in Vienna in 1878 by the well-known historian Fraknói Vilmos (1843-1921) in the original Latin version, and the Hungarian translation appeared during the same year in Budapest. Around the same time when Schwandtner published the letters, in the climate created by the development of culture in the direction of the Enlightenment, although deeply anchored, within the Hapsburg monarchy, in the erudite spirit of the previous century, Georgius Pray[3] published, in Vienna, his book entitled *Annales Regum Hungariae,* whose second and third parts refer to the epoch of John Hunyadi. The methodological conception of the book sets it at the border between a collection of documents and a historical work, in the modern sense.

Organized in a strictly chronological order, the book reproduces in extenso the documents known up to that time. Between documents, the author makes comments, sometimes interpretative, sometimes strictly pragmatic, sometimes only to establish a connection between one document and another.

The first one to gather all the documents regarding John Hunyadi that were known up to that time, accompanied by passages from narrative sources, was Georgius Fejér (1766-1851), under the title *Genus, incunabula et virtus Joannis Corvini de Hunyad, regni Hungariae gubernatoris.*[4] Not long afterwards, another collection of documents centered round John Hunyadi's activity appeared in volume X of the work of Teleki József, *A Hunyadiak kora Magyarországon,*[5] which we shall discuss later on. In time, the number of the documents that were discovered and printed in various publications increased. Among these publications, one should mention the monumental Hurmuzaki collec-

---

[2]The first edition of the collection appeared in Vienna in 1746-1748, and the second edition appeared in Trnovo and Vienna in 1765-1766.

[3]Famous historian, with a rich activity, concerned in part with the past of the Romanian principalities (1723-1801).

[4]Buda, 1844.

[5]Pesta, 1853.

tion, especially volume I, part 2,[6] and volume XV, part 1.[7] An addition to the publication of documentary sources regarding John Hunyadi was brought by J. Hajnal, who published 87 registers under the title "Kivonatok Hunyadi János kormányzöi okleveleiból, 1446-1452," in *Levéltári közlemények,* Budapest, 1923. It is useful to consult the volumes published by Mályusz Elemér under the title *Zsigmondkori oklévеltár*[8] which, although they refer to a previous epoch, contain documentary sources necessary for understanding the historical phenomena of the time of John Hunyadi.

Given the European proportions of the personality and activity of John Hunyadi and the diplomatic correspondence which he kept with the main European courts of the time, there are also numerous external documentary sources which contain information about him.

From the point of view of the epoch, this category may also include the documents originating from the chancelleries of the Romanian principalities of Wallachia and Moldavia, in which we are interested first of all, since they reflect a major aspect of the activity of John Hunyadi – his relations with each of the three Romanian principalities.

Besides the volumes in the Hurmuzaki collection, one should also consult the last edition of the documents of Wallachia, *Documenta Romaniae Historica, seria B. Ţara Românească,* volume I (1247-1500),[9] the older edition published by Mihai Costăchescu, *Documente moldoveneşti înainte de Ştefan cel Mare,*[10] and also volumes I and II of *Documenta Romaniae Historica, seria A. Moldova,* 1975-1976.

Valuable sources from foreign archives, both documentary and narrative, were published by Nicolae Iorga in the collection *Notes et extraits pour server a l'histoire des croisades au XVe siècle.*[11] Infor-

[6]Edited by N. Densuşianu, Bucureşti, 1890.

[7]Edited by Nicolae Iorga, Bucureşti, 1911.

[8]Volumes I and II, parts 1-2, Budapest, 1956.

[9]Edited by P.P. Panaitescu and Damaschin Mioc, Bucureşti, 1966.

[10]Volume II, Iaşi, 1932.

[11]Series IV, Bucureşti, 1915.

mation on John Hunyadi can also be found in Ioan Bogdan, *Documente privitoare la relaţiile Ţării Româneşti cu Braşovul şi cu Ţara Ungurească în secolele XV şi XVI.*[12]

The internal narrative sources begin with the well-known and Important chronicle by John Thuróczi, entitled *Chronica Hungarorum,* which first appeared in 1488 in two almost simultaneous editions, one in Brno and the other in Augsburg. The edition which has been commonly used until today is the one published by Schwandtner in volume I of the collection *Scriptores Rerum Hungaricarum,* mentioned above.

The chronicle was written in the time of King Matthias Corvinus, the son of John Hunyadi. Consequently, it has an obviously favorable attitude toward John and the Hunyadi family in general. Although it belongs to the internal narrative sources which were almost contemporary to the epoch and many of its accounts are admitted as basic information, the chronicle of Thuróczi is not free of errors. Some of these were deliberate, originating from the laudative intention of the author, others resulted from deficiencies – distortions and confusions of facts – of the sources he used.

Another chronicle favorable to the Hunyadi family, older than the one by Thuróczi, but briefer, was written by an anonymous author and is known under the title of *Chronicon Budense.* It first appeared in Buda in 1473 and was the first book printed in Hungary.[13]

A chronicle written not much later after the events is that of the Italian Marco Antonio Bonfini (Bonfinius),[14] who arrived in Hungary in 1486, in the entourage of Beatrice of Aragon, the second wife of Matthias Corvinus. His chronicle entitled *Historia Pannonica sive Hungari carum Rerum Decades IV et dimidia* and finished in 1495,

---

[12]Bucureşti, 1905.

[13]The first critical edition was published by Fraknói Vilmos, under the title of *Chronica Hungarorum*, Budapest, 1990.

[14]1434-1503.

under King Ladislas II, was published in many editions, beginning in the sixteenth century.[15]

Following to a great extent the information given by Thuróczi, Bonfinius amplifies the latter's accounts, especially in the description of the events, partly by adding new information, partly by inventing, with panegyric and rhetorical tendencies, in the spirit of humanistic historiography and imitating the Roman historians, especially Titus Livius.

That is why the chronicle of Bonfinius must be examined critically before accepting its statements, especially when it comes to details.

The chronicles written in the sixteenth century, like that of Gáspár Heitai,[16] follow Bonfinius to a great extent, and thus cannot be considered primary sources. The Moldavian and Wallachian chronicles, written – even the older ones – after the period of John's activity, contain brief information about him, preserving the concise character of the annals contemporary with the events on the basis of which these chronicles were composed.

Thus, the two versions of the Putna Chronicle limit themselves to mentioning the fact that Peter II, prince of Moldavia for a short time, a protégé of John Hunyadi, ceded Chilia to the Hungarians. They continue by relating the ephemeral reign – information which is actually erroneous – of a Voievod "Ciubăr," which could be the distorted name of a Hungarian army commander, Csupor, sent by John to Moldavia. The Moldavian-Russian chronicle provides the same information, while the Moldavian-Polish chronicle attributes the act of ceding Chilia to Voievod Alexăndrel: "he gave Chilia to the king of Hungary to protect

[15]The first edition at Basel, 1543, published by M. Brenner; another – the first complete edition – was published by J. Sambucus also at Basel, 1568. Other editions were published at Köln, 1690, and Vienna, 1744. The most recent, in four volumes, was published by J. Fógel, B. Iványi, and L. Juhász in the collection *Bibliotheca scriptorium medii recentiorisque aevorum*, Budapest, 1936-1941.

[16]Transylvanian scholar of Saxon origin, promoter of the Reformation and typography in Transylvania. His chronicle, written in the Magyar language, appeared in 1575.

him from the Turks, to which king it is not known."[17] The Serbian-Moldavian chronicle contains brief pieces of information, short mentions about the battle of John against Mezid-bey and about his victory on the Ialomiţa, but with errors of place and time.[18]

The great Moldavian and Wallachian chronicles written only in the seventeenth and the beginning of the eighteenth century do not have, for the epoch of John Hunyadi, the value of direct sources, as they are based, except for the inclusion of summary data from older internal sources, on the compilation of information from external sources.

There are numerous external narrative sources which contain extensive references to the life and actions of John Hunyadi, as well as to his epoch. One of these, especially interesting, detailed, and with veridical information, is that of Jean of Wavrin, based on the accounts of his nephew Walerand of Wavrin, the commander of the Burgundian fleet during the campaign in the Straits and on the Danube in the years 1444-1445. First published in the nineteenth century under the title *Anchiennes chroniques d'Angleterre, par Jehan de Wavrin, seigneur du Forrestel,*[19] the fragments which are of interest for our book were reproduced by Nicolae Iorga in *Buletinul Comisiei istorice a României*, VI, 1927. This chronicle is also very important for the history of Wallachia around the year 1445.

The great Polish chronicler Jan Długosz (1415-1480),[20] in his essential work *Historiae Poloniae libri XII ab antiquissimis temporibus usque ad annum 1480*, also has numerous references to our subject, manifesting however an unfavorable attitude toward John, although he recognizes, on the whole, his merits as an army commander. His

[17] *Croniciile slavo-române din sec. XV-XVI publicate de Ion Bogdan*, edition revised and completed by P.P. Panaitescu, Bucureşti, Editura Academiei, 1959, pp. 48, 61, 70, 161, 177-178.

[18] Ibidem, p. 192.

[19] Paris, 1859.

[20] Canon of Cracow and bishop of Lvov, having an important political and diplomatic role as well.

chronicle was first published in 1615, then in Leipzig in 1712, and in 1863 it appeared in Cracow as part of the first edition of the complete works of Długosz. For us, a useful work is *Informaţiile româneşti ale cronicii lui Jan Długosz* by Ilie Minea.[21]

We can also consider as a Polish source the chronicle of the humanist of Venetian origin, Philippus Callimachus Buonacorsi da Gemignano (1437-1496), who emigrated to Poland in 1472, entitled *Historia de rege Vladislao Hungariae, seu Clade Varnensi anno 1444 libri tres*.[22] Andrea del Palatino, papal tax collector, also wrote an account of the Varna disaster under the title *Litterae de clade Varnensi ad Ludovicum Cardinalem datae*.[23] Mention should also be made, this time as a German source, of the rhyming chronicle of Michael Beheim (1416-1474), a soldier who participated in the campaigns against the Turks, published by Th.G. Karajan in *Quellen und Forschungen zur vaterlandischen Geschichte*.[24] This chronicle was thoroughly treated in Romanian historiography by Gr. Conduratu, *Gedicht über den Woivoden Wlad II Dracul*[25] and by C.I. Karadja, "Poema lui M. Beheim despre cruciadele împotriva turcilor din anii 1443 şi 1444."[26] The so-called chronicle of the counts of Cilli, *Die Freien von Saneck und ihre Chronik als Grafen von Cilli*,[27] published by Fr. Krones, is written in a spirit clearly hostile to John Hunyadi.

The Byzantine chronicles also represent an important source. They are rather well informed and what makes them especially valua-

---

[21]Iaşi, 1926.

[22]The first edition was published in Augsburg, 1519; others were published in Frankfurt, in 1573 and 1578, and in Cracow, 1582-1584. It was also edited by J. Bongars, in *Rerum Hungaricarum Scriptores varii*, Frankfurt, 1600, in the eighteenth century by Schwandtner, and, finally, by S. Kwiatkowski, in *Monumenta Poloniae Historica*, vol. VI, Cracow, 1891.

[23]Edited by A. Prochaska, Lemberg, 1882.

[24]Vienna, 1849.

[25]Bucureşti, 1903.

[26]In *Buletinul Comisiei istorice a României*, XV (1936).

[27]Vol. I-II, Graz, 1883.

ble is the fact that the information they provide on this epoch is based on the knowledge of the realities in Southeastern Europe and in the Ottoman Empire. Thus, they present a picture from the perspective of the opposite side of the mobile barricade on which the great battles against the Ottoman expansion were fought.

An Important Byzantine chronicler of the fifteenth century was Doukas,[28] author of *Decline and Fall of Byzantium to the Ottoman Turks,* which treats the events between 1341-1462. This chronicle appeared in two "classic" editions, one in Paris in 1649, and the other in Bonn in 1834, edited by Immanuel Bekker, in the well-known collection *Corpus Scriptorum Historiae Byzantinae.* In 1958, Vasile Grecu published a critical edition of the chronicle, which contains the original text and the Romanian translation.

Laonikos Chalkokondyles,[29] in his *Historical Chronicles,* provides valuable information as well, especially concerning the great campaigns of John Hunyadi in the Balkans. Although it is difficult to make a judgement, given the uncertain coordinates to which we are limited, we consider, with reservation, that Chalkokondyles appears to have been more precisely informed and more moderate and realistic in his affirmations than Doukas.

The chronicle of Chalkokondyles, which was also published in the above-mentioned *Corpus* in Bonn, in 1843, can also he consulted in the critical edition of Eugen Darkó, published in Budapest, volumes I and II, parts 1 and 2, between 1922 and 1927. In Romanian historiography, the same Vasile Grecu published, also in 1958, an edition similar to that of the chronicle by Doukas. As for Georgios Sphrantzes,[30] a third remarkable Byzantine chronicler of the epoch, his chronicle entitled *The Fall of the Byzantine Empire* contains, in general, less infor-

---

[28]His first name was probably Michael. He lived between 1400 and 1470.

[29]Both the years of birth and death are unknown. He was contemporary with the events that interest us and therefore could have been born approximately in the first quarter of the fifteenth century and died after 1465, the date when he recorded the last events presented by his chronicle.

[30]1401-1477.

mation on John than the works of his two contemporaries. However, here and there, Sphrantzes completes our documentation with veridical information, for which he remains the only source, such as, for instance, on the question of relations between John and Byzantium on the eve of the fall of Constantinople, and, in general, on the attitude of the Byzantine court toward the battles against the Ottomans[31] led by John Hunyadi.

Further information, especially referring to the siege of Belgrade in 1456, can also be found in the work of another Byzantine chronicler, Michael Kritovoulos, who wrote, in a pro-Ottoman spirit, a biography of Mehmed II.

When referring to external narrative sources, one must mention the Turkish ones as well. They began circulating throughout Europe due especially to the translations by the German Hans Löwenklau, better known under his Latinized name, Leunclavius.[32] In 1588, he published in Frankfurt *Annales Sultanorum Othmanidarum,* and in 1590, also in Frankfurt, an Ottoman history in the German language, followed a year later by a Latin version entitled *Historiae Musulmanae Turcorum de monumentis ipsorum escrpitatae libri XVII.*

Subsequently, the Turkish chronicles were published in different countries, in the original or in translation, but no unitary collection was created, such as the one dedicated to Byzantine historiography. Dimitrie Cantemir, Hammer, Zinkeisen used these sources when writing their great Ottoman histories. Of the more recent publications we mention, in Hungarian historiography, the volumes published by Thúry József, *Tórök történetirók*, volumes I-II.[33] They reserve all important

[31]Until the abolition of the sultanate (1 November 1922), the Turks called themselves, throughout their history, Ottomans, a term which had a different connotation than the ethnic-national one of Turks, and corresponded to a different political conception than the contemporary one.

[32]Originally from Westphalia, he lived between 1533 and 1593. After working as a professor of Greek and law at Heidelberg, he traveled to Hungary and the Ottoman Empire, learning the Turkish language and becoming an expert in Turkish history.

[33]Budapest, 1893-1896. They were continued with a third volume published by Karácson Imre, in 1916, but containing chronicles from a later period.

space to references to Magyar history. After World War I, Fr. Giese published a partial edition, as it is shown by the title: *Die Altosmanische anonymen Chroniken,* Breslau, 1922 (original text), and Leipzig, 1925 (translation). An important work of historiography was published by the famous Orientalist Franz Babinger, *Die Geschichtsschreiber der Osmanen und ihre Werke,* Leipzig, 1927.

In Romania, a valuable first step was taken by Mihail Guboglu and Mustafa Mehmet who published *Cronici turceşti privind ţările române, sec. XV-mijlocul sec. XVII (Turkish Chronicles Regarding the Romanian Principalities, from the Fifteenth Century to the Mid-Seventeenth Century),* Bucharest, 1966, containing passages in Romanian translation accompanied by biographical introductions, observations regarding the value of the chronicles, and explanatory notes. Unfortunately, the Turkish chronicles do not have the value we might expect. Undoubtedly, they contribute to the clarification of certain data and to the completion of certain information, but they suffer from an uncertain chronology, exaggerations of the facts, a laudatory attitude toward the sultans, and, without exception, a tendentiously denigrating attitude toward their enemies. Their rhetorical style obscures even more the grain of truth they contain. The life and deeds of John Hunyadi became permanently established in scholarly works beginning in the nineteenth century, namely when a modern historiography was developing in the cultures of the peoples in that part of Europe, mainly the Romanians and the Hungarians.

The coordinates of the dominant ideas of nineteenth century historiography are obvious in the manner in which the epoch and personality of John Hunyadi are presented in this historiography. In the first half of the century there was romantic climate, followed by the development of a positivist spirit which led to the broadening of documentation and to a more serious critical consideration of it, with the intention of establishing the facts with exactness. This evolution was marked, however, by the social and political conditions of the development of society – and therefore of culture as well – in Central and Southeastern Europe. It was the period of the struggle for regaining independence, for the formation of national states of the peoples in that part of the world. Taking place under the leadership of the bourgeoisie and of some elements of the nobility with more advanced ideas, the struggle for the independent national state was represented in culture in the colored images of bourgeois nationalism. The mentality created by this environment of historical development had repercussions on the interpretation of the events of the more distant past as well. The prevailing concern for the "political" determined a corresponding selectivity in the concerns of historiography at that time. The struggle for independence was searching for bases and traditions in the past: it found them in the evocation of the anti-Ottoman struggle, and the victories and defeats of John Hunyadi were viewed with Romantic enthusiasm. His life, his ascension from an obscure social rank to the highest dignities and to a wide European notoriety made him an ideal subject for those with Romantic propensities, yielding to hero worship. This perspective also included the intentions of both Romanian and Hungarian historians to demonstrate, through the exceptional personality of John Hunyadi, the capacity of their own people "to create history," and, consequently, to justify certain political aspirations, the recognition of a prominent place in the eyes of the world. All these, however, were conjugated with the beginnings of positivist historiography, with the publication, critical or less so, of a considerable amount of documentary material.

The factors mentioned above, excepting the use of a wide range of documentary materials, characterize the first modest monographic attempt in Romanian historiography, about John Hunyadi. It was written by Damaschin Bojincă[34] and appeared in *Calendarul romånsec de la Buda* in 1830 under the title "Description of the Birth and the Deeds of

[34]A jurist, professor, and cultural figure, he worked both in Transylvania and in Moldavia (1803-1896).

the Famous Hero, Celebrated by the Entire Europe, John Corvinus Hunyadi."[35]

The author claims that the monograph is a translation and, indeed, his main source seems to have been the work of Kovács Mátyás,[36] *Biographia Joannis Hunyadi...*, published in Eger in 1818. It is obvious, however, that at least partially we are dealing with the rewriting and not simply the translation of Mátyás's work, the author having declared it a translation for purpose of facilitating its approval by the censors, given the spirit in which it was written. Half of the article is dedicated to the origins of John Hunyadi and contains a passionate pleading, in a polemical spirit, for his Romanian origin. Citing the main narrative sources (Thuróczi, Bonfinius) and some general historical works (Benkö, Pray, Engel, Fessler, etc., as well as Istoria pentru începutul românilor în Dacia *(The History of the Beginnings of the Romanians in Dacia* by Petru Maior), Damaschin Bojincă closes the first part of his article in this way:

> Should there be someone who, for whatever reason, would dare deny the true and indubitable Romanian origin of John Hunyadi, he must be shown the documents cited here and taught that the entire history of the country is based mainly of Thuróczi and Bonfinius; and if they are not believed, having lived in those times, and if there is no confidence in the words of other patriotic historians who, being Hungarian, recognize the Romanian origin of John Corvinus, then the entire history of the country will have no credibility, and everyone will believe whatever he wants.
>
> But no one has said that John might have been anything other than Romanian, except those who, having embraced the above mentioned legend that he was supposedly the illegitimate son of Sigismund[37] and a Romanian maiden, want to revel in the idea that they might be able

---

[35]"Descrierea naşterii şi a eroceştilor fapte a mult vestitului şi de toată Europa minunatului erou Ioan Corvin de Huniad," pp. 44-141 of the above-mentioned publication, printed, in parallel, with Latin and Cyrillic characters.

[36]High Catholic official in Eger (1790-1861).

[37]Sigismund of Luxembourg, king of Hungary and Roman-German emperor (1387-1437).

> to take away from the Romanian people the praise that it deserves due to the deeds of this famous hero and to the glory of his son, King Matthias Corvinus; some prefer to ignore the fact that the Romanian nation produced a very famous Hungarian king.

These conclusions prove that the article of Damaschin Bojincă was a rewriting with important personal contributions. They also demonstrate our previous considerations on the spirit in which a number of the first studies on John Hunyadi were written.

The second part of the article is a concise narration of the deeds of John Hunyadi, written in a dithyrambic tone and having lacunas and errors of information. Consequently, its value is inferior to that of the first part.

In Magyar historiography, a work of special importance is that of József Teleki,[38] *A Hunyadiak kora Magyarországon.* Conceived as a work of large proportions, only six volumes appeared during the life of its initiator. It was continued by others, among whom was Csánki, Dezsö, who published as part of it a valuable historical geography of Hungary during the time of the Hunyadi family.

Volumes 1 and II of this great work, published in Pesta in 1825, cover the period until the death of Ladislas Posthumous V (the end of year 1457). They are a detailed political history, based on a considerable effort of erudition. The numerous and extensive footnotes contain, very often, whole or partial reproductions of the original sources, remarkable being the considerable proportion of documentary sources, which in those days were still novel to a great extent. The intention of Teleki was a critical one, especially on a methodological level, as he tried to solve the possible contradictions of the sources and to establish the exact dates of the events. The contribution of this work to the knowledge of the life and activities of John Hunyadi was fundamental for that time and, to a certain extent, it has remained valid until today.

---

[38] A nobleman with certain liberal ideas (1790-1855), governor of Transylvania (1842-1848); in this position, he promoted the nationalist policy of the Hungarian nobility and supported the forced union of Transylvania with Hungary (29 May 1848), ignoring the revendications of the Romanian people.

Possibly inspired by Teleki's work, but certainly as a result of the interest in the peoples that had brought their contribution to the revolutionary cause in 1848, a French work dedicated to John Hunyadi appeared, written by Charles Louis Chassin.[39] It constitutes the second part of a popularization work about Hungary; the presentation of the life and deeds of John Hunyadi, entitled significantly "a story from the fifteenth century," has the same character.[40] Two decades after Teleki's work began to be published, there appeared the monograph by Pór Antal, *Hunyadi János. Elet-és korrajz,*[41] which caused Romanian historiography to hark back to John Hunyadi, through an important study by George Bariţiu, "John Corvinus Hunyadi. His Origin, Genealogy, and Immortal Deeds."[42]

Bariţiu resumes, although better informed, the ideas that Damaschin Bojincă had maintained in his time. He demonstrates, polemicizing rather vehemently with contrary opinions, the indisputable Romanian origin of John Hunyadi. He rejects with indignation the legends according to which Hunyadi might have been the illegitimate child of Sigismund of Luxembourg, seeing them – an erroneous opinion – as an intentional fabrication meant to contest the Romanian origin of John Hunyadi. Bariţiu declares clearly that the intention of his study is to prove that the Romanian people are capable of giving great personalities to world history through which it has brought an important contribution to the evolution of society, therefore deserving the same respect as any other people.

"The affirmation of our *genetic* nationality before the Areopagus of the European peoples," wrote Bariţiu, "is one of the main problems that we need to solve. The world asks not only about the ancientness of the origin of a people, but it rightfully wants to learn about the power

[39]1831-1901.

[40]*La Hongrie, son genie et sa mission, suivi de Jean Hunyad, récit du XV-e siècle,* Paris, 1855; second edition, 1859.

[41]*The Description of the Life and Epoch of John Hunyadi*, Budapest, 1873.

[42]"Ioan Corvin de Hunedoara. Originea, genealogia, faptele sale imortale," published in *Transilvania*, VI (1873), nos. 5-24 and VII (1874), no. 1.

of life and the productive power of our nation, productive not only in the physical but also in the spiritual sense. This can be proved especially by enumerating those individuals born within our genetic nation, who, through their deeds or writings, exerted a great, maybe even decisive influence, on the destinies of our nation or country, or even on other peoples or countries...[43] Among the monographs that appeared until the end of the nineteenth century, one should mention the work of Fraknói Vilmos, a well-known historian of the Hunyadi period, entitled *A Hunyadiak és a Jagellók kora (1440-1526).*[44]

In the second half of the nineteenth century and the first decades of the twentieth century, a large number of detailed studies were published, made possible by the more and more complete publication of the documentary sources.

These studies had a special preference for the campaigns of John Hunyadi, therefore for the military history of the epoch. Gradually, with all the profusion of derails allowed by the sources, there appeared studies, some with a character of small monograph, about the battles of Varna (especially),[45] of the Field of Blackbirds, of Belgrade, and also of others, like the battle with Mezid-bey or the less known campaigns in Serbia. There also appeared general studies on the anti-Ottoman campaigns of John Hunyadi, some of them insisting on the battles between 1440-1444, which was preeminently the offensive phase of these campaigns.

The study of the organization and tactics of Hunyadi's army, elements in which scholars tried to find an explanation for his successes, also intensified. These studies, dealing with military history, appeared mostly in the pages of the journal *Hadtörténelmi Közlemények,* which began to be published regularly in 1888. They were gathered later in a

[43] *Transilvania*, VI (1873), no. 5, p. 52.

[44] Budapest, 1896. It constitutes volume IV of the so-called "jubilee history" of Hungary, *A Magyar Nemzet története*, vol. I-X, edited by Sándor Szilágyi, Budapest, 1895-1898.

[45] At least six special studies, between 1854 and 1892.

monograph on all the military aspects of John Hunyadi's activity.[46] In more recent Romanian historiography the questions of military history regarding the epoch of John Hunyadi are focused on in the book of T. Nicolau, *Ioan Huniade Corvin,*[47] and especially in the valuable study of Mihail Dan, "The Army and Military Art of John Hunyadi (Based on Contemporary Chronicles)."[48] At the end of the nineteenth century there appeared the first Romanian monograph about John Hunyadi published as a separate work, not in the pages of a periodical.[49] The author, Iosif Bălan, did not have a special education as a historian, and his attempt is therefore tributary to the works that were in circulation at the time. A much better monograph is one written later by Teodor Popa, entitled *Iancu Corvin de Hunedoara.*[50] It is based, to a great extent, directly on the sources and succeeds in making a valuable presentation of the life of John Hunyadi, predominant being, however, the political and genealogical questions. Unfortunately, the author confused certain information. Mention should also be made of the article by Ioan Lupaş, ''The Transylvanian Voievod John Hunyadi – 'fortissimus athlete Christi'"[51] and the monograph by I. Lespezeanu and L. Marcu, *Ioan Corvin de Hunedoara,*[52] the latter placing the hero in a larger European context, dealing with the social basis of his power, and being written in a pleasant style, adequate for the purpose of popularization intended by the authors. Of great importance in Romanian historiography is the studies by Ilie Minea regarding the epoch of Vlad

---

[46]Doberdói Bánlaky József, *Hunyadi Janos*, Budapest, 1936, forming volume I of part X of the collective work *A Magyar Nemzet Hadtörténelme* (*A Military History of the Magyar People*). The book is written in a nationalist spirit and contains denigratory comments on the role of the Romanian element in Hunyadi's campaigns.

[47]Bucureşti, 1925.

[48]"Armata şi arta militară a lui Iancu de Hunedoara (pe baza cronicilor contemporane)," in *Studii şi cerecetări de istorie*, Cluj, VIII (1957), nos. 1-4.

[49]Iosif Bălan, *Iancu de Hunyad*, Caransebeş, 1897.

[50]Hunedoara, 1928.

[51]"Voievodul transilvan Ioan Huniade – 'fortissimus athlete Christi,'" in *Studii, conferinţe şi comunicări istorice,* vol. II, Cluj, 1940.

[52]Published in 1957, in *Colecţia Societăţii pentru răspândirea ştiinţei şi culturii.*

Dracul and his immediate predecessors or descendants, which reveal the political relations between Transylvania and Wallachia during the time of John Hunyadi.[53] During the years before World War I, the historians insisted on a few aspects of John Hunyadi's activity about which previously only vague information, provided by the sources, had been recorded. Thus, on the one hand, the period of Hunyadi's youth was analyzed more closely, by trying to separate the incontestable elements from the interweaving of reality and legend in which it was enveloped. In this context, they studied the relations of Hunyadi and his family with the military commander of Italian origin Filippo Scolari, also known under the name of Pippo de Ozora or Pippo Spano, who was in the service of King Sigismund of Luxembourg for many years and also occupied the dignity of equerry of Timişoara. Also, they worked on classifying the years that John, also in his youth, spent in Italy.[54]

In the same period, Francisc Pall published his first of many studies, bringing important contributions to the chronology and details of certain episodes in the life of Hunyadi which had remained obscure up to then. He elucidated the question of the fictitious character of a correspondence between King Ladislas I of Hungary and the Albanian hero Scanderbeg, in 1443-1444, and pointed out the certainty of relations between John Hunyadi and Scanderbeg on the eve of the anti-Ottoman campaign of 1448. The studies by Francisc Pall also brought a contribution to the controversial question of the Seghedin Peace and its hasty denunciation by the King of Hungary in the summer of 1444. They demonstrated the indubitable existence of a formal peace treaty,

---

[53]*Din trecutul stăpânirii româneşti asupra Ardealului. Pierderea Amlaşului şi a Făgăraşului (On the Past of the Romanian Rule in Transylvania. The Losing of Amlaş and Făgăraş)*, Bucureşti, 1914; *Principatele române şi politica orientală a împăratului Sigismund (The Romanian Principalities and the Oriental Politics of Emperor Sigismund)*, Bucureşti, 1919; *Vlad Dracul şi vremea sa (Vlad Dracul and His Times)*, Iaşi, 1928.

[54]Bánfi Florio, "Filippo Scolari és Hunyadi János," in *Hadtörténelmi Kozlemények*, 1930; "Hunyadi János itáliai tartózkodása" in *Erdélyi Muzéum*, XXXIX (1934), nos. 7-12.

concluded by Hungarian messengers in Adrianople in June 1444, and confirmed afterwards on the occasion of the visit of Turkish representatives to Seghedin at the end of July of the same year.[55]

In the last decades, historiography has broadened the perspective from which the personality of John Hunyadi, the results of his activities, and their significance are considered and explained. After studies that were oriented mainly toward political and military questions, there followed studies that emphasized a general consideration of the epoch of Hunyadi, its specific economic, social, and institutional aspects. The mutual conditioning and determination of such factors provided a solid basis for understanding and explaining Hunyadi's personality, establishing his contribution and role in world history at their correct dimensions. Operating with the same coordinates, certain particular aspects of the life and activity of this great army commander were able to be revealed. Studies that intended to elucidate certain details at a factual level also continued. The Hungarian historian Elekes Lajos wrote a monograph of great dimensions and, on the whole, considered of unquestionable value, entitled *Hunyadi.*[56] Using a number of novel documents, reconsidering the interpretation of many of the known ones, clarifying certain chronological and factual questions, this monograph centers at the same time around the idea of state centralization as the pivot of Hunyadi's politics. Lajos tries therefore to outline the adverse social forces representing the tendencies of feudal anarchy and those of order and authority – realizing, in this sense, a valuable study. But the author appears to be too dominated by certain schemes, he connects Hunyadi too exclusively to the categories of the lower nobility and townspeople, attributes too profound a significance to his relations with the peasants and workers, all these with the intention of finding a

[55]Cf. "Les relations entre la Hongrie et Scanderbeg," in *Revue historique du Sud-Est européen,* X (1993), nos. 4-6; *Ciriaco d'Ancona e la crociata contro I Turchi,* Vălenii de Munte, 1937; "Autour de la croisade de Varna: la question de la paix de Szeged et de sa rupture (1444)," in *Bulletin de la Section Historique de l'Académie Roumaine,* volume XXII, 2, Bucureşti, 1941. In this last study, the author defends successfully his points of view against the opinions of the Polish historian Oscar Halecki.

[56]Budapest, 1952.

complex of great social forces which would have represented powerful and consistent support for Hunyadi in his struggle with the higher nobility and against the external danger.

The valuable study of institutional history by Mályusz Elémer, "A magyar rendi állam Hunyadi korában,"[57] deals with the same sphere of problems – the basis and structure of power and the state institutions in fifteenth century Hungary – appearing more flexible, more nuanced in their treatment in comparison with the previously mentioned study. 1956, when 500 years from the death of Hunyadi were commemorated, marked an occasion to resume research of his epoch.

There appeared a study by the Romanian historian Ştefan Pascu, "The Role of the *Cnezi* in Transylvania in the anti-Ottoman Struggle of John Hunyadi."[58] Besides the gathering and presentation of the documents that attest to the permanent presence of this social class and of the Transylvanian Romanian element in the campaigns led by John Hunyadi, what makes this study interesting and valuable is the fact that it explains the ascension of the Hunyadi family, establishing an undeniable relation between its evolution and that of the class of the Romanian *cnezi* in Transylvania. The author presents the origins and ascension of John Hunyadi's ancestors from a sociological perspective, reaching plausible conclusions and innovating in matters of method. In the following years, the most constant Romanian historian of the epoch of Hunyadi remained Francisc Pall, author of thorough studies which brought several new contributions: they proved that in 1438 the Ottomans organized a second campaign in Transylvania, short but violent, in Ţara Bârsei; they elucidated the problem of the duration and character of Hunyadi's domination over Chilia; they specified the exact interval of the campaigns of Hunyadi in Wallachia and Moldavia, between

---

[57] In *Századok*, an. 91 (1957), no. 1-4 and 5-6.

[58] "Rolul cnezilor din Transilvania în lupta antitomană a lui Iancu de Hunedoara" in *Studii şi cercetări de istorie*, Cluj, VIII (1957), nos. 1-4.

1447 and 1448; and, finally, they clarified the obscure question of the Wallachian interregnum of 1442-1443.[59]

In Hungarian historiography, the distinguished medievalist Pál Engel also published several important works: *Kiraly hataloru éarisztokrácia vitzonya a Zoigmond Korbau, 1387-1437* (Budapest, 1977); "János Hunyadi: The Decisive Years of His Career, 1440-1444," in *From Hunyadi to Rákoczi: War and Society in Medieval and Early Modern Hungary* (New York, 1982). A contribution of American historiography was made by Joseph Held with *Hunyadi: Legend and Reality* (Boulder, New York, 1985), 268 pages, with an extensive bibliography, it, however, ignores many recent studies and it neglects Romanian historiography, except for Nicolae Iorga. In the light of what we have shown above we can consider that historiography has extensively covered the life and times John Hunyadi. The documentation of his epoch may yet contain unknown pieces, but it is unlikely that they might conceal sensational revelations and thus determine an essential change of perspective, either in the general considerations, or in the detailed knowledge.

Nevertheless, research on this subject does not find itself in front of a closed case. The way for reconsidering the interpretation of many phenomena of the epoch is still open, especially in the area of the economic and social basis of the activity of Hunyadi. And the personality of John Hunyadi, a firm defender of the political freedom of the peoples in this part of the world, will always deserve the homage of posterity, through the agency of historians.

---

[59]"Ştiri noi despre expediţiile turceşti sin Transilvania în 1438," ("New Evidence about the Ottoman Campaigns in Transylvania in 1438"), in *Anuarul Institutului de istorie din Cluj,* I-II (1958-1959); "Intervenţia lui Iancu de Hunedoara în Ţara Românească şi Moldova în anii 1447-1448," in *Studii,* XVI (1963); "Stăpânirea lui Iancu de Hunedoara asupra Chiliei şi problema ajutorării Bizanţului," in Studii, XVIII (1965); "Iancu de Hunedoara şi confirmarea privilegiului pentru negoţul braşovenilor şi al bârsenilor cu Ţara Românească în 1443," in *Anuarul Institutului de istorie din Cluj*, IX (1966). See also: "Byzance a la veille de sa chute et Janco de Hunedoara," in *Byzantinoslavica*, Prague, XXX (1969); "Skanderbeg et Ianco de Hunedoara," in *Studia Albanica*, Tirana, 1968.

Chapter II

"The Crescent's Furious Storm..."

Almost one thousand years ago the life of the peoples of Europe and Asia was becoming more peaceful, after it had been for a long time full of unrest and struggles that had determined the collapse of the old slave-owning society and of the Roman Empire, creating, in their aftermath, the new feudal society.

One after another, coming from the north or the east, German, Slavic, and Asian peoples had penetrated the weakened borders of the Roman state, had overthrown its domination, and had thus opened the possibility for European society to develop, in difficult conditions, but freer than those before. This was the time known as the period of the great migrations and of the barbarian invasions.

The last invasions that upset the east of Europe and the Near East took place in the tenth and eleventh centuries.[60] Among the peoples that, beginning with the eleventh century, appeared east of the Mediterranean Sea and at the boundaries of Europe, playing a long-term role in the history of this continent, the most important were the Turks.

The Turks, coming from Central Asia, penetrated into Iran and Iraq in the middle of the eleventh century, occupying successively the small Arab states and even Baghdad, the capital of the last Arab caliphs.

---

[60]In the thirteenth century, the Mongols and the Tartars also appeared.

They threatened for a long time the eastern borders of the Byzantine Empire. In 1071, the armies of the Byzantine Empire suffered a severe defeat by the Turks, who took the emperor himself, Romanos IV, prisoner. As a result, in less than twenty years they conquered Asia Minor, Syria, and Palestine. The Byzantine Empire was in great difficulty, as were the economic ties between the states in the west of Europe and the eastern regions of the Mediterranean Sea. To stop the powerful expansion of the state of the Seljuk Turks – as they were called after one of their leaders –, the Western states – France, the Holy Roman Empire, England, the Italian cities, and others, organized the crusades which succeeded in taking back from the Turks some territories in Asia Minor and on the eastern shore of the Mediterranean Sea.

As the Seljuk sultan and the army commanders around him – the emirs – took possession of vast lands, of riches resulting from the spoils of war, and from the exploitation of subject populations, these representatives of the ruling class of the Turkish tribes began to carry out their own policies; they would not submit any longer to the authority of one sultan. The Seljuk state was divided up into a few smaller states, among which a rather important one was formed in Asia Minor, around the city of Iconium *(Konieh* in the Turkish language).

In the thirteenth century, the Seljuk states were threatened by the danger of a new invasion which was making its way toward them from the east, through the south of the Caspian Sea. They were the Mongols, who in their immense expansion conquered the principalities of Kievan Rus' and penetrated into Central Europe, while, after 1250, another branch made its way to the Near East. Most of the states of the Seljuk Turks were conquered by the Mongols or became dependents of them. The sultanates and emirates in Asia Minor were somewhat better protected, but even they were considerably weakened following the Mongol incursions.

The Mongol invasion pushed another branch of Turks further west, not very numerous, simply a tribe of shepherds and warriors. Later on, also after the name of one of their leaders, they would be called Ottoman Turks or Osmanlis, a term which would acquire a political significance, defining the relations between the sultan and his subjects. According to tradition, this tribe, headed by a leader with the name of Suleiman, left its native land in central Asia sometime at the beginning of the thirteenth century, forced out by a Mongol invasion. That was probably the campaign of the Mongols led by Genghis Khan against the Horezmian state, around the years 1219-1220.

This tribe settled, in those years, east of Asia Minor, northwest of lake Van, and then between the cities of Erzerum and Erzigean. In the following years, it made its way into northern Syria but, while crossing the Euphrates, the leader of the tribe, Suleiman, supposedly drowned (around 1227). After this accident, a part of the tribe, overcome by nostalgia, was thought to have returned to their native land. However, around 400 families, under the leadership of Ertoghrul, the son of Suleiman, started west and entered in the service of the Seljuk Sultan Ala-ed-Din Kai-Kobad. The latter established as their settlement the region of Kara-Dag, near Ankara. After they proved themselves meritorious in a war with the Mongols, probably at the time when the latter conquered Persia, forming a khanate there (1258), the Turks of Ertoghrul were rewarded by another sultan with a region in northwestern Asia Minor, around the city of Soyut (whose Greek name was Thebasion).[61] He gave them this small territory as a kind of fief, instructing them to defend in return the borders of the sultanate against the Byzantines and giving them total freedom to undertake incursions into the Byzantine lands near the sea. These were the modest beginnings of the future Ottoman Empire.

The Ottoman Turks were at the time a people of shepherds. Even their leaders were still living in tents. When they organized a plundering incursion, they would form bands led by the so-called *alps* or *gha-*

[61]M. Guboglu, "Turcii osmanlîi," in *Hrisovul*, VII (1947), pp. 56-57. The Ottoman historical tradition, registered by Laonikos Chalkokondyles, claims that they took possession of the city of Söyüt during the time of Ala-ed-Din Kai Kobad, therefore between 1219-1220 and 1236-1237. However, this tradition is vague and contains numerous confusions and chronological inversions, cf. Nicolae Iorga, *Geschichte des Osmanischen Reiches*, I, Gotha, 1908, pp. 150-151.

zis, who formed an aristocracy of the tribe. Following the conquering and plundering campaigns that they led everywhere, they acquired fortunes, took possession of lands, and gradually became feudal proprietors, whose permanent incomes came from taxes on the subject populations. Their authority was now grounded on fortune and not on the prestige of the bravery shown in battle. The historical circumstances in which such social classes and the Ottoman state came into being determined its founders to create a powerful military organization which allowed them to conquer relatively easily the regions in the west of Asia Minor and in Europe. Everywhere they encountered and subjugated populations which were, compared to them, on a superior level of economic and social development: they had been practicing agriculture and trades from ancient times, while the Turks were just surpassing the pastoral stage. The Ottoman ruling class realized soon that the plundering and subjugation of more developed peoples could represent a productive source of revenue. That is why the wars of expansion and plunder became a fundamental feature of the policy of the new Ottoman state. The Turks did not and were not able to bring any contribution to the development of the production of material goods or to the cultural progress of the territories they conquered. On the contrary, they were the ones who had things to learn from the more advanced peoples. The Turks limited themselves to imposing different taxes on the conquered population, exploiting it, and keeping it subjugated with the help of the army. As a result, a somewhat different feudalism formed in the Ottoman state, namely one with a pronounced military character, based first of all on the conquest of territories and the subjugation of other populations, exploited through taxes, while the ruling element contributed nothing to the organization and development of production. The expansion of the Ottoman state in the second half of the thirteenth century was facilitated by the fact that the incursions of the Mongols had weakened and divided up the Seljuk sultanates in Asia Minor. The Ottoman Turks, more protected through their geographical location from the Mongol invasion, became more powerful than their rulers and began the conquest of the sultanate of Iconium which, eventually, they would subject entirely.[62]

To the west, the circumstances were also favorable for them. The Byzantines had succeeded in reconquering Constantinople in 1261, which had been taken away from them in 1204 during the Fourth Crusade, and were now busy reestablishing their authority in Europe, neglecting the Asian part of their possessions. According to tradition, around 1281 the semi-legendary Ertoghrul died, at the age of 90. He was succeeded by his son Osman, a character with whom the history of the Ottoman Turks begins to be more precise. He is thought to have begun his reign around the year 1300.[63] In his time, until around 1326, the Ottomans already extended their conquests in the Byzantine territories. Osman's son and successor, Orkhan (1326-1359), occupied the important cities of Brusa and Nicaea. The former became the capital of his state.

In the middle of the fourteenth century the Byzantine state was going through a period of internal unrest caused by the conflicts among different parties that supported rival pretenders to the imperial throne. One of the rival parties called upon the assistance of the Ottomans, especially against a popular uprising which broke out in the city of Thessalonika and in Thrace. Thus, the Ottomans had the welcome opportunity to intervene in Europe as well. At that time, around the year 1350, they possessed a powerful and well-organized army. The elite corps of their infantry, called *janissaries*, had been created, they had a numerous and fast cavalry which numbered up to 16,000 soldiers. In addition, they also had the troops of the small land owners, called *spahis*, who were obligated to serve in the military for the sultan. Crossing

[62]But on the territory of the former sultanate of Iconium, the so-called emirate of Carmania was formed, which, in the fifteenth century, caused many difficulties for the Ottoman sultans through their revolts.

[63]Tradition attributes the assumption of the title of sultan to Osman, or to Orkhan at the latest, but historically the fact is only proven under Murad I (1359-1389), or even Bayezid I (1389-1402). "Sultan," a word of Arabic origin, appears in the Koran with the meaning of "power," but it also has other meanings. Cf. M. Guboglu, *op. cit.*, p. 61, note 1.

into Europe, the son of Orkhan, Suleiman, occupied the port of Gallipoli in 1356-1357. In 1361, the great city of Adrianople and the surrounding region fell to the Ottomans. Sultan Murad I moved his capital to this city and began a series of attacks in Bulgaria, Thrace, and Macedonia.

The states in the Balkans, alarmed by the unexpected appearance of this new enemy, tried to prevent its advance. In 1371, the Serbians had an encounter with the Ottomans near the Maritsa River, which was won by the Ottomans. In 1385-1386, they reached as far as Sofia and Niš. In 1387, they were defeated in Plocnik by a united army of Bulgarians, Serbians, and Bosnians, but without serious consequences for their later expansion. On the contrary, in the following year they entered eastern Bulgaria again and forced Tsar Šišman to conclude a peace treaty under difficult conditions, with the obligation to pay annual tribute. On 15 June 1389, the Ottomans obtained a new great victory at Kosovopolje, in Macedonia. There, they faced an army made up of Serbians, Hungarians, Bulgarians, and Albanians. At the beginning of the battle, fate seemed to be against them, as the Serbian hero Miloš Oblich made his way to the tent of Sultan Murad I and killed him. The son of the sultan, Bayezid I, nicknamed "the Thunderbolt," then took command of the troops and transformed the momentary rout into a great victory, which seriously threatened the independence of Serbia and Bulgaria.

The Ottomans conquered the last possessions of the Byzantines in northwestern Asia Minor and occupied Bulgaria all the way to the Danube River in 1393. Their expansion in the Balkan Peninsula began to worry Wallachia, Hungary, and even the states in Western Europe. They organized a campaign north of the Danube. Although they were stopped at Rovine in 1394[64] by the Wallachian Prince Mircea the Old, their numerical superiority and the treason of a group of boyars threatened for a time the independence of Wallachia.

---

[64]The opinion of some Romanian historians is that the battle took place in May 1395.

It appears that the first Ottoman incursion in Transylvania and Ţara Bârsei[65] took place around 1395 and was probably made by a detachment of the army that had attacked Mircea, who was at the time in a short exile in Braşov. Under the leadership of the king of Hungary, Sigismund of Luxemburg, a great united Christian campaign against the Ottomans was organized in 1396. The European army encountered the army of Bayezid at Nicopolis, south of the Danube, on 28 September 1396. The Western soldiers were not familiar with the military tactics of the Ottomans. The latter were fighting in an organized, disciplined manner, the movements of their troops were well coordinated, and the orders of the sultan were respected precisely. The Westerners could not oppose such an army with anything more than the individual bravery of a few of them, which lost much of its value through the lack of discipline which hindered their efforts. Mircea the Old, who had regained his country, vainly urged them to prudence.

The Ottomans were victorious once more. They would have attacked Hungary at that time if a serious event for them had not occurred. Another great state which had been formed in the second half of the fourteenth century in Central Asia, under the leadership of Timur Lenk, or Tamerlane, and which manifested the same tendencies of expansion and plunder of other peoples, had extended its domination, around the year 1400, all the way to Asia Minor. Sultan Bayezid I tried to oppose the new invaders, but he was defeated and taken prisoner during the battle of Ankara in 1402. Timur conquered almost the entire Asian part of the Ottoman Empire. After the death of Timur, in 1405, the power of his state weakened and the Ottomans regained their lost provinces, but the struggle for the throne among the descendants of Bayezid undermined the Ottoman state for over ten years and even permitted the intervention in these struggles by the Byzantine Empire, Serbia, and Mircea the Old. The latter, supporting successively the two pretenders to the throne, Musa and Mustafa, became at one time almost an arbitrator of the political situation in Southeastern Europe. Unfortu-

[65]G. Gündisch, "Die Türken Einfälle in Siebenbürgen bis zur Mitte de 15 Jahrhunderts," in *Jahrbücher für Geschichte Osteuropas*, II, 1937, pp. 404-407.

nately, his protégés were able to maintain themselves only for a short time at the head of the Ottoman state, reunified by Mehmed I.

After reestablishing internal order and the authority of a single sultan, the Ottomans were able to resume their aggressive politics, beginning especially with the reign of Murad II (1421-1451). In 1430 they conquered the great city of Thessalonika and launched systematic attacks against Serbia, Bosnia, Albania, Wallachia, Transylvania, and Hungary. Among these states, Hungary was the largest and most powerful. Together with the other countries we have mentioned, Hungary fought a long series of defensive wars against the Ottomans, which, in the fifteenth century, despite many defeats, managed to delay for almost a century Ottoman expansion to the north, across the Danube and the Carpathians. Beginning with the year 1387, the Hungarian state had been headed by King Sigismund of Luxemburg, who became, after 1410, German emperor,[66] and, in 1419, also king of Bohemia. These monarchical titles forced him to be away from Hungary for many years, a time which the noblemen in this country used to consolidate their economic and political power and weaken royal authority. Sigismund of Luxemburg was concerned, nevertheless, with stopping the Ottoman advance. An example of this was the campaign that ended in defeat at Nicopolis in 1396. He tried, beginning in 1410, and especially during the third decade of the fifteenth century, to strengthen the domination of Hungary in Bosnia, Serbia, and the Romanian principalities, with the intention of using the armed forces of these countries in support of Hungary. The policies of Sigismund of Luxemburg did not lead to the formation of a solid united anti-Ottoman front because it was combined with the annexation tendencies of Hungary toward these countries. As a result, the leaders of the respective countries would be encouraged to hesitate between Hungary and the Ottoman Empire. For example, Sigismund of Luxemburg attacked Bosnia in 1410 to enable the coming to power of a ruler favorable to Hungary. In 1427, he de-

---

[66]Until his formal coronation as emperor, in 1433, Sigismund only held the title of "king of the Romans."

manded of Serbia the cession of the important fortresses of Belgrade and Golubato.

The king recognized, to a certain extent, the hesitant attitude of the higher nobility within his country concerning the question of the anti-Ottoman struggle. The higher nobility, concerned with its own local interests, preferred to avoid the risks of a decisive encounter with the Ottomans and to buy peace with them rather than win it in battles. It was inclined to leave the actual fighting, when it was necessary, to its vassal states at Hungary's southern borders. Sigismund also understood the deficiencies of the system of military tactics and organization of the Hungarian state and tried, through the agency of the diet, to impose certain reforms and regulations meant to oblige the nobility to provide the king, in certain cases and under certain conditions, with military contingents, and to allow a wider participation of the population in the army. He also resorted to mercenaries for the defense of the fortresses. The noblemen did not like these measures and they opposed their application. Because of his long absences from the country, Sigismund did not have the courage and necessary independence to impose his will on them. Therefore, Hungary remained, during his reign, without any reliable allies, and its military organization was not sufficiently adapted to the difficult task of confronting the Ottoman Empire. That is why Sigismund failed to achieve a decisive victory in the series of battles that he fought, with rather long interruptions, over a period of forty years.

The influence of Hungary in Wallachia was becoming more and more counterbalanced by Ottoman influence. They took advantage of the rivalries among the boyar parties and among their pretenders to the throne. Thus, in 1420, they managed to overthrow the son of Mircea the Old, Michael, who had Hungarian support. The continuous battles between Dan II, supported by Sigismund of Luxemburg, and Radu II "Praznaglava," helped by the Ottomans, characterized the following years in Wallachia. The attitude of the ruling class of Wallachia began to reveal increasingly obvious tendencies toward duplicitous politics, in the sense that the princes, without interrupting their economic and political ties with neighboring Transylvania and the Hungarian kingdom, could not ignore Ottoman might and the possibility that they might intervene in their country at any time. This was the case of Alexander Aldea, prince between 1431 and 1436, who was a subject of the Ottomans but at the same time he informed Braşov of their actions. Vlad Dracul, another son of Mircea the Old, did the same. He was enthroned in 1436, also with the support of Hungary, where he had spent many years as a pretender in exile. However, shortly afterwards, he had to submit to the Ottomans and wait for a more favorable moment to reveal his feelings of hostility toward them.

West of this Danube front, which Sigismund of Luxemburg was unable to consolidate, he tried to strengthen the defense of northern Serbia by conquering the fortress of Golubato. Sigismund had tried to prepare these offensive actions in the Balkans on a diplomatic level as well, carrying on negotiations with Venice, in 1425, for its fleet to contribute to the blocking of the Straits, to stop the crossing of the Ottomans from Asia into Europe if the king of Hungary would advance in the Balkans "toward Greece." The negotiations led to no practical results.[67]

At the end of April 1428 Sigismund of Luxemburg wanted to occupy the fortress of Golubac with an army of about 20,000 to 25,000 soldiers, among whom were Romanians sent by Dan II. On 3 June 1428, the Ottomans took his army by surprise under the walls of the fortress and defeated it. After this failure, Sigismund concluded a peace treaty with the Ottomans and concentrated his attention more on defense.

Between 1429 and 1432 he sent a group of Teutonic Knights to the Banat of Severin, offering them considerable revenues and assigning them the defense of the fortresses in that area: Severin, Orşova, Mehadia, Saan (Ada-Kaleh), as well as other fortresses in Serbia, as well as along the Danube. However, the Teutons, besides the fact that

---

[67] I. Minea, *Principatele române şi politica orientală a împăratului Sigismund*, Bucureşti, 1919, pp. 178-179.

they were not content with the revenues offered by the king, proved themselves incapable of posing any resistance to the Ottomans, being seriously defeated in the summer of 1432 and forced to leave their possessions on the Danube, which were plundered by the Muslims.[68] In the same years the Ottomans invaded Transylvania and Moldavia. They returned the next year, as well as in 1435-1436, with incursions into Wallachia, southern Transylvania, the Banat of Severin, and some localities in Serbia.

In this last country, the despot George Branković carried on an obvious a politics of duplicity in the anti-Ottoman struggle. In 1433, he arranged for the marriage of his daughter Mara to Sultan Murad II, and of another daughter to Ulrich of Cilli, a member of a powerful noble family at the border of Austria, related to the imperial family of Germany. Around the same time, in 1434-1435, Branković also expressed his intention to join Hungary in the struggle against the Ottomans. In fact, he was trying to keep his possibilities open for any future contingency.

During the time of Sigismund of Luxemburg (1387-1437), the main political coordinates of Central and Southeastern Europe were established for the entire fifteenth century: the permanence of the Ottoman threat, the necessity for the internal strengthening of the threatened states, attempts at alliances among them, the role of the Romanian principalities being already profiled, appeals to Western help, etc. Sigismund outlined many of the diplomatic and military solutions that would be adopted after his death and verified their necessity in the anti-Ottoman struggle.

In the summer of 1437, the Hungarians had some local successes in Serbia. On the other hand, in 1438, the sultan led a great campaign in Transylvania, while another branch of his army again plundered Serbia. The Ottomans crossed into Wallachia through Nicopolis or, more probably, through Vidin, forcing Vlad Dracul to accompany them to Transylvania, which was not at all prepared for defense. The

---

[68] I. Minea, *op.cit.*, pp. 215-219.

province had been weakened by a great peasant uprising in 1437-1438, and the nobility had been concerned only with suppressing it. The Ottomans also crossed through Severin and entered Transylvania probably through the Iron Gates, in Haţeg, where they devastated the estates of the Romanian nobleman Cândea, crushing any local resistance. Afterwards, they advanced along the valley of the Mureş toward Sibiu, burning and pillaging everything in their way. At the siege of Sebeş, Vlad Dracul arranged for the surrender of the city, promising the leaders their quick return from the captivity that awaited them. It appears that he kept his word. Due to the intervention of the Romanian prince, the prisoners from Sebeş were given a milder treatment, being allowed to return from captivity. The rector, Anton of Sebeş, and a few other officials were not allowed to return by the king of Hungary who regarded them traitors.

The Ottomans also plundered the towns of Mediaş and Sighişoara; they could not conquer Sibiu or Cetatea de Baltă, nor could they penetrate the walls of Braşov, but they burned the districts outside of them. They returned to Wallachia through the Bran Pass with many prisoners and loaded with plunder.

According to more recent research, the main campaign ended in the middle of June, having lasted for around 45 to 60 days. In the fall, probably after 10 September, they organized a new, quick campaign in the Szeckler region. It is possible that Braşov might also have been affected in this second incursion. In total, the sources speak of 30,000 to 40,000 captives taken during the campaigns in Transylvania in the summer and autumn of the year 1438.[69]

These constant incursions, which could not be effectively opposed by the feudal states of Eastern Europe, show very clearly that a great and permanent threat had appeared in the life of the peoples in this region. Their economic life, the development of their cities, of trade relations, and the people themselves were in continuous uncertainty. The

---

[69]Francisc Pall, "Ştiri noi despre expediţiile din Transylvania în 1438," in *Anuarul Institutului de istorie din Cluj*, I-II (1958-1959), pp. 17-22.

example of the brutal subjugation of Bulgaria, Greece, and of some parts of Serbia and Albania showed what was going to be in a short time the fate of Hungary and the Romanian principalities. The peoples of these countries, subjugated or threatened with subjugation, were faced with a task of fundamental historical importance: to gather all their forces and employ them in the defensive struggle; to leave aside their hesitation, to find in their midst a personality able to lead this domestic and foreign struggle. The Romanian people, in alliance with the other threatened peoples, engaged in the collective effort demanded by the gravity of the moment. Among other things, it also produced a powerful political and military personality, worthy to lead the great struggle for the defense of Christendom – John Hunyadi.

p̄meditat⁹ē: paucos post dies mĺtis eū muneribꝰ (vt ip̄e sp̄abat) placatū regni hūgarie trāssiluanas traducere fecit in partes.

De electione dn̄i iohānis wayuode in gubernatorē: ⁊ de talione per eundē a drakul wayuoda exacta.

Post hāc tādē belli tēpestatē: postq̄z regis wladislai lugubrem interitū: ne quis in regno in alterius offensā moueretur: per dominos prelatos ⁊ barones regni interdictum est. ⁊ nihilominus vt̄ adueniente festo pē/

Depiction of John Hunyadi
from a Fifteenth Century Hungarian Chronicle

CHAPTER III

UNDER THE SIGN OF THE RAVEN WITH A RING

Toward the end of the fourteenth century, increasingly troubled times were threatening the fate of Wallachia and its inhabitants. South of the Danube, after they had defeated the Serbs and their allies at the battle of Kosovopolje in 1389, the Ottomans ruled. They were coming ever nearer to the great river. In 1393, the last traces of the Bulgarian state fell under the attacks of the Ottomans who occupied its capital, Trnovo. In the fall of the following year, 1394, or in May of 1395, an Ottoman army crossed north of the Danube. The prince of Wallachia, Mircea the Old, confronted them with his army, somewhere on the Jiu or the Argeş, at a place called Rovine. That was where the first battle took place in which the Wallachians fought to defend their freedom against the Ottoman invaders. The Ottomans suffered great losses and could not pride themselves on adding another quick victory to the series of those that had brought Bayezid I the nickname of "the Thunderbolt."

Something happened then which would be repeated in the history of the struggles of the Romanian principalities against the Ottomans and which the chroniclers would later render in the bitter ascertainment that "the few need to stop the many." There was an overwhelming disparity of military resources between the powerful and vast Ottoman Empire and the small state north of the Danube. Even though they were defeated for the moment, Ottoman forces remained overwhelming. Resistance proved all the more difficult to maintain as part of the Wallachian boyars, afraid for their estates and well-being, supported the enthronement of a boyar by the name of Vlad, who favored peace with the Ottomans. The agreement was not difficult to conclude as long as a tribute was promised. In return, the boyars were hoping to be able to keep their ranks, their situations, and their estates. Submission to the Ottomans was convenient to some of the boyars, being for them an easier and seemingly more secure way than that of resistance which, in case of a defeat, would have caused them to lose their fortunes and flee abroad to escape captivity or death.

For the peasants, however, free or in bondage, submission to the Ottomans meant an increase in their obligations, especially in the taxes in kind, through which they had to cover not only the claims of the boyars and the Church, but also those entailed by the payment of the tribute. Submission also meant the opening of the southern border for the crossing of the Ottoman armies on their way toward various targets, armies which had to be fed, and which, during their transit, would take to pillage and violence.

Nevertheless, not all the boyars capitulated, especially in the early epoch of struggles against the Ottomans. Part of them understood the consequences of Ottoman domination and could foresee a time when the fate of the country would be at the mercy of the sultan and those surrounding him. They were not in favor of the idea of dividing power within the country between the domestic ruling class and a suzerain foreign power because such a situation would have meant impairing their material interests. Thus, two points of view, two possible conclusions, two ways of defending the same interest, caused some of boyars to submit and others to place themselves in the opposite position, that of supporting the defensive struggle. Also, influenced by the Church, an institution which, naturally, could not have adopted anything but a hostile attitude toward the Muslim Turks, the boyars who decided to fight claimed that the main reason for their struggle was the need to defend the Christian faith against the "pagans."

When Mircea the Old, overwhelmed by Ottoman strength and betrayed by part of his nobility, had to retreat on the roads that led through the mountains to Transylvania, many of the boyars remained loyal to their prince and accompanied him to Braşov, together with their troops. Their presence there is mentioned in the treaty of alliance against the Ottomans that Mircea the Old signed with Sigismund of Luxemburg, the king of Hungary, on 7 March 1395.[70] They participated in the next campaign against the Ottomans in 1395, following which, with Hungarian help, the western part of Wallachia was liberated. One year later, on the eve of the battle of Nicopolis that took place in September 1396, Mircea the Old was able to regain the throne of the entire Wallachia, the usurper Vlad and his acolytes being banished.

Wallachia had been through two years of crisis, during which its land had been crossed many times by Ottoman armies as well as by Hungarian and Wallachian ones. Battles had been fought, pillage and devastation had been perpetrated, the uncertainty of life and wealth had appeared, which inhabitants of the principality would have to face as long as the Turks were along the Danube. That is why some families, especially of lesser boyars, who did not have great material interests in Wallachia, preferred to move to Transylvania, which, for the time being, was better protected from Ottoman attacks, both due to the range of the eastern Carpathians and the greater military power of the feudal Hungarian kingdom.

The refuge taken by some Wallachian boyars in Transylvania represents the starting point of one for the versions provided by sources regarding the origins of the family of John Hunyadi. According to this version, among the lesser Wallachian boyars who took refuge in Transylvania there were two brothers, of whom one, by the name of Şerbu, had distinguished himself through military merits, together with his sons: Voicu, Mogoş, and Radu. The other brother, whose name is not known, also had a son by the name of Radu. Their reputation as good soldiers of the members of this family attracted the attention of King Sigismund who enabled their settlement in Transylvania and took them into his service. The older son, Voicu, was the one who especially distinguished himself as a "soldier of the king's court." He probably

[70]Hurmuzaki, I, 2, pp. 359-361.

fought in the army that defended southern Hungary and Transylvania because he enjoyed the appreciation of the general of Florentine origin, Filippo Scolari – known in Hungary under the name of Pippo de Ozora or Pippo Spano –, who had been assigned for a time with the command of the military defense of those regions.[71] Many Romanian *cnezi* from the Banat and Ţara Haţegului fought on the same front, and one might consider that those Wallachian exiles felt the need to be in a region closer to the country they had been forced to leave. The resettlement of this family from Wallachia to Transylvania is a fact stated in certain chronicles,[72] but in reality, we are not certain that this is what actually happened. The information of the chroniclers could have been derived from the fact that Voicu and his brother were of Romanian origin and thus it was thought that they must have come from the south of the Carpathians. However, that was not a necessary conclusion. They could very well have come from among the Romanians of Transylvania, from a region where the Romanian population living in Transylvania had preserved for a long time an autonomous local organization, respected both by the king and his noblemen.

The villages and the armies of Hunedoara, like those of the Banat, Maramureş, and other regions, were headed by representatives of the local population, called *cnezi.* Some of them were recognized by the

---

[71]Lajos Elekes, *Hunyadi*, Budapest, 1952, pp. 89-90.

[72]Thuróczi, *Chronica Hungararum*: "...nobili et claro transalpinae gentis de gremio natus, Johannes de Hunyad...," in Schwandtner, *Scriptores Rerum Hungaricarum*, I, Tyrnavia, 1765, p. 397; also *Cronica familiei de Cilli*: "...aus dem Land Walachey bürdig;" probably Thuróczi also inspired Gáspár Heltai in his *Cronica Hungarorum*, written in the sixteenth century, who considers Voicu a refugee from Wallachia; John Hunyadi is considered to have been born there as well. For a discussion of this question see Ştefan Pascu, "Rolul cnezilor din Transilvania în lupta anti-otomană a lui Iancu de Hunedoara," in *Studii şi cercetări de istorie*, VIII (1957), nos. 1-4, Cluj, p. 25, note 1. The expression of Phillipe de Commines, who named John Hunyadi "*le chevalier blanc de la Valaquie*," does not support the hypothesis mentioned above. Commines knew Western narrative sources, which refer to Hunyadi as a Romanian, and, consequently, he associated his person with Wallachia (Ţara Românească – "The Romanian Land"), because he was not aware of the ethnic realities in Transylvania. On the other hand, the French chronicle of Jean de Wavrin presents Hunyadi as defender of Wallachia on the Danube, in 1445, which could have again inspired Commines.

king as leaders of local communities and were given certain rights. They were the so-called royal *cnezi* Many of the royal *cnezi* distinguished themselves through the military services brought to the king and were rewarded with estates, thus becoming lower noblemen. The ascension of the family of Voicu, the son of Şerbu, through military services at the royal court was part of the larger process of ascension to the nobility of part of the *cnezi* of Hunedoara. This would explain better the later kinship of this family with *cnezi* and the lesser nobility of Hunedoara and Caraş.

Other arguments plead in favor of this hypothesis as well. Thus, some very well informed narrative sources from the fifteenth century (Aeneas Sylvius Piccolomini, Długosz, Bonfinius) mention the Romanian and "obscure" origin of the family, without saying anything of their coming from Wallachia, a fact which, through its exceptional character, would have normally drawn attention. Also, the diplomatic sources do not contain any hint of such an event. Chronicles from the fifteenth and the sixteenth centuries (Laonikos Chalkokondyles, Anton Verancsic) state clearly that Hunyadi was originally from Transylvania, and even from Haţeg. A document from 2 June 1360 allows, with necessary precaution, a deeper analysis of this hypothesis. At that time, Stoian and Boian, the sons of "Musana," as well as their cousins, Balotă, Boiu ("Boy" = Voicu ?), Şerb, and Nan, the grandsons of Costea, won a trial for the villages of Răchitova and Lunca, in Haţeg, where they stood accused of having allegedly taken possession of them by violating the *cnezial* right, because the respective villages had been founded – the trial proved – by their grandfather and father. Could Şerb in the above-mentioned document be the same person as the father of Voicu, the later beneficiary of the royal gift through which he became the owner of the castle and domain of Hunedoara? This is not impossible, but it is not certain either. Admitting it as true would allow the placing of the origins of John Hunyadi in Haţeg and the tracing of his *cnezial* ancestry back to the mid-fourteenth century.[73]

Either originally from Wallachia or a descendant of the *cnezi* of Hunedoara, it is certain that Voicu was in the service of the king of Hungary and that in the first years of the fifteenth century he married a young woman of the lesser nobility of Hunedoara. Different hypotheses were put forward regarding this young woman, whose name was Elizabeth Morsinai. Her name indicates a very probable Romanian origin: Morsina, Musian, Musana could be distortions of the word Marginea due to the writing of the documents in the Latin language by Hungarian scribes. Returning to the document from 1360, in which a "Musana" is mentioned, one may deduce that Elizabeth was one of his descendants, which would imply that she and Voicu, the son of Şerbu, were related. Another hypothesis was that she was of Hungarian and Catholic origin, which was argued with the religion in which her children were raised, as well as with the name of Clara – not common for the Romanians – given to one of her daughters. From this marriage, a son by the name of Iancu (John) was born in 1407,[74] who would become the great army commander John Hunyadi, the most outstanding fighter against the Ottomans in the first half of the fifteenth century.

[73]See this hypothesis, argued minutely by Ştefan Pascu, op. cit., p. 26, note 1, and p. 32. The document from 1360 was first used by the historian Wertner Mór in a study published in 1990.

[74]For a long time, because of a misinterpretation of a passage in the letter sent by John to Pope Nicholas V on 17 November 1448, it was thought that he was born sometime in 1386-1388. Later sources, like Gáspár Heltai, from the sixteenth century, consider 1392 as the year of his birth, which, because of certain evidence, could be corrected to 1395-1396. In a Western chronicle, published in Frankfurt in 1614, the date of 30 March 1390 appears. In favor of placing the birth of John around the year 1407 pleads the indisputable fact that his younger brother was born after 1409, and a 15 to 20 year difference between them would be unlikely. The marriage of John around 1428-1430 and the birth of his first son in 1431 also indicate a date only slightly prior to 1409. The fact that his ascension to important positions began only in 1438 and that his wife was born for certain after 1409-1410 are also arguments in the same sense.

He had a brother whose name was Ioan (John) the Young,[75] born after 1409, who would later stand next to him during his military career, dying in battle near Belgrade after 1441. Another younger brother, Voicu, died very young, after 1419. One of his sisters, Clara, married the nobleman John Székely, and the other married Pancraţiu de Dindeleag. Some sources mention another sister, married to Peter II, the prince of Moldavia in 1448-1449, and one – even more uncertain information – married a boyar from Wallachia, named "Manzilla" from Argeş, through whom the family was related to the princes of Wallachia.[76] In both cases, they were at most distant relatives and not sisters.

An important moment in the ascension of this family occurred in 1408 when, on 18 October, King Sigismund of Luxemburg offered a gift to Voicu, his brothers Mogoş and Radu, his cousin Radu, as well as his son John, consisting of the castle of Hunedoara and the lands attached to it, which included the city and 35 villages, custom points, salt, gold, silver, and iron mines. This was an important gift through which the family of Voicu became the owners of a feudal domain which was about as large and rich as that of the fortress of Deva. As a result, the family of John Hunyadi already occupied a high position among the provincial nobility, of medium condition. By rewarding this family, as well as others, for their military services, King Sigismund intended to strengthen the defense of the Transylvanian border against the Ottomans, connecting these families, through material interests, to the regions that were beginning to be directly threatened.

---

[75]In the medieval Latin documents both brothers are named Ioan (Joannes, Johannes) because in Latin there is no equivalent for Iancu. The Serbian and Greek sources use the names of Janko, Jangos for Iancu.

[76]This was claimed in the sixteenth century by the great humanist of Romanian origin Nicolaus Olahus. According to him, "Manzilla" from Argeş, of the Dănesti ruling family, was married to Marina, John's sister. He had two sons, Stanciu and Stoian. The first one fell victim to the persecutions of Vlad Dracul, or rather Vlad the Impaler, and the second one, who took refuge in Transylvania, married and had four children, one of whom was Nicolaus Olahus. This version, however, contains so many conflicting elements that its authenticity is doubtful. Cf. Ştefan Bezdechi, *Nicolaus Olahus*, Aninoasa-Gorj, 1939, pp. 34-45.

On this occasion, the Hunyadi family also received its nobiliary coat of arms, which was comprised of a raven with its wings slightly open and carrying a ring in its beak. After John Hunyadi gained his reputation as a hero in the struggles against the Ottomans, and his son Matthias became king of Hungary, this coat of arms inspired many legends referring to the origin of the family it represented. Its resemblance to the coat of arms of Wallachia – a royal eagle with a cross in its beak – served as an argument for the Wallachian origin of the family and for its kinship with the royal Wallachian families.

However, a better known legend is the one claiming that Sigismund of Luxemburg, passing through Transylvania toward Wallachia, fell in love with the daughter of a Romanian boyar in the region of Hunedoara, to whom, before their parting, he offered a ring as a sign of recognition for the child that was to be born out of their love and whom his mother was supposed to send to the royal court when he grew up. In the haste imposed by the circumstances, the young woman was married to a Wallachian boyar, who had taken refuge in Hunedoara, by the name of "Woyk Buthy." Once, during a hunting trip, a raven tempted by the sparkling ring with which little John was playing – that was the name of the child, whose stepfather had died in the meantime – stole it from him and flew away with it, stopping on the branch of a tree. Alerted by the cries of the little boy, an uncle realized what had happened and shot the raven with an arrow, recovering the ring that was important for the future of the family. Thus, young John was able to present himself at the royal court where he was recognized due to the ring, and was taken under the protection of the king and given vast estates. Finding out about the incident in John's childhood, the king gave him as his coat of arms a raven with a ring.[77]

---

[77]This is the legend recorded by the Transylvanian chronicler Gáspár Heltai, who claimed (in 1575) to have heard it from "those whose parents had been John's servants." This old legend has circulated in the folklore with a few different versions of details; cf. *Heltai Gáspár válogatott munkái*, edited by Székely Erzsébet, Editura de Stat pentru Literatură şi Artă, Bucureşti, 1957, pp. 278-282, or Gáspár Heltai, *Magyar Krónika*, vol. I, Györ, 1789, pp. 336-341.

Another legend, which deserves no credence, is the one invented by the Italian humanist Bonfinius, the official historian of the court of King Matthias Corvinus. With the intention of flattering his sovereign, he strove to fabricate a genealogy according to which the Hunyadi family (or the Corvinus family, as they began to be called, also in connection with their coat of arms) were descendants of the Roman royal family Valeria Corvina. In this also legendary history of this family, a raven is said to have helped one of its members to defeat a Gallic warrior. Later, during the time of Emperor Augustus (31 B.C.-14 A.D), a descendant of this family, Valerius Messala Corvinus, was sent to Pannonia to suppress an uprising. Croatia owes its name to him (Corvatia, in Latin), and his descendants moved to Transylvania, bringing with them the name of Corvinus.

The story of Bonfinius does not deserve to be discussed. It was not believed – either by the author or by the one he was trying to flatter – and it had no circulation in folklore. Despite his tendency toward laudatory fabrication, Bonfinius had to adopt a more moderate tone when he speaks of the immediate ancestors of John. About his father, he says that he was a Romanian, one of those "who now live on the lands of the Getae and the Dacians, being the descendants of the Roman colonists, as is proven by the similarity of the languages." He was "not a common" man, having enjoyed the esteem of his people. About John's mother he says that she was a Greek of imperial blood.[78]

The illustrious origin of John Hunyadi, regardless of its nature, is only an illusion. For example, the documentary information does not confirm any special treatment given to him by Sigismund. His real ascension began only in the time of Sigismund's successor, Albert of Austria, after the year 1443, and the circumstances of this ascension are rather well known and easy to explain. In fact, had John Hunyadi been the illegitimate son of the king, he would not have had any reason not to declare this fact himself, which in those days was not at all de-

[78]Antonii Bonfinii, *Historia Pannonica sive Hungaricarum Rerum Decades IV et Dimidia*, IIIrd decade, IVth book, Köln, 1690, p. 304.

grading, but, on the contrary, it would have justified, in certain circumstances, even claims to the throne, which John never expressed.

The theme of a ring or another object through which people with an obscure situation, but of noble origin, were able to be recognized by their high protectors is very common in medieval literature. It appears, for instance, in connection with an episode in the life of King Matthias Corvinus, after the defeat he suffered at Baia against Stephen the Great.[79]

The nobiliary emblem and the name of "Corvinus," which was later given to the family, gave birth to the erroneous opinion that they were originally from a village with the name of Corbi, Corbeni, either in Haţeg or in Argeş.[80]

John Hunyadi was born either at the royal court, or in Hunedoara, where he grew up in the castle that his father had received as a gift in 1409. His father, Voicu, died sometime between 1414 and 1419, and his brother Radu remained head of the family. Radu is mentioned in documents, in 1419, under the Magyarized name of Ladislas, which could mark a further step in the process of assimilation of the family by the Hungarian and Catholic nobility.

On the estate of Hunedoara, the future hero was able to learn already as a child about the life of the peasants in that region. He knew his relatives, of course, who were *cnezi* and local lesser noblemen. He must have seen, on the mountains that were guarding the southern horizon of the castle of his parents, the fires that announced in the night the coming of Ottoman armies to the region of Haţeg around 1421. His sympathy for the *cnezi* and the free peasants, the family ties on which he would count in the course of his political career, and the Ottoman threat were ideas that grew with him, from the first observations that life offered him. Growing up in Transylvania, the idea of a

[79]I. Lupaş, "Voevodul transilvan Ioan Huniade – 'fortissimus athlete Christi'," in *Studii, conferinţe şi comunicări istorice*, vol. II, Cluj, 1940, p. 80, and note 1.

[80]The confusion starts again with Bonfinius, who says about John: "In Corvino viconatus" (Born in the village of Corvin). In fact, what the chronicler says is only that John was born in the place of residence of his family, namely in Hunedoara.

common struggle of the Romanian and Hungarian peoples against the Ottoman invasion became deeply rooted in his mind, and he also acquired a great tolerance in matters of religion.

He did not receive a great education. He was probably tutored by the rector of Hunedoara, or "the chaplain of the castle" but he never learned Latin very well. When he was very young, he left his home, being sent, according to the tradition of the lesser nobility, to achieve his military education in the service of a great baron. The information on his youth is scarce and vague, recorded in later narrative sources which are prone to errors due to the oral tradition on which they are based.

Among these errors is one that attributes to John a short period of service in the Ottoman military, in the service of Evrenosbeioglu Alibey, during which he learned the Turkish language and "everything about the artifice of the Ottomans."[81] Other sources present him – unverifiable, but plausible information – in the service of some Hungarian noblemen, for instance the Csáky and Csanádi families; with the latter he remained in very good personal relations. Afterwards, for a long time, he was in the service of the Serbian despot Ştefan Lazarević, probably on one of the estates that he had in the south of Hungary. This could explain the Serbian popular traditions about a courageous deed of John, who, during a hunting trip, killed a ferocious wolf, or even about his being a descendant of the Serbian despot.[82]

---

[81]"Cronica lui Orudj-bin-Adil," in *Cronici turceşti privind ţările române*, vol. I, edited by Mihail Guboglu and Mustafa Mehmet, Editura Academiei Republicii Socialiste România, Bucureşti, 1966, pp. 53-54; the information is also found in Laonikos Chalkokondyles, *Expuneri istorice*, in Romanian by Vasile Grecu, Bucureşti, 1958, p. 157, where the Ottoman land owner is named "Ali of Brenez." This story was certainly invented to explain his successes in the battles with the Ottomans.

[82]More information in Bonfinius, *Historia Pannonica*, IIIrd decade, IVth book, Köln, 1690, p. 304, about the service to the Serbian despot and the episode of the killing of the wolf. Also, Chalkokondyles, *op. cit.*, p. 156.

Leaving Ştefan Lazarević, he entered into the service of the Ujlaki family and afterwards into that of a bishop of Zagreb.[83] Now he was not just a simple soldier, but the commander of a small detachment of 6 to 12 cavalrymen. His first military actions took place in the south of Hungary, near those inconstant Ottoman borders, where he would later win his glory. At that time, he met Pippo de Ozora, who had also supported his father.[84]

Around 1428-1430, John Hunyadi married Elizabeth Szilágyi, of a noble family from Slavonia, or from the county of the middle Solnoc. The Szilágyi family was among the ones that were supporting the reign of Sigismund of Luxemburg. The father of Elizabeth, Ladislas, was a well-educated man. He had participated in fights against some pretenders that had threatened the ascension of Sigismund to the throne of Hungary.

Two sons were born from this marriage: the older, Ladislas, in 1431, and the younger, Matthias, in Cluj, on 24 February 1443.

In the summer or fall of the year 1430, John Hunyadi entered, like his father previously, into the direct service of King Sigismund. The chronicles say that at that date he was still young. They even describe his physical and moral portrait, to which they add, of course, features deduced from his later brilliant successes. He was a man of medium height, well-built, with a strong neck, shiny chestnut hair, large eyes, red cheeks, and with a serious countenance. He liked arms more than anything else. The life of a soldier, say the chronicles, meant for him

---

[83]The narrative sources (Bonfinius) even give the name of the bishop: "Demetrius, episcopus Zagrabiensis." But, in Zagreb, there was a bishop by the name of Dumitru only between 1376-1379, and another one as late as 1465-1466. However, the majority of the studies incline to identify the supposed patron of John with this second bishop, Dumitru Csupor, who, in 1466, became bishop of Györ. We believe that this was Bonfinius's basis when he introduced the name of a bishop of Zagreb about whom he had heard for certain. If the information has a grain of truth, then John was either in the service of one of the bishops of Zagreb between 1420-1430, or in that of the Csupor family, to which a future bishop of Zagreb belonged.

[84]Florio Banfi, "Filippo Scolari és Hunyadi," in *Hadtörténelmi Közlemények,* 1930, pp. 130-132; Elekes, *op. cit.*, pp. 89-90.

what water means for fish, or what the shady woods mean for swift stags.[85]

In the service of the king, John was able to enhance his knowledge, especially in the military area. He met people, saw places, enriched his experience. In the fall of the year 1431, he accompanied Sigismund of Luxemburg to Italy, being among the soldiers whom the king had promised to assist the duke of Milan, Filippo Visconti, against Venice.

This rich country, in full economic and cultural development, must have made a deep impression on the young soldier. In Milan, the great trade and commercial center in the north of Italy, John Hunyadi stayed for two years. He wandered its streets enlivened by people, although many of them were narrow and dirty. He saw the colorful crowd of people come from everywhere and the multitude of things brought there by merchants from all over the world. Sometimes he was surprised to hear phrases in his native tongue, and maybe this is how he met the clergyman John of Zredna,[86] who, as a result of the long years he spent studying in Italy, would become one of the first representatives of humanist culture in Hungary. His friendship with John Hunyadi helped him ascend to the rank of bishop of Oradea and chancellor of the kingdom. On 25 November 1431 John was, together with other soldiers, in the crowd that had gathered in the square to watch the coronation of King Sigismund with the iron crown of the Lombard kings, an act which preceded his coronation as emperor, which had to take place in Rome, being performed by the pope himself. However, John did not go to Rome where Sigismund went in the May of 1433 for his coronation. He remained in his military service in Milan and the north of Italy, having the opportunity to study the organization of the Italian armies, their fighting methods, seeing some of the commanders of the time, like Francesco Sforza, from whom, as well as from others, he was able to learn military science, without ever coming close to the

---

[85] Thuróczi, *op. cit.*, p. 397.

[86] Elekes, *op. cit.*, p. 99. It is a supposition more than anything else.

spirit of adventure and the doubtful character of those Italian *condottieri.*

His stay in Italy was also useful to young John from another point of view, apart from that of enriching his knowledge about the world, people, and his profession. We do not know through what means, but we find that in Milan John gathered somewhat of a fortune, being able, in the following years, to lend more than once important sums of money to King Sigismund, for which he received as guarantees villages and estates around Arad, Cenad, and in the county of Békés.

Upon the return of Sigismund from Italy, John Hunyadi left the service of the duke of Milan and accompanied the king to Basel, in Switzerland, where he is mentioned on 17 January 1434. At that time, meetings of a general assembly of the high representatives of the Catholic Church were being held in Basel. During the works of the council a great part of the European religious and political activity was concentrated around this city, as during any important diplomatic congress, with the participation of the outstanding personalities of the time. It is possible that John Hunyadi might have looked in the face of the one who, in his purple robes, was presiding over that great assembly: the delegate of the pope, Cardinal Giuliano Cesarini. He did not know then that ten years later he would see this cardinal die near him on the battlefields in Bulgaria on which they would fight together.

The council of Basel discussed, among other things, an important matter for King Sigismund of Luxembourg: the means to suppress the movement of the Czechs to free themselves from German domination, known as the Hussite movement. In 1415, another council of the Church, also held in Switzerland, at Constance, had tried to put an end to this movement through a barbarous act: they had attracted its leader, Jan Hus, there and had burned him at the stake as "heretic." The result had been an even more embittered struggle of Czechs against their oppressors: the empire and the Roman-Catholic Church. That is why the council of Basel was now trying to adopt a different, more indirect approach. They entered into negotiations with the Czech townspeople and noblemen, who represented the moderate Hussites and who, alarmed by the uprisings of the masses, were willing to accept German rule again.

As a result of the betrayal by these elements of the leadership of the Hussite movement, Sigismund of Luxembourg was recognized as king of the Czech lands, and, in the following years, he would go to Bohemia to take possession of his throne, from which the Hussites had overthrown him in 1419. In 1436-1437, always in the entourage of his sovereign, but already in command of a detachment of 50 heavily armed cavalrymen, plus their aids, John Hunyadi participated in the campaign of Sigismund of Luxemburg in the Czech lands.[87] The occupation of the new kingdom was not easy, although Sigismund had been officially recognized as its king. Many Czech peasants and even part of the townspeople opposed the return of German rule and tried, in certain regions, to oppose it with arms. Their isolated resistance had to be defeated and John Hunyadi participated in these confrontations, some of them rather severe, putting his life in danger. Fighting by his side was his younger brother, John, who, in the time of the campaign of Italy, had remained home and fought against the Ottomans in the regions neighboring Wallachia in 1433-1434.[88]

The battles John Hunyadi fought in the Czech lands contributed to the enrichment of his political experience and the formation of his knowledge of the military arts. He was faced with an army composed of common people, peasants, tradesmen, miners, who had been opposing the feudal armies sent to suppress them for almost twenty years. Harassed in long wars, with their numbers made scarce by so many bloody campaigns, those common people were able to find nevertheless the moral strength to make an effort for their cause, even though lost. John Hunyadi appreciated the value of those Hussite elements that he would later hire to serve in his army against the Ottomans.

---

[87]Elekes, *op. cit.*, p. 100.

[88]József Teleki, *A Hunyadiak kora Magyorországon*, vol. I, Pesta, 1825, pp. 224-225, note 5; cf. also Elekes, *op. cit.*, p. 78.

Hunyadi also observed closely the military tactics employed by the Hussites: the extensive use of the infantry and light cannons, and especially the use of wagons as means of transportation and improvised defense. When they fought on open field, the Hussites rapidly disposed their wagons in a square formation, tied them together with chains and reinforced the empty spaces with beams and planks. Protected by such an improvised fortification, the Hussite army was able to defeat the disorderly charges of the cavalry. John Hunyadi would later on apply the Hussite tactics in his campaigns against the Ottomans.

The borders of the Czech lands were also being threatened in those times by Poland. The Jagiello dynasty that ruled there hoped to occupy the Czech throne as well. Their hope was shattered by the coming of Sigismund of Luxemburg. In this theater of war, the two Hunyadi brothers once again risked their lives for their sovereign.

In December 1437, Emperor Sigismund of Luxemburg died. In the same month, John Hunyadi was in Székesfehérvár for the coronation of Albert of Austria, the new king of Hungary. Afterwards, he returned to the Czech lands, where he remained for almost all of 1438. It is certain that neither he, nor his brother, participated in the struggles of the Transylvanian nobility against the insurgent peasants in 1437-1438.

The new sovereign of the empire and of Hungary, Albert, was recognized as king of the Czech lands by part of the nobility, but the Hussites opposed him, electing Casimir, the brother of the king of Poland, as their king. Albert was crowned in Prague on 29 June 1438, but a Polish army entered the Czech lands and, in alliance with the Hussites, tried to overthrow him. The new king, with quite a numerous army, besieged the Hussite center at Tabor to no avail in August and September 1438. He did, however, manage to drive back the Poles, concluding an armistice with them in Wroclaw in November of the same year. In all probability, John Hunyadi participated in these military operations. During the armistice negotiations with the Poles, taking into consideration the Ottoman threat, the king named Hunyadi as *ban* of Severin, together with his younger brother. The two brothers entered upon their new job at the end of the year 1438 or the beginning of the next year.[89] They had under their protection the fortresses of Severin, Gureni, Orşova, and Mehadia. In May of 1439 they committed themselves to serving the king with one hundred cavalrymen, at their own expense, for which they were given as a guarantee a few localities in the county of Bodrog.[90]

It was around this time that the king, with the consensus of the Diet, adopted a decision to organize a campaign against the Ottomans. Their threat to the southern border of Hungary had intensified. The devastating invasion of the summer of 1438, through Severin and Haţeg, in the south and east of Transylvania, and a powerful attack against Serbia in the first months of 1439, represented a clear indication in this sense. The Turkish chronicles record, between 24 June 1438 and 13 June 1439, the pillaging of the fortress of Mehadia by the army of Evrenosbeiogly Ali-bey, also mentioned, without foundation, in relation to an episode from Hunyadi's youth. The incursion ended in the killing and capturing of a great number of "infidels," among whom a few of high rank.[91]

These were the difficult times that John Hunyadi faced when he was named ban of Severin.

---

[89]Doberdói Bánlaky József, *A Magyar Nemzet Hadtörténelme*, part X, *A Hunyadiak kora*, vol. I, *Hunyadi János, 1437-1456*, Budapest, 1936, pp. 4-9.

[90]Pesty Fr., *A Szörény bánság története*, III, Budapest, 1878, pp. 35-36.

[91]*Cronicele turceşti privind ţările române...*, p. 53.

Fifteenth Century Woodcut Depicting
John Hunyadi

CHAPTER IV

BETWEEN TWO ENEMIES

After traveling through so many countries, John Hunyadi began his activity on the theater of war where he would gain renown as a soldier, ascending to the highest dignities.

He was still young at the time, around 32 years old. For fifteen years, he had dedicated his life to a military career. In that time, he had seen many things that could serve an army commander well in perfecting his art. He had participated in minor confrontations with the Ottomans, had seen what a developed country from the point of view of trade and commerce was like, as Italy was, he had realized the material resources that such a development offered to the state and the army, had learned something of the military art of the Italian *condottieres*, had possibly already drawn conclusions on the advantages presented by mercenary armies and on the conditions one had to meet to be able to hire them and maintain their loyalty: money. In the atmosphere of political intrigues of the Italian city-states, and in the equally complicated one characterizing the Council of Basel, he had become initiated in the intricate subterfuges of the diplomacy of the European courts, which, through their lack of sincerity hidden under empty promises, would disappoint him so many times. In the Czech lands, he had learned the value that the belief in a social and political ideal gave to an army. He had observed the skill with which the Hussites applied new battle methods, in accordance with the specific features of the social elements that formed the army, and superior to the tactics, or often to the lack of military tactics, of feudal troops. For the constant and valuable services brought to the kings of Hungary he had been rewarded with many estates, through which he rounded off the initial fortune of his family, reaching, in terms of his material situation, almost to the level of the upper nobility.

Before 1439, John Hunyadi had the possibility to enrich his experience, to become a politician, and especially a military commander. While the Ottoman threat was becoming more and more serious, the higher noblemen of Hungary and other neighboring countries were becoming increasingly indifferent to the danger and more concerned with their personal interests. The defensive mission that the peoples of Hungary, the Romanian principalities, Serbia, Albania, and Bulgaria were facing required the energy, intelligence, and skill of a leader who was up to the difficulties that could be foreseen. John Hunyadi was one of the best trained people for that mission.

When he was named *ban* of Severin in 1438-1439, Hunyadi obtained his first important dignity in the kingdom of Hungary. Besides the military role that he had played up to that time, and which continued to remain his main mission in that border area, from that moment on he also had to play a political role. The circumstances of his ascension after the year 1439 were initially connected to the internal events that were taking place in Hungary at the time, namely the internal power struggles among certain parties of the nobility.

In the first half of the fifteenth century, Hungary was a country in with a developing feudal system. Agriculture was making slow but steady progress, as were trades in the cities. The commercial ties between the latter and neighboring areas, or even between regions far away from each other, were becoming stronger and more frequent. Commercial ties with the Holy Roman Empire, Italy, Wallachia, Moldavia, and other countries were also developing. The same elements characterized the development of Transylvania.

The development of economic life was taking place to the advantage of the class that held the economic and political power, namely the landowners. They had in their possession the greatest part of the lands. On their estates, they exploited the serfs, requiring them to work a certain number of days without payment, to give up part of the crops that resulted from the small plots they had in use, as well as taxes in money. The landowners also exploited the peasants and the townspeople through the mediation of the taxes due to the royal treasury, through the taxes on commerce – the customs at the borders and at the market locations within the country –, through the military obligation of the townspeople and free peasants, and through numerous other obligations that derived from the administrative and judicial rights that the noblemen had over the peasants.

Profiting from all these forms of enrichment, the nobility was always trying to extend the material and "legal" basis of their power: the ownership over the lands and the political, judicial, and administrative rights. Therefore, the development of the feudal regime took place in close connection with the expansion of property, with the tendency to concentrate in the possession of higher noblemen ever vaster estates, which eventually reached the size of small states. The upper nobility also tried to obtain more and more rights to rule over the immense domains they kept accumulating: rights of administration, of judgement, of tax collection, of organizing their own "defense" forces (which they could use to attack and plunder their neighbors). In short, they tried to obtain full authority over their lands. In this, they opposed even the power of the king and his administrative authorities. They considered themselves strong enough to solve their own problems related to ruling the land and keeping the serfs subordinated. The policy of the upper nobility was therefore one of dividing the state and thus strengthening their own power. The conflicts among the noblemen were often solved through small local wars, which meant plundering each other's estates. They often attacked the cities and the merchants traveling with their goods. They devastated the fields and houses of the peasants under the pretext of being in conflict with the owner of the estate. They wanted a weak king at the head of the state, incapable of opposing their will. This feudal anarchy, convenient for the upper nobility, was detrimental to economic development, as well as to the life of the townspeople and the peasants. To be able to carry on their work, the peasants, craftsmen, and merchants need peace and order within the country, and, therefore, they preferred a powerful and energetic central government, able to put an end to the anarchy of the upper nobility.

The upper nobility was not seriously concerned with the threat of Ottoman expansion. Absorbed by their personal interests, by the rivalries of internal politics, and by repressing revolts, they did not concentrate their attention on the struggle with the Ottomans.[92] They often preferred negotiations and offering gifts, in the hope that they could direct the attacks of the Ottomans somewhere else, thus avoiding the threat to their domination and prosperity. The internal conflicts among the landowners weakened the resistance power of the entire country and hindered the organization of the defense against an enemy whose intentions of conquering and plundering other peoples were obvious to the entire world. This is how the Hungarian upper nobility was depicted in the writings of those times: "...they do not fear God, but care only about their bellies, they will not go to war where the Ottomans are threatening, they do not defend the country and the people."[93] A nobleman from Dalmatia admitted in a letter to the king that he preferred to offer gifts to the Ottomans, lest they should devastate his estates.[94]

The common people, however, depended upon the defense of the borders from the Ottomans, or any other enemy, and were interested in establishing a regime of peace and order within the country. The Ottoman incursions, more frequent all the time, were devastating villages and cities, and thousands of people were taken into slavery. Merchants avoided entering the regions under constant threat. Economic life was troubled, poverty was worsening. We can also add the fact, which the people in those days could not yet realize, as it became evident only from a historical perspective, that Ottoman domination was exerting a negative influence on the life of the occupied peoples, because the Ottomans had a military-feudal regime, which was very little concerned

[92]Fr. Pall, *Ştiri noi despre expediţiile turceşti din Transilvania în 1438*, p. 17.

[93]Elekes, *op. cit.*, p. 52.

[94]Ibidem.

with the organization of production, did not take measures to encourage it, but only to exploit the subject population. The Ottoman army and civil servants were dishonest and corrupt, and committed many abuses against the people, thus worsening their poverty and cultural backward state.

The defense against Ottoman expansion was thus a vital mission for the fate of the peoples of Eastern Europe, for the protection of their prospects for progress: it meant the defense against an even more oppressive form of feudal exploitation than the one that was ruling, in general, throughout Europe. The peoples in the eastern part of the continent instinctively understood the danger that threatened them. They opposed the Ottoman invasions unhesitatingly and gathered around those leaders who favored a politics of resistance. The simple and justified wish of the common people was peace inside and outside of their country.

The lesser nobility in Hungary and Transylvania, like those in many other countries, were discontented with the growth beyond limits of the power of the upper nobility. The former did not have vast estates nor very substantial revenues. Some lesser noblemen were truly poor. It was very difficult for them to extend their estates because they were surrounded by the immense domains of the higher noblemen. In this situation, the lower noblemen took up a military career and entered into the service of the great barons or the king, hoping that they would become rich as a result of their military exploits. Their condition of subordination, their reduced political power, the lack of certain privileges,[95] the difficulty to obtain great dignities in the state, their modest material situation in comparison to that of the higher noblemen, all these made the lesser nobility a social class that was to a certain extent opposed to the upper nobility and a possible ally of the cities and, in rare cases, even of the peasants. The lesser nobility wanted to ascend to the same economic and political situation of the higher noblemen: they

[95]For example, the lesser noblemen, who did not have serfs, were not exempted from the tithe until the mid-fifteenth century. Cf. D. Prodan, *Iobăgia în Transilvania în secolul al XVI-lea,* vol. I, București, 1967, p. 29.

wanted political equality for themselves, and not for the common people, on whom they only relied to give more power to their claims. The fact that elements of the lesser nobility and the townspeople participated in the 1437-1438 uprising of the Romanian and Hungarian peasants of Transylvania shows clearly the structures of the parties (not in the modern sense, but with a more general meaning) involved in the political life of Hungary and Transylvania in the first half of the fifteenth century: on the one side there was the upper nobility, that included the high prelates as well, on the other side there was the lesser nobility, seconded by the townspeople and having the possibility, in certain conditions, to attract the peasants as well. The peasants would join the lower nobility not because they had a direct interest in fulfilling the latter's aspirations, but instead driven by their hate toward the aristocracy, against whom they would have allied with anyone.

However, the lesser nobility did not have, under normal circumstances, the power or the courage to openly address the question of a "redistribution of power" in the feudal state, to directly claim political leadership. To accomplish their goal, they resorted to the method of supporting royal power. They struggled to strengthen the authority of royal power so that all noblemen, of any condition, would be equal with each other before the king, and have the same rights and obligations toward the king. With regard to the main problem of foreign policy – the anti-Ottoman struggle –, the lesser nobility, generally having military careers, were more favorable to an armed opposition, although with certain reservations: in general, they were not willing to fight outside the borders of the kingdom.

Contrary to the general political line represented by the upper nobility – territorial division, anarchic manifestations, weak central power, inconstancy in foreign politics –, the lower nobility was in favor of strengthening the king's power, of strengthening the ties among provinces, of ending the anarchy of the upper nobility, and of a more resolute defense of the state's borders. This second political line was more in agreement with the interests of the townspeople and peasants, and more able to ensure the future development of society and of the states in Southeastern Europe.

John Hunyadi, as a member of the lower nobility, ascending to high dignities almost exclusively as a result of military services performed for the king, shared the point of view of his social class and acted in this sense during the political events that took place in Hungary after 1439. Although in the meantime he had acquired vast estates that placed him close to the upper nobility, the latter never recognized him as one of their own: they regarded him with contempt, considering him an "upstart." Throughout his career, Hunyadi was always confronted with the hostility of the great barons. Even when he became the most powerful nobleman, his program and political activity remained loyal to that of the lesser and middle nobility, and, indirectly, to the common people. The victories he obtained in his battles with the Ottomans, soon after he was named to the position of *ban* of Severin, attracted attention to his talent and bravery. Both at the level of domestic events, as well as of the struggles for the defense of the kingdom, John Hunyadi proved himself to be the right man to represent the interests of the party of the lesser nobility and, gradually, he rose to become its leader.

In 1439, the activities of the Ottoman troops increased in Serbia, near the southern borders of Hungary. In the spring of the same year, Sultan Murad II attacked and conquered the region east of the Morava River. At the same time, some of the vassals of the Ottomans were devastating the western parts of the Serbian kingdom. The sultan besieged the capital of Serbia, Semendria (Smederevo). The Serbian despot, George Branković, entrusted the defense of the fortress to his son, Gregory, and the latter's uncle, Toma Cantacuzenus, and took refuge in Hungary, taking with him his youngest son and all the possessions he could transport. He was accompanied by many noblemen and priests. Branković asked for the assistance of the Hungarian nobility. The latter, during the meeting of the Diet held in Buda on 29 May 1439, decided to organize a campaign against the Ottomans to eliminate the danger that threatened Belgrade, rather than to help the Serbians. The Diet established that the king would go to battle only with his personal armies and those of the upper nobility and prelates, not having the right to call the entire nobility to arms, except in an extreme emergency, nor to demand general taxes for the hiring of mercenaries.[96]

The campaign was prepared slowly, the noblemen showed no enthusiasm, trying to escape the responsibility for gathering soldiers. A few thousand people, poorly prepared, gathered with difficulty in the camp of Seghedin, and their departure was long procrastinated. On 27 August 1439, the fortress of Semendria fell to the Ottomans, who tortured cruelly the relatives of Branković who were taken in captivity. The sultan left a garrison in Semendria and started toward the south of Serbia where he conquered the rich mining center of Novobrdo. Probably in connection to these events, John Hunyadi and his brother doubled, in 1439, the forces for the defense of the fortresses in Severin. Now they had 200 heavily armed soldiers, plus auxiliary troops.

Only at the end of July, when Semendria could no longer be saved, did the king of Hungary, Albert, decide to take action. The army was advancing very slowly, toward the south, on the valley of the Tisza River; with it was the son of the former Wallachian prince, Dan II. Dysentery broke out, the soldiers and the noblemen refused to obey the orders of the king, desertions increased in number, and, therefore, the advance had to be halted. John Hunyadi was among the few who remained firmly loyal to the king. They decided to retreat. The army scattered more and more. John Hunyadi returned to Severin where he had several confrontations with the Ottomans in which he did not limit himself to defense, but also initiated local attacks in the region of Vidin.

The king, who was ill, returned to Hungary, reaching as far as a locality near Esztergom, where he died on 27 October, widowing his queen, Elizabeth, who was expecting a possible heir to the throne. This is how this less than glorious campaign ended, followed by an event that generated complications: Hungary had remained without a king

---

[96] Bánlaky, *op. cit.*, p. 12, note 28.

and without a positive heir. The child the queen was expecting had to be a boy to inherit the throne. This was a very grave problem at a time when Hungary, after the fall of Semendria and, in fact, of the entire Serbian kingdom, was being seriously threatened. Solving the problem of the succession to the throne was an immediate necessity for resistance against the Ottoman Empire to be organized. This problem revealed the difference in opinions between the upper and lesser nobility. The barons gathered around Queen Elizabeth and were defending the rights to the throne of her future son. Only if she gave birth to a girl, a new king would have to be elected. The upper nobility liked the idea of having a sovereign only in name, a child under their tutelage. The main magnates who supported this candidature to the throne were: the dukes of Cilli, the Garai, Ujlaki, and Szécsi families; Dionysius Szécsi, the archbishop of Strigoniu, was a member of the latter. However, Queen Elizabeth also had many powerful adversaries, like Palatine Lawrence Hédervéry, or the bishop of Eger, Simion Rozgonyi. She was also opposed by the majority of the lesser and middle noblemen who wanted a king who would govern effectively. Part of the higher noblemen in the regions neighboring Serbia, concerned about their estates in the south of Hungary, or harboring designs of expansion in the Balkans, also needed a powerful king under the leadership of whom they would concentrate their forces against the Ottomans. Such were the Tallóczi and the Marczali families, as well as others.

At the meeting of the Diet held in Buda on 1 January 1440, Queen Elizabeth asked the Hungarian noblemen to support her in ruling the kingdom until the birth of the legal heir. The majority of the noblemen appeared to be in favor of this temporary solution, either for the previously discussed reason, or out of respect for the idea of dynastic continuity. John Hunyadi participated in the meeting of the Diet as well. He presented there the seriousness of the Ottoman threat, the conflict between Hungary and Poland for the Czech crown, for Galicia, and for Moldavia, and showed how dangerous it was for Hungary to remain isolated because the sultan had already proposed to the Polish King Ladislas III Jagiello a military alliance against Hungary. He drew the conclusion that there was an immediate need for a king of age, with real authority to rule the state, and for the strengthening of Hungary's ties with the neighboring countries, especially with Poland (the lower nobility and the townspeople were not favorable to German influence, and that is why relying on the empire was not taken into consideration by Hunyadi). He concluded by expressing his support for the candidature of the king of Poland to the throne of Hungary. Along with the throne, the latter would also be offered the hand in marriage of the widow Queen Elizabeth, the rights of the child she was expecting remaining in force, but only after the death of Ladislas. The speech of John Hunyadi had a convincing effect and his proposal was adopted by a majority of the members of the Diet, so that the queen agreed, reluctantly, to send a delegation to the Polish court.

Between 23 and 30 January the delegation left for Cracow where they began negotiations with the Polish court. The delegation was made up of Matko Tallóczi, the *ban* of Dalmatia, Croatia, and Slovenia, John, bishop of Segno, also in Dalmatia, and three other great dignitaries. During the time of the negotiations, on 22 February, Queen Elizabeth gave birth to a son, who would be known by the name of Ladislas the Posthumous. She sent letters to Cracow immediately, ordering the Hungarian delegation to withdraw the invitation made to the Polish king. But the delegation, prompted by Hunyadi and others, continued the discussions, and, on 6 March, King Ladislas accepted the throne of Hungary.

He promised that at his coronation he would confirm by oath the rights, freedoms, and traditions of Hungary (meaning of the nobility), and that he would defend Hungary and Poland against the Ottomans. A few days later, the Hungarian diet confirmed the election of Ladislas as king, which opened the way to civil war between the supporters of Queen Elizabeth and her son, on the one hand, and the supporters of the new king, on the other. Unhappy about the baffling of her plans, the queen arrested the members of the delegation upon their return from Poland and confiscated and destroyed the documents they were bringing. Ladislas Garai, the keeper of the royal treasury in the fortress of Visegrad, secretly gave her the crown of the kings of Hungary, with which the underage Ladislas the Posthumous was crowned, in Székesfehérvár, by the archbishop of Strigoniu, Dionysius Szécsi. Duke Ulrich of Cilli took the oath of loyalty in the name of the noblemen present, and Nicholas Ujlaki, another great baron, symbolically enkindled the sword of the king in the cradle. The child was officially placed under the tutelage of Duke Albert of Austria, to thus persuade the Hapsburgs to support Elizabeth. They were also given a few cities on the western border of Hungary.

Detained in Poland by the revolt of a Lithuanian prince, Ladislas was not able to arrive in Hungary before 21 May, when he entered Buda with an imposing Polish retinue, welcomed by Palatine Lawrence Héderváry, by John Hunyadi, by members of the Marczali, Frangepán, Csáky, and Losonczi families, and by delegates of the king of Bosnia and of Despot George Branković. The coronation of Ladislas was set to take place on 17 July 1440, in Székesfehérvár. The archbishop of Strigoniu was compelled by the Diet to agree to perform personally this second coronation also. Because the real crown had been given by Garai to Elizabeth, Ladislas was given the crown that had until then adorned the relics of King Saint Stephen, in Székesfehérvár. After his coronation, Ladislas was accompanied, according to tradition, to the church in the square of the town, where he appeared on the throne, dressed in the royal attire, receiving the ovations of the crowd. Afterwards, he rode his horse throughout the streets of the town, stopped in front of another church, climbed up into the tower and, at the highest window, one could see his sword flashing in the sunlight, as he crossed the air in the direction of the four cardinal points, as a symbol of his determination to defend the borders of the country against enemies from any direction.

After the crowning of Ladislas, the conflict between the two sides deepened. The western and northern parts of the country remained on the side of the queen and the upper nobility – Cilli, Garai, Archbishop Szécsi. The eastern parts of Hungary, as well as Transylvania, were on the side of Ladislas and his partisans, among whom figured John Hunyadi. On 9 August 1440, Ladislas gave John Hunyadi and his brother four estates in Hunedoara, and one in the county of Timiş, as a reward for their services, among these the battles fought by John the Young against the Ottomans, *"in partibus Transalpinis,"* during which he was wounded.[97]

To ensure her domination over the rich mining counties in Slovakia, Queen Elizabeth hired troops of Hussite mercenaries from Bohemia, under the leadership of Jan Jiskra. He occupied the mining towns and the main fortresses in northern Hungary. Although he came as a mercenary for the party of the upper nobility, the population in those parts supported him, out of sympathy for the former fighters in the Hussite wars for freedom. Unable to pay these mercenaries, the queen pawned to King Frederick III of Hapsburg the "holy" crown of Hungary, which was set in 53 sapphires, 50 rubies, one emerald, and 338 large pearls, for the sum of 2,500 ducats. She also transferred to him the rights of tutelage over her son, "King" Ladislas V, the Posthumous.

In the fall and winter of 1440-1441, the queen pawned to Frederick of Hapsburg some of her estates in Austria and even the city and region of Sopron, in Hungary,[98] to obtain more money for the civil war. All these actions contrary to the interests of Hungary drove the majority of the nobility and the population even farther from the queen. One of the resounding defections from the queen's camp was that of Nicholas Ujlaki, *ban* of Macva.

In the western parts of Hungary, the party of the queen relied mostly on the power of the Cilli family, the owner of an immense domain in the south of Austria, the north of Croatia, and in modern Slovenia, on which there were about 70 fortresses and fortified localities. Not only through the dimensions of their properties and through their political influence, but also through their family ties, the dukes of Cilli were among the most powerful landowners in central Europe. They

---

[97]Teleki, *op. cit.*, X, p. 90.

[98]Ibidem, pp. 95-96.

were related to the Jagiello family, the Luxembourg family, to George Branković, one of whose daughters was the wife of Ulrich of Cilli.

John Hunyadi, named commander of the troops of the party of King Ladislas I,[99] first attacked the fortress of Györ, which had been handed over to Queen Elizabeth by the bishop of the city and fortified by Cilli. Hunyadi and his troops were not able to conquer the fortress, but they cleared the regions around the cities of Buda and Székesfehérvár of enemies. Ulrich Cilli was caught by a Polish detachment while he was trying to run away to Poszony (Bratislava) and handed over to King Ladislas. The latter held him in an honorable captivity and, after a few months, in January 1441, gave him his freedom, asking in return for an oath of loyalty and a number of hostages. The king was hoping that through the mediation of Cilli he would be able to make peace with the opposing party. In the meantime, in the south of Hungary there broke out a revolt of the nobility loyal to Queen Elizabeth, led by Ladislas Garai. The army under the command of John Hunyadi and Nicholas Ujlaki set out against them. The confrontation of the two armies took place in the south of Hungary, not far from the right bank of the Danube, near Báttaszék, on 10 September 1440. Moving his army rapidly, giving orders to his troops to spare the region and the population, John Hunyadi defeated and cleared the south of Hungary of adversaries. Ladislas Garai fled to Austria.

In this battle, John Hunyadi attracted the attention of the young king and the entire party whose troops he was commanding, through his military talents. Consequently, as a reward for his services, he was named to one of the highest dignities: voievod of Transylvania and *comite* of Timişoara, also keeping his position as *ban* of Severin. He was also given a few estates in Hunedoara, among which was Şoimuş. He was named voievod of Transylvania together with Nicholas Ujlaki, but the presence of the latter was mostly formal: in actuality, the digni-

[99]As king of Poland he was Ladislas III, but on the throne of Hungary he was the first one with this name.

ty was exerted by Hunyadi.[100] He occupied his new position only in the spring of 1441, because in the fall and winter of 1440 he was assigned with organizing the defense of the fortress of Belgrade.

The need for a skillful army commander was being felt again along the southern borders. The Ottomans, led by Murad II, had concentrated in the summer of 1440 in the vicinity of Belgrade. There, before launching an attack against the fortress and beginning hostilities with Hungary, the sultan waited for the results of his offer of military alliance which he had made to Poland. But, when he heard that King Ladislas had accepted the Hungarian crown, seeing his plans baffled, he began the siege in July. The garrison of the fortress, composed mainly of German mercenaries, was under the command of the nobleman of Croatian origin, John Tallóczi. The Ottomans surrounded the fortress on land and blocked it with ships on the two rivers, the Danube and the Sava. Both on land and on their ships, they had war machines, with which they were bombing the walls of the city. The garrison had to rebuild at night the parts of the walls that the besiegers had knocked down during the day.

To make their assault easier, the Ottomans secretly began to dig an underground gallery, on the southern side of the walls, from where they intended to begin a surprise attack. An anonymous person in the Ottoman camp informed the garrison of Belgrade about this plan by means of a note tied to an arrow which he shot over the wall. Because of this, measures to mine the threatened area could be taken. When the Ottomans attacked, they were decimated by explosions and thus their onslaught was severely weakened. They managed to climb over the walls at certain points and to enter the city, but the garrison made a powerful counterattack and drove them back.

In September, the delegates of Ladislas I went to the sultan, reminding him of his previous offer of cooperation and asking him to stop the siege. Murad realized he no longer had enough troops to con-

---

[100]Cf. Francisc Pall, "Iancu de Hunedoara şi confirmarea privilegiului pentru negoţul braşovenilor şi al bîrsenilor cu Ţara Românească in 1443," in *Anuarul Institutului de istorice din Cluj*, IX (1966), pp. 64-65.

quer Belgrade, and thus he agreed to negotiate. He was willing to stop the siege for the moment, but for the conclusion of peace he set the condition that Belgrade be ceded to him later. In case this condition was not respected, he threatened that he would return and devastate everything in his way. For the time being he left Ishak, the bey of Semendria, to raid along the Danube border and the surroundings of Belgrade, while the sultan set out with the bulk of the army toward the south, through Macedonia. On their way, they took so many captives that, according to the chronicles, the Ottoman soldiers "would offer a beautiful girl for a boot."

The new campaign of the sultan terrified the Serbians and the rich commercial city of Ragusa (Dubrovnik), on the coast of Dalmatia. George Branković, knowing the situation in Hungary and realizing that he could not expect any help from there, had gone already in May 1440 to Venice to ask for the help of the republic. However, he did not receive any assistance, as the Venetians disliked him because he ruled over some territories in the vicinity of the coast of the Adriatic Sea. The civil war that troubled Hungary in the summer and fall of 1440 prevented John Hunyadi from lending any support to Belgrade, which defended itself heroically, with its own resources.

Hunyadi arrived in the city after the siege had ceased and dedicated himself promptly to the reconstruction of the fortress, which lasted until the end of 1440. After finishing this project, having unknowingly prepared a foundation for the victorious battle he would fight there fifteen years later, Hunyadi went to Transylvania the next spring, where he entered upon his dignity as voievod.

In the fall of 1440-1441 the civil war was continuing in the western parts of the country. The brother of the archbishop of Strigoniu besieged Buda, and the troops of the king replied by attacking the residence of the archbishop. Bloody confrontations took place in both places, without a decisive result. However, Archbishop Dionysius Szécsi agreed to conclude a truce, ending the siege of the capital.

In the same winter, Cilli, breaking his oath of loyalty in return for which he had been given his freedom, sent an army led by one of his captains, John Vitovec, which devastated Slovenia, defeated the royal troops sent against it, and advanced as far as Buda. Then the king took command of the army personally, drove back the troops of Cilli as far as the outskirts of Szombathely, and compelled the turbulent magnate to sign, on 19 April 1441, a peace treaty, according to which he renounced his support for Ladislas the Posthumous and Elizabeth, being promised in return to receive the good graces of the king and to be treated like the other higher noblemen. Cilli's gesture was also determined by the fact that the queen had grown closer all the time to her Austrian relatives, namely the Hapsburg family, with whom Ulrich Cilli had disputes over certain estates in Austria.

In this way, through the renunciation of the conflict by the partisans of Elizabeth, the struggles in the west ceased, and Ladislas was able to set out against Slovakia, where Jan Jiskra ruled. The latter had already defeated several armies sent against him. This time he was victorious again, defeating the army of the king in October 1441, near the town of Košice. The civil war did not end, therefore, with a total success for the party of King Ladislas. Jiskra, the man of Queen Elizabeth and the Hapsburgs, was still ruling over the northern parts of the country. He was already beginning to show intentions of personal domination in those regions, which he would reveal even more in the following years.

The state of domestic uncertainty generated by the rivalries among the nobility and dynastic ambitions in the Hungarian kingdom, so detrimental to the consolidation of anti-Ottoman defense, persisted.

CHAPTER V

IN TRANSYLVANIA AND WALLACHIA

The year 1441 was an important moment in the career of John Hunyadi. After he had distinguished himself the year before through his military talent in the civil war, he now consolidated his reputation through a resounding success he obtained against the Ottomans. Having been invested as voievod of Transylvania, he began to apply the measures required by the situation, necessary for a more stable organization of the defense against the Ottomans and for the consolidation of royal power. In this he proved himself to be also a good and energetic organizer in matters of finance and administration. These qualities were combined with those of a good politician, who had the sense of reality and balance. He would attack his adversaries when he needed to, but he would also deal tactfully with them when this second method helped him accomplish his goal sooner.

The mission that John Hunyadi had in Transylvania was not an easy one. The higher noblemen were powerful there. The peasant uprising of 1437-1438, against which they had fought with their own resources, had given them the opportunity to conclude a treaty of alliance with the ruling class of the Szecklers and the Saxons, through which the three parties promised to help each other in time of need. This alliance was known as the *Unio Trium Nationum.* The power of the noblemen had been consolidated as a result of this treaty. One of the stipulations of the treaty was that the noblemen, the Szecklers, and the Saxons would not oppose the king with arms if he had a dispute with any of them. However, they would be able to intercede with the king in favor of each other. Solidarity among them was therefore a characteristic feature of their treaty of alliance and it was not certain that, in relation to the king, it would remain within the limits of a peaceful and respectful attitude, especially after the mutual enmities provoked by the coronation of Ladislas I and the civil war that began in 1440. The voievod preceding John Hunyadi, Deziderius Losonczi, was a partisan of Queen Elizabeth. In January 1441, he was still taking measures for the collection of annual taxes from the cities for the queen. He even committed hostile acts against King Ladislas I. He devastated the estates of some of the king's partisans and caused damages to the office for the administration of salt in Dej, granted on lease to some administrators of Italian origin. Ladislas I declared him disloyal and confiscated some estates from him in the county of Dobâca (in the region of the Someş River), and then gave them to another nobleman. In March 1441, the king ordered the new voievods, John Hunyadi and Nicholas Ujlaki, to investigate the complaint of the administrators in Dej against Laszocki.

Hunyadi adopted a cautious attitude toward the powerful nobleman. He preferred to persuade him, through a lenient treatment, to no longer support the opposing party. He convinced the king to give back to Lasonczi the estates he had confiscated from him.[101] At the same time, Hunyadi tried to attract partisans in Transylvania, thus to strengthen his position and that of the king, and to be able, when necessary, to take firmer measures against their adversaries. He strengthened ties with the lesser noblemen on his lands, or in the vicinity of his personal domains, of whom a considerable number were his *familiares,* namely a kind of vassal. As a result of his intercession, undoubtedly, in March 1441 – around the same time when Hunyadi entered upon his dignity of voievod – the king gave 25 villages of the counties of Hunedoara and Alba to some lesser noblemen. He supported the *cnezi* in Hunedoara, granting them certificates of property, confirmations of their *cnezial* rights, or interceding with the king for this purpose. He

---

[101]Elekes, *op. cit.*, pp. 134-135.

was in good relations with the Cândea family, living in the south of Hunedoara, whose members had been and would be among the most loyal participants in the campaigns against the Ottomans.[102]

Another basis for the strengthening of the position of John Hunyadi in Transylvania were his family ties. In the south of the country he was supported by the relatives of his wife, the Geréb of the Vingard family. In the north, in the region of Sătmar, he was supported by his brother-in-law, the nobleman Pancraţiu of Dindeleag, whom he named vice-voievod. But he also kept the previous vice-voievod in his position, Nicholas of Ocna Sibiului, who in this way became one of his *familiares*.[103]

The new voievod also concerned himself with the consolidation of the material basis of his administration. He encouraged those areas of economic activity that were bringing important revenues to the royal treasury, such as salt and other mines in Transylvania. He exerted a stricter control over the exploitation and administration of the salt mines. He established close relations with the cities where there functioned offices for the administration of salt mines, such as Dej and Turda. In general, he left the numerous Italian leaseholders of the salt mines in their positions, but he also placed his reliable people there. Later on, he named two of his main vassals, who lived in Turda, as administrators of the salt mines in that town. The royal documents recognize Hunyadi's merits in organizing the administration of the salt mines.

The consolidation of his revenues and relations allowed him to act more firmly toward the unruly noblemen. One example is his attitude toward the nobleman Dionisie of Sfăraş, who, in 1437, had been a representative of the nobility in the negotiations with the peasants. Taking the side of Elizabeth, he was declared disloyal by King Ladislas. Some noble families adopted special tactics during events like those that took

---

[102]See, for details, the cited study of Ştefan Pascu, "Rolul cnezilor...," pp. 25-67.

[103]Francisc Pall, "Iancu de Hunedoara şi confirmarea privilegiului pentru negoţul braşovenilor...," p. 65.

place in Hungary in 1440-1441. Having strong relations with each other, they would choose the side of one party or the other. The families that had supported the victorious party then interceded afterwards in favor other families that had fallen into the king's disgrace. This is what happened in the case of Dionisie of Sfăraş, who was absolved by the king as a result of the intercession of another nobleman who had been loyal to him.

John Hunyadi, however, did not accept these eschewals of the nobleman. He confiscated three villages from Dionisie of Sfăraş, waiting for actions and not words from him in the support of the royal party. Thus, he forced him to participate in the battles with the Ottomans which followed.[104]

It was also in this initial period of his activity as voievod that he achieved a better organization of the army that he would lead against the Ottomans. The strengthening of the army would remain one of his constant concerns.

Like all important landowners, John Hunyadi had his own army, composed especially of *cnezi* and lower noblemen from the counties of Hunedoara and Caraş. Many of the *cnezi* who joined his army, on the basis of their military obligations, were given properties and ennobled by Hunyadi. The sixteenth century chronicler Anton Verancsis recorded that the Romanians in Haţeg were ennobled during the time of John Hunyadi.

Even from the beginning, Hunyadi's army was considerably different from the usual type of feudal army. The experience of his campaigns in Italy and the Czech lands and the fact that he could not count – especially given the domestic circumstances in Hungary at that time – on the presence of the noblemen and their armies determined him to rely more on an army of mercenaries. It is probable that already at that time he began hiring Czech, Polish, German, and even Hungarian mercenaries.

---

[104]Elekes, *op. cit.*, p. 137.

He paid the mercenaries out of the revenues of his position and those of his personal estates. His resources were not great in comparison with the expenses necessitated by an army of mercenaries. An estate that included a hundred villages brought in at that time an annual revenue of approximately 1,000 florins, and for a heavily armed horseman one had to pay between 4 and 7 florins a month, or even as much as 8 to 10 florins. He did not obtain much money from the king for this purpose. In general, the king was indebted to him for the maintenance of the mercenaries and pawned certain estates to him. The incapability of the royal treasury to ever pay these debts led, in many cases, to the transfer of some of these estates into the full ownership of Hunyadi or of others in similar situations. This was a means by which he consolidated even more his fortune and personal power. He trained his army with special care. We cannot ignore, although we cannot establish exactly to what extent, that the explanation for his victories also lies in his less conspicuous work of training of his army.

The cavalry continued to be the main weapon of Hunyadi's army. However, he was one of the first in Eastern Europe to attach importance to the infantry, introducing it to fire arms, which were still a novelty. For a faster movement of the infantry, less mobile than the cavalry, he adopted the Hussite method of transporting it by wagons, and for strengthening it he introduced into the arsenal of his army light cannons. Until then, cannons had been considered mainly siege weapons, or they had been used for the defense of fortresses, therefore occupying fixed positions. Hunyadi studied carefully the battle tactics of the Ottomans and, to be able to defend against the quickness of their movements, he created numerous detachments of light cavalry, which he placed on the flanks of his army, to hinder, through their quick counter-attacks, the enemy's outflanking maneuvers. He was aware of the plans of conquest of the Ottomans and understood that limiting himself to defense meant to expose the country to constant incursions and plunders and to harassment that would eventually lead to exhaustion. That is why he preferred to take the offensive, involving deep penetration into enemy territory, to defeat the adversary decisively on his own territory, thus putting an end to the war that had been going on, with interruptions, for more than half a century. His preference for the offensive was also justified by the support that he was certain he would find in Ottoman lands from the subject populations: Romanians, Serbians, Bulgarians, who were waiting for help to come from the north for their liberation.[105]

To be able to carry on this offensive struggle, he used mainly his army of mercenaries, who, if they were paid, would follow him anywhere, while the noblemen, having to maintain the army at their own expense, refused to fight far from the borders of the kingdom.

In this manner and for these purposes, John Hunyadi built, through hard work and with patience, the basis of his political and military power. To the organization and command of the army he brought with him the experience of many years of battle on the plains of Europe. He also brought a great deal of theoretical military knowledge. Through the mediation of some of his friends, who knew Latin better than he did, Hunyadi studied the military writings of Caesar. He was highly conscious of his mission as a soldier. He often told those around him: "the profession of the arms is not as easy as some might think; one must acquire a great deal of knowledge and experience."

As a result of the sustained work that he carried on in Transylvania during the spring and summer of 1441, John Hunyadi was able to intervene again, in the fall, before 8 October, in the theater of war in Serbia, where Ishak, the bey of Semendria, was constantly raiding the surroundings of Belgrade and the valley of the Sava River. In his turn, with the intention of putting an end to the incursions of Ishak, Hunyadi and his army entered the Serbian territory occupied by the Ottomans, a three-day journey. When he was returning, the bey of Semendria attacked him. Opposing him, Hunyadi placed the heavily armed infantry in the center of his line, together with the archers and the auxiliary sol-

---

[105] See the detailed study by Mihail Dan, "Armata şi arta militară a lui Iancu de Hunedoara (pe baza cronicilor contemporane)," in *Studii şi cercetări de istorie*, VIII (1957), nos. 1-4, Cluj, pp. 68-118.

diers. On the flanks, in front, he had the light cavalry of lancers, and in the back of it he placed the heavy cavalry, supported by mounted arbalesters. Part of the heavy cavalry remained in reserve. It had an important role in the countering this Ottoman attack.[106] The army of Hunyadi obtained a complete victory. The Ottomans were pursued almost as far as Semendria, and only few of them were able to escape. The victors, loaded with spoils, returned to Transylvania, through Belgrade and the Banat.[107] His fame increased. In Buda, King Ladislas celebrated Hunyadi's victory, thanking him in a letter, and giving him new estates in Hunedoara.

In these battles, however, the voievod suffered the loss of his younger brother, John, his faithful companion since their youth, together with whom he had climbed the difficult steps of the first dignities. He buried him with all honors, at the episcopal church in Alba Iulia. In the memory of his brother, he donated to the episcopal church a few estates in the county of Alba, choosing, in his turn, the same church for his resting place.[108]

He did not have much time for mourning. His skill and courage belonged now to the country and to the peoples that were beginning to put their hopes in him. They were calling him again to lead their struggle against dangers that became more threatening all the time.

An important problem for the defense of Transylvania was also the fate of Wallachia. Did it have a prince determined to defend his country? If so, the Ottoman armies could be stopped or much delayed on their way north. Did it have a prince who was hesitant or a treacherous boyar? In this case, the passes of the Carpathians were open, the Ottoman troops could find the defense of Transylvania unprepared at any time, and they would even be helped in their incursions. Sigismund of Luxemburg had been concerned many times with the question

---

[106]The description of the battle according to Bonfinius, the IIIrd decade, the IVth book, p. 309.

[107]On 16 October 1441, he was near Timişoara; cf. Francisc, *op. cit.*, pp. 66.

[108]Georgius Fejér, *Genus incunabula et virtus Joannis Corvini de Hunyad*..., Buda, 1844, pp. 46-50.

of ensuring a loyal prince in Wallachia: in the time of Mircea the Old, of his son Michael, and during the struggles between Dan II and Radu Praznaglava (1421-1427). Vlad II Dracul, another son of Mircea the Old, had ascended to the throne in 1436 also with the help of this monarch, but he could not entirely maintain his loyalty toward his protector. The Ottomans were too close and too powerful. He could not hope for help against them from Transylvania which, from the summer of 1437 until the spring of the next year, was shaken by a powerful peasant uprising. Despite his own feeling and those of his people, Vlad Dracul had no choice but to join the Ottomans in their campaign against Transylvania, in 1438, and to continue to cooperate with them. But whenever he had the opportunity, he declared his true convictions, keeping friendly relations with Transylvania. His attitude made him suspicious in the eyes of the Ottomans. Different commanders and dignitaries of the sultan accused him of dis-loyalty. The Ottomans fortified Giurgiu, placing a strong garrison inside the fortress, to supervise the prince in Târgovişte. As suspicions about him grew, after 11 October 1441 the Ottomans invited him to the Porte. Against the advice of his boyars, Vlad accepted the invitation. He was received with honors in the capital of the sultans, Adrianople, but not long afterwards he was detained and taken to Gallipoli. The boyars who accompanied him were allowed to return to Wallachia, however, two of the voievod's sons, Vlad and Radu,[109] also invited to the Porte, were confined in Egrigöz, a locality in Asia Minor. A third son, Mircea, who was only a child, remained formally to rule in Wallachia, where the Ottomans sent an army of 12,000 soldiers, probably under the command of one the Ottoman beys along the Danube. It appeared as if the sultan had the intention to transform Wallachia into a simple Ottoman province.

From here, the Ottomans launched a campaign against Transylvania in the spring of 1442, under the leadership of Mezid, the bey of Vidin. Already in September 1441, news from Ragusa informed King Ladislas about the preparations of the Ottomans against Hungary. They

---

[109]Both of them would later ascend to the throne of Wallachia. The first was the future Vlad III Dracula, and the second was Radu the Handsome.

could have referred to the preparation of this expedition[110] (which would imply a long and thorough premeditation), or, more likely, to the incursions launched from Serbia, as was that of Ishak, bey of Semendria, defeated by John Hunyadi at the beginning of October 1441.

They went through Turnu Roşu and entered the valley of the Mureş, while part of them besieged Sibiu, a well-fortified city, which was able to resist them again, as it had resisted the Ottoman attacks of the previous years.[111] Due to the immediate vicinity of the place from which they launched their attack, the Ottomans found the army of the Transylvanian voievod unprepared. John Hunyadi had just returned to Alba Iulia from the battlefield in Serbia. Faced with the unexpected danger, he did what few noblemen or army commanders in his time dared to do: he ordered a general circumscription.

This results from the chronicles, which report that Hunyadi sent messengers throughout Transylvania, who were carrying a bloody sword as a sign of danger. He gathered men from villages and towns, he ordered the Szecklers to take up arms, and he ordered everyone, villagers and townspeople, to serve in the army, through a public decree, for the salvation of all.[112]

The Ottomans appeared before Alba Iulia while the army of the voievod was not yet gathered. He decided to confront them anyway, hoping for the quick arrival of assistance. The Ottomans were at a small distance north of the city. Their right flank was the heights west of the Mureş River, and their left flank was in the village of Sântimbru, on the bank of the river, where their reserve troops were also hiding. It was 18 March 1442. The army of the voievod marched out of Alba

---

[110]Francisc Pall, "Le condizioni e gli echi internazionali della lotta antiottomana del 1442-1443, condotta da Giovanni di Hunedoara," in *Revue des études sud-est européenes*, volume III (1965), nos. 3-4, pp. 442-443.

[111]The itinerary of this Ottoman attack, as well as other information about this campaign, as, for example, the place where Hunyadi's victory took place, are vaguely presented by the sources; they commit obvious contaminations between the events of the expedition led by Mezid and those of the previous Ottoman invasions, especially that of 1438.

[112]Bonfinius, the IVth decade, the Vth book, p. 311; and Elekes, *op. cit.*, pp. 150-151.

Iulia, toward the north. Faithful to his offensive tactics, John Hunyadi tried to take initiative and attacked with his right flank. The Ottomans made a powerful counterattack and the center of the Transylvanian army staggered and retreated. During the rout, the bishop of Alba Iulia, George Lepeş, was killed. He was the one who, by introducing onerous taxes, had led to the outbreak of the peasant uprising of 1437.

Following this defeat, Hunyadi retired to the fortress of Alba Iulia, and the Ottomans scattered about the neighboring areas for plunder, after which they made their way toward Sibiu, to reinforce the troops that were besieging it. In the meantime, reinforcements from all the counties came to Alba Iulia: from Cluj, Turda, Târnave, and Hunedoara. Szeckler and Saxon troops came, commanded by the royal *jude* Anton Trautenberger. With his army considerably reinforced, Hunyadi set out to pursue the Ottomans, who were not far away. At the news of the voievod's approach, the Ottomans drew up in battle array. Mezid-bey had given instructions to his army to try to kill Hunyadi at any cost. With a view to this, the Ottoman soldiers had been given detailed descriptions of his armor and his appearance. The intention of the enemy became known in the Transylvanian camp. A lesser nobleman, one of Hunyadi's servants by the name of Simion Kamonyai, offered to change his armor with that of the voievod, for the latter to be better protected in the battle.

The confrontation began on 22 March. The location where it took place could not be established with certainty. The most probable hypothesis is that the battle was fought near Sibiu. The army of Hunyadi, this time more numerous and more animated, shook heavily the lines of the adversary. In the middle of the troops, Simion Kamonyai, dressed in the armor of the voievod, seemed to be leading the attack.

The Ottomans saw him and, following their orders, they did everything to get near him. In the turmoil that occurred, Simion Kamonyai was killed, and the Ottomans were already rejoicing, hoping that the Transylvanians would lose courage and retreat in a hurry. But the voievod, dressed in the armor known only by his men, kept leading the battle unhesitatingly.[113]

Far from weakening, the attacks of his army became more powerful. The captives taken by the Ottomans rose in arms. Panic broke out among the Ottomans, causing general retreat. Mezid and his son lie dead on the battlefield. The remainder of the Ottoman army tried to escape by fleeing toward Turnu Roşu. They were pursued especially by the detachment commanded by Basarab, the son of Dan II, whom John Hunyadi wanted to enthrone in Wallachia.

He managed to annihilate groups of fugitive Ottomans in the mountains of Transylvania and Wallachia. Hunyadi also entered Wallachia with his army. A source dating not much later than these events shows that the inhabitants received him well, gathered in great numbers, and elected him as their prince.[114] In reality, this described the enthronement of Basarab with the support of Hunyadi.[115] In July 1442, the voievod informed the king in Buda about his victories. The news about them spread all the way to Germany and Italy. More celebrations took place in the capital where the victor was overwhelmed with gifts and royal promises.

Through this victory and its immediate consequences, John Hunyadi manifested for the first time his intention to fortify the anti-Ottoman front, creating an alliance between Transylvania and Wallachia which were under a common threat. The Serbian despot, George Branković, stimulated by the news of the victory, began to join with more courage the forces opposing the Crescent.

---

[113]Many historical sources, from many places and times, mention this type of event. We could be dealing in this case as in others, with the repetition of a frequent motif of medieval chronicles.

[114]"Cronica lui Wavrin şi românii," in *Buletinul Comisiei istorice a României*, VI, 1927, p. 63.

[115]The Serbian annals say that this change in reign took place only in the fall of 1442; cf. Francisc Pall, "Iancu de Hunedoara şi confirmarea privilegiului pentru negoţul braşovenilor...," p. 78, note 70. It was probably the confirmation of the reign of Basarab, following a new victory won by Hunyadi on the Ialomiţa River.

The Ottomans became concerned about the successes of John Hunyadi. The sultan held council in Adrianople and, according to some sources, in July he sent a delegation to Buda to offer a peace treaty. The conditions were the ceding of Belgrade, or the payment of an annual tribute. The Ottoman offer was rejected as a result of the recent victory of John Hunyadi. The sultan, disappointed in his expectations and threatened with the loss of his influence in Wallachia, wishing to avenge the defeat of Mezid-bey, sent in August a powerful army (the chronicles mention up to 80,000 soldiers), commanded by the beylerbey of Rumelia,[116] Shehabeddin. He was accompanied by six high beys and sandjaks[117] from Anatolia. He had received the order to remove or to kill the prince of Wallachia, to transform the province into a pashalik, and to invade Transylvania as well.

The Ottomans crossed the Danube near Nicopolis. Basarab could not resist them alone and, therefore, took refuge in the mountains waiting for John Hunyadi's help. The latter came to Wallachia. The Ottomans had probably occupied Târgoviște and advanced toward the north, along the valley of the Ialomiţa, with the intention of crossing the mountains. Part of them had separated from the bulk of the army and scattered about the country for plunder. Hunyadi attacked the Ottoman troops on 2 September 1442, on the Ialomiţa River, in mountainous and narrow places.[118] The battle lasted until dark. It was a great victory for John Hunyadi. One sandjak and four beys fell in battle. Shehabeddin fled across the Danube and the detachments of his army, scattered for plunder, were annihilated one after another. The spoils that fell into the hands of the victors were huge, consisting of flags, tents, about 5,000 camels, horses, and mules, expensive clothes, and

---

[116]The European part of the Ottoman Empire was called Rumelia, and the Asian part was called Anatolia. *Beylerbey* was the title of the military commander of each of those to regions.

[117]Titles of military commanders in the Ottoman army.

[118]"*Ad locum qui Waskapu dicitur…*" Thuróczi, the IVth book, chapter XXXVIII, in Scriptores, I, p. 412. The Iron Gates is not, evidently, the straits of the Danube. If it is not a confusion of the chronicler, it suggests a similar place.

many other things, creating the rumor that everyone in Wallachia had become rich. The sultan dismissed Shehabeddin from his post, replacing him with Bey Hassan.

In November-December, John Hunyadi crossed south of the Danube, drove away the Ottoman troops that were trying to resist, attacked Vidin – but did not initiate a siege – and returned through Serbia, where, also in November, the Hungarians managed to defeat another Ottoman army, commanded by Bey Turakhan.

The victory on the Ialomiţa River represented a turning point in the history of the battles of John Hunyadi against Ottoman aggression. Until then, his successes had been obtained in defensive battles. In the limited space of the battlefield, he had applied offensive tactics, but from the point of view of his strategy, of his plans regarded as a whole, he had limited himself to defending himself or to responding to attacks.

In August-September 1442 he no longer waited for the enemy to approach. He was the one who crossed the mountains, confronted the adversary army outside his borders, and pursued it all the way across the Danube.[119] For a few years, this remained the manner in which he fought the Ottomans. He tried to put an end to the war, to obtain a decisive victory, assuming the offensive, penetrating deeply into Ottoman territory. His ultimate goal became that of driving the Ottomans out of Europe, to thus free the oppressed peoples in the Balkans and Byzantium, thus ensuring the peace of his own country. The Ottomans, impressed by their defeats, would show themselves more willing to make peace in the future. Wallachia consolidated its relations with Hunyadi.

[119] "*Invadere potius hostem, quam invade ab illo praeoptans*" ("Preferring to attack the enemy instead of letting himself be attacked"), comments the chronicler Thuróczi, in the IV book, chapter XXXVIII, p. 412. Chalkokondyles, in *Expuneri istorice* (*Historical Chronicles*), Bucharest 1958, p. 157, notices the same change in the character of the struggles between the Christians and the Ottomans, beginning with the victory of Ialomiţa.

Chapter VI

Toward the Heart of the Balkans

In Hungary, the victories of the Transylvanian prince ensured the superiority of King Ladislas over his adversaries. All of Europe was deeply impressed. In Venice, the victory over Shehabeddin was celebrated on 4 November 1442 with a procession in St. Mark's Square, headed by the doge himself. Hopes of a coalition that would drive the Ottomans out of Europe were reborn. The Ottomans, influenced by these events, called off the siege of Constantinople, which they had begun in April 1442, and concluded a peace with the Byzantines.[120]

While the voievod of Transylvania was winning these victories, and to a certain extent under their influence, the domestic struggle between the two parties in Hungary was moving toward settlement. Already in 1441 some of the noblemen in the entourage of Queen Elizabeth were advising her to show herself more favorable to a reconciliation.[121] Most of all, they were advising her to reclaim her child, Ladislas the Posthumous, who had been entrusted to the tutelage of Frederick III of Hapsburg, and to regain the crown of Hungary, pawned to the same sovereign. The first of these acts was meant to give the impression of a wide liberty of action for the party of the queen. It was meant to eliminate the suspicions about an overwhelming German influence –

[120]Francisc Pall, *Le condizioni...*, p. 438.

[121]On 9 September 1441, King Ladislas was also designating delegates for negotiations with Elizabeth; cf. Teleki, *op. cit.*, X, pp. 104-106.

unpopular in Hungary – to which the queen and the country would have been subjected in the eventuality of the assertion of the rights of the minor king. The pawning of the crown had offended the Hungarian nobility very deeply, and this cause of disagreement had to be eliminated as well. They began discussions with Frederick III, but he refused to give up any of his rights as tutor. It became clear then that Frederick intended to extend his domination over Hungary. The relations between him and the Hungarian noblemen in the entourage of the queen grew cold. Frederick went so far as to arrest Ladislas Garai, the most redoubtable enemy – next to Cilli – of King Ladislas. Thus, the party of the great barons became even weaker. From a military point of view, Ladislas I also held an advantage. In the late fall and in the winter of 1441-1442, the troops of the king resumed the attacks against Jiskra and conquered a few fortresses in Slovakia, including Roznava (Rosenau) and Trnava (Tyrnavia). Finally, they besieged Pojon, which resisted only due to help received from Vienna, from which 1,000 infantrymen, firearms, cannons, and gunpowder were sent on 1 February 1442. The infantrymen were hired at the expense of the queen. The strengthening of the king's situation allowed him to send home the Polish troops, which he had brought along two years earlier, on the occasion of his arrival in Hungary for his coronation.

In March 1442 the papal legate, Cardinal Giuliano Cesarini, left for Hungary with the mission of mediating the reconciliation between the two parties. The negotiations proved rather difficult as a result of the queen's obstinacy to maintain her claims and certain political acts that she had committed during the civil war. John Hunyadi was also consulted with regard to the prospects for a reconciliation. His reply is proof of his broad political outlook, beyond personal rivalries, embracing the national interest. He maintained that, considering the relations with the Ottomans at that time, the conclusion of peace within the country should not be refused. But it should not be begged for either, although peace is always better than war. That is why, if the queen persisted in her conditions, which meant that extensive areas of the country's territories would be alienated forever, Ladislas should oppose it with determination, because there existed both the will and the necessary force to win a less costly peace. Hunyadi alluded first of all to the ceding of certain cities in the west of Hungary to the Hapsburgs, but, probably, also to certain political clauses through which the Polish entourage of Ladislas had sacrificed the interests of Hungary and especially of Transylvania in favor of Poland, which wanted, among other things, to establish its complete domination over Moldavia. Eventually, Ladislas and Elizabeth met at Gÿor on 23 November 1442. The exact conditions of the reconciliation that took place are not known, because they were never applied. The queen died unexpectedly, on 19 December, and therefore the status quo remained in effect: her son, Ladislas, with claims to the throne, supported by his tutor, Frederick of Hapsburg and Jiskra as ruler of Slovakia, a conflict ready to break out, in more serious forms. The only result was an armistice for two years, in the summer of 1443, which allowed Hungary to intensify its efforts on the anti-Ottoman front during 1443 and 1444. These efforts were also supported by propaganda for a new European crusade against the Ottomans. Pope Eugenius IV had managed to obtain superficial successes for Catholicism at the Council of Florence held in 1439. The Byzantine emperor and the representatives of the Orthodox Church who participated in this council formally recognized the union with the Western Church. Their gesture was determined only by the hope of obtaining aid against the Ottomans.

Indeed, immediately after the council, the pope communicated to Emperor John VIII Palaiologus his plan to organize, in the spring of 1440, a double military action – naval and terrestrial – to help Byzantium. However, this plan was never put into practice. The pope continued, nevertheless, to insist in favor of an anti-Ottoman crusade. His conflict with the Council of Basel, which in November 1439 had elected an anti-pope, Felix V, determined Eugenius IV to pursue a major European political success to consolidate his own position.[122] Encouraged by the recent victories of John Hunyadi, the pope tried again to

---

[122]Francisc Pall, *Le condizioni...*, p. 435.

organize “support” for Byzantium. His intention was to extend his influence over the East, as it became more and more obvious that the “union” of Florence had remained a simple declaration, because the majority of the population in Byzantium and Eastern Europe would not renounce Orthodoxy. The sending of Cesarini to Hungary as mediator of domestic peace was also a stage in preparation for this European alliance. The official convocation to the organization of a common campaign was formulated in a papal bull on 1 January 1443. Eugenius IV was offering a fifth of the annual revenue of the Apostolic Chamber to equip a fleet whose mission was, besides defending Byzantium and the islands of Cyprus and Rhodes, to reestablish the security of navigation on the Mediterranean Sea, which was infested by the piracy of the Moors of North Africa.[123] The papal appeal initiated an intense diplomatic activity at various European courts. The delegates commissioned with spreading propaganda for a war against the Ottomans met in Poland. Cesarini concerned himself with this problem in Hungary and within the empire. The duke of Burgundy, Philip the Good, was approached numerous times. Besides the papal delegates, he was visited, from May through October 1443, by three Byzantine delegations that had also gone to Venice, Rome, and Naples. It was in the interest of Burgundy to defend Eastern Europe, which was importing fabrics made in the Low Countries (today Belgium) that were under its domination. The duke was willing to contribute with 9 or 10 ships to a fleet that would block the Straits – the Bosphorus and the Dardanelles. However, the Burgundians were less willing to participate in a campaign on land. They did not have much confidence in the success of such a campaign because, even though they were aware of the victories of John Hunyadi, they were of the opinion that the Hungarian army was poorly trained and lacked the necessary equipment: “if a soldier has a bow, he will not have arrows, and another will have a sword, but not a sheath.”[124] Especially with a view to forming a fleet, negotiations

[123]Francisc Pall, *op. cit.*, p. 441.

[124]Iorga, *Istoria românilor*, IV, p. 76.

were carried on with the greatest naval power of the day, Venice, which was also interested in defending the strategic points on the Greek coast that were under its control. Venice promised, in principle, 10 galleys, but fitted out at the expense of the pope; it refused categorically to engage the fleet it had on the Adriatic Sea in the campaign, as it deemed it necessary to maintain the security of the waters surrounding it. In fact, Venice conditioned its participation on the reconciliation between the papacy and the Duchy of Milan, whose interests it favored. The hesitant attitude of the republic of the lagoons was caused by fear of the expansion of the Hungarian kingdom and of the Serbian states toward the Dalmatian coast, as well as by certain financial disagreements with the pope. In August 1443, Venice, after various objections and delays, refused to equip the promised ships during that year.[125] King Alphonse of Aragon, who also ruled over the south of Italy, manifested his intention to support the campaign with 6 ships. But in August 1443 he began a war with Milan, which rendered his previous engagement unlikely and complicated even more the political relations among the Italian states, favoring the reservations of Venice concerning an anti-Ottoman campaign.[126]

All this turmoil in the West brought only words meant to cover the scantiness of their actions. The tithes promised by the Church for the "crusade" were gathered, but part of the sum was used for other purposes. Venice manifested its discontent toward the insufficiency of the sums received for equipping the fleet against the Ottomans. The Byzantine scene did not look any more encouraging for a potential campaign of liberation. Fighting amongst each other, different claimants to the imperial throne would go so far as making an alliance with the Ottomans, seeking their help in their attempts to obtain the crown. One of the princes of the Byzantine imperial house, a claimant to the throne, participated alongside the Ottomans in the unsuccessful siege of Constantinople that the latter carried on from the spring until the fall

---

[125]Francisc Pall, *op. cit.*, pp. 445-446, 450-453.

[126]Ibidem, p. 449.

of 1442. Under those circumstances, the organization of the project for the Western campaign and the sending of a fleet to the Straits were postponed. But the nations of Eastern Europe did not renounce the fight. They were ready to fight alone. Their ruling class was forced to put an end to its hesitations and adopt a more decisive attitude. The Serbian Despot George Branković was now among the most ardent supporters of the campaign against the Ottomans. He had tried to win their benevolence, he had even given his daughter's hand to the sultan, but the results of this policy were the loss of his country, the occupation of Semendria, and the capturing and blinding of two of his sons.

In Hungary, after the armistice concluded with Frederick of Hapsburg and with Jiskra during the Diet held in June 1443, it was decided that a campaign be organized in the Balkans. On the 28th of the same month, King Ladislas informed the emperor that he was busy with the preparations and consequently proposed the postponement of their meeting until the February of the following year, when he was hoping to have returned from the campaign. Already in January, the king gave strict orders to the counties to pay the taxes due to the treasury on time.[127]

In Transylvania, John Hunyadi was ahead of him in terms of preparations. In March, he requested wagons and gunpowder from Braşov, renewing in the same month its privilege of trade with Wallachia. This reflects the good relations between Transylvania and Wallachia, which was probably ruled at the time by Basarab II.[128] In April and June he repeated his requests to Braşov, asking for cannons as well. He used money received from Branković, but also his own money, to gather an army, which consisted of many Czechs, Poles, Serbians, Romanians, and, certainly, his own Transylvanian troops. The recruitment of up to one-third of the army that was going to participate in this campaign was a result of Hunyadi's personal efforts. He also al-

---

[127]Fejér, op. cit., pp. 52-54.

[128]Cf. Francisc Pall, *Iancu de Hunedoara şi confirmarea privileguilui pentru negoţul braşovenilor...*, pp. 78-79.

lowed a number of serfs to join the army. He managed to gather around 10,000-12,000 men who, together with royal troops, Serbian and Wallachian help, and volunteers from among the liberated populations who had joined the army during its advance, raised the total number of the soldiers to 35,000. John Hunyadi tried for the first time to use on a large scale the transportation wagons, equipped "in the Czech way." But the Hungarian noblemen were against it and, therefore, not even all of the 600 wagons that had been prepared were used. Sometime in June or July of 1443 news came to Hungary of a severe defeat suffered by Murad II in Asia Minor in his attempt to suppress the rebellious emirate of Carmania, which had even offered an alliance with Hungary.[129] The time appeared, therefore, favorable to the opening of hostilities. The king left Buda on 22 July, accompanied by the royal troops and those of a few magnates, by a Polish cavalry detachment and units of Czech mercenaries, which also included adventurers from other countries. There was also a small detachment of crusaders brought by Cesarini. At Kubin (Keve), on the Danube, the army of John Hunyadi met with the small army gathered by George Branković. The entrance into the territory occupied by the Ottomans was put off until the end of September. This delay, which the historical sources attribute to the prolongation of the negotiations for an armistice with Jan Jiskra (until 1 September),[130] and which caused the hostilities to take place in the fall and winter, was later generally considered a mistake. Indeed, it caused great difficulties for the campaign, but John Hunyadi did not permit such a delay without certain calculations. He knew that wintertime would render difficult the movements of the Ottoman army, maybe even more so than those of his own army. Usually, the Ottomans did not fight in the winter, nor did they expect to be attacked any longer during this season. Therefore, Hunyadi took into consideration the element of surprise when, only at the end of September, he ordered his army to cross the Danube. The army advanced toward the southeast.

---

[129]Francisc Pall, Le condizioni..., pp. 456-459.

[130]See the text of the armistice, valid until 29 September 1444, in Teleki, *op. cit.*, X, pp. 135-139.

John Hunyadi was leading the vanguard. He encountered no resistance until the Morava River. At the crossing of this river, the bey of Semendria, the same Ishakbey whom Hunyadi had defeated two years earlier, tried to stop his advance but was overcome and forced back across the Morava. With 12,000 better cavalrymen, as well as with his Transylvanian troops and those of Nicholas Ujlaki,[131] Hunyadi crossed the Morava and sets to pursuing the Ottomans, with the purpose of impeding the arrival of troops of different Ottoman beys from the regions of Vidin and Niš, who wanted to stop his progress toward Sofia. Advancing quickly, his vanguard occupied the city of Niš, and in the neighboring area it defeated, one after the other, three Ottoman detachments whose mission had probably been to reunite in Niš; but the impetuous advance of John Hunyadi took them by surprise.[132] When he was in Niš, Hunyadi received the news that the sultan had personally left Adrianople to confront him. Murad II had managed to conclude a peace with the emir of Carmania. Hunyadi went back to the bulk of the army, which was advancing slowly upstream along the Morava, because it had been announced that another Ottoman army, "coming from the left,"[133] was approaching the royal army. This Ottoman army was joined by the detachments that had been defeated by Hunyadi in the previous days. Hunyadi's letter from 8 November 1443, addressed to Ujlaki, enumerates 10 beys whose units formed the army. The return of the voievod to the north proved opportune. He arrived in time to contribute to the defeat of that Ottoman force as well, capturing and killing more beys and afterwards presenting the king with prisoners and enemy flags. His victories gave rise to great enthusiasm, which was immediately expressed in ornate letters to the pope and the Euro-

---

[131]"...et vestra, simul nobiscum familia...," says Hunyadi in a letter to Nicholas Ujlaki dated 8 November 1443, an important source for the first part of the campaign, Hurmuzaki, I. 2, p. 687.

[132]The letter indicates a certain Esebec (recte Ezembeg – Hassan-bey?), a Turkanibeg (= Turakhan-bey), and a "*novus bassa*," whose name is not mentioned, as commanders of the detachments that were defeated by Hunyadi on the banks of the Morava, in the vicinity of Niš.

[133]Hurmuzaki, I. 2, p. 687.

pean courts. The exaltation that had seized the camp could not be shaken by the news of the sultan's approach.

During its advance toward Niš the royal army was joined by numerous contingents of Serbians from the occupied territory who wanted to participate in driving the Ottomans from their lands. A small Wallachian detachment also came to the region, probably led by Mircea, a son of Vlad Dracul. Under circumstances that are still unclear, Vlad Dracul had regained the throne, probably sometime between March and October 1443.[134] By setting him free from his captivity, the sultan was hoping, to all appearances, to prevent Wallachia from joining the anti-Ottoman campaign that was being prepared. However, Vlad Dracul immediately inclined in favor of John Hunyadi, but it appears that he did not want to participate personally, nor to engage himself too much. He was probably afraid of a defeat which would have been fatal to him. He was also held back by his concern for the fate of his sons, who had remained hostages of the Ottomans. The sultan, trying to convince him not to participate in the campaign, had offered to set the two boys free.

Resuming his advance beyond Niš on 20 November, the Transylvanian voievod won a new victory. 2,000 Ottomans lay dead on the battlefield; Hunyadi's army took 4,000 prisoners and rich spoils. The remainder of the enemy army, scattered in the mountains and in the woods, had to suffer the fury of the local population. The road to Sofia was thus opened and the city was occupied. The Balkan peoples became excited by the hope of their liberation which appeared close. In the previously-mentioned letter to Ujlaki, Hunyadi mentions that the local population welcomed them everywhere with gifts and food, so that the soldiers hardly used the supplies they had brought along. The camp of the king became filled with Bulgarians, Bosnians, Serbians,

[134]Francisc Pall, *Iancu de Hunedoara şi confirmarea privilegiului braşovenilor…*, p. 78.

and Albanians.[135] The Ottomans could no longer trust the Bulgarian villages in the Balkans which, invested by them with certain privileges, had the mission to defend the mountain passes. Certain towns in Bulgaria surrendered willingly to John Hunyadi. According to the sources from that time, the population was very much set against its oppressors.

In Albania, some local leaders rebelled. An Albanian nobleman who had been taken hostage by the Ottomans when he was young and had been educated in their language and their religion, was serving in the Ottoman army. His name was George Castriota. His father had been the ruler of the region and the fortress of Croya, in Albania. The young man had distinguished himself in the eyes of the Ottomans through his military qualities. They called him Scanderbeg. He now served in the Ottoman army which was headed to confront John Hunyadi. At the news of the defeats that took place in November, Scanderbeg, taking advantage of the confusion that seized the Ottomans, found the opportunity, for which he had waited for seven years, to escape to Albania, to Croya, where he took possession of his father's fortress and became the leader of the fight for the liberation of the Albanian people, which he led for more than twenty years. The Serbians in the mining region of Novobrdo rebelled as well. In the south of Greece, Despot Dragas, the future emperor of Byzantium, Constantine XII Dragases, was preparing to attack the Ottomans.[136] From Sofia, the mission of the army of Hunyadi was becoming more and more difficult. It was wintertime, provisioning was difficult, and the roads were in bad condition. Ahead of them there rose the snowy peaks of the Balkans. Their steep and narrow passes, well-protected by the Ottomans, who had

---

[135]Hurmuzaki, I. 2, pp. 687-688. The ending of this letter reveals the hesitation of certain higher noblemen, one of whom was Ujlaki, to participate in this campaign. Hunyadi, finding out that Ujlaki "was feeling somewhat better" (probably a pretext invoked by the latter for not going to fight), urges him insistently to join the army, to thus do his duty toward the king; he warns him not to listen to those who might advise him otherwise, because they are traitors.

[136]Francisc Pall, "Un moment décisif de l'histoire du sud-est européen: la croisade de Varna," in *Balcania*, VII (1944), p. 106.

concentrated there the bulk of their army under the command of the sultan, had to be crossed for them to be able to penetrate toward Adrianople and Constantinople. Always in the vanguard, John Hunyadi was already advancing, on 3 December, toward the passes. He did not take the shortest route, toward Philippopolis and Adrianople, through the valley of the Maritsa, where he expected a more aggressive resistance, but headed east, through the Balkan range proper and Sredna Gora. The sultan managed to close the passes in this direction as well. An important war council was held in his camp. Murad II was for a decisive battle. Kasâm-pasha, the beylerbey of Rumelia, supported him. Turakhan, the bey of Thessaly, had a different opinion. He argued that the morale of the army was very weak, with the exception of the janissaries, who were risking though to remain fighting alone, "like a bird without wings." That is why Turakhan proposed that they retreat, devastating everything in their way, and waiting for the lack of supplies and the cold to gradually make Hunyadi's army easier to defeat. A third Ottoman commander proposed that they resist on the spot, using their position in the mountains, and, when the enemies would be forced to retreat, to harass and destroy them, using the cavalry. This last plan was adopted. On 12 December 1443, the army of Hunyadi was in the village of Zlatitsa, facing a pass fortified by the Ottomans with dirt, stockades, and cut down trees.[137] Seeing the small number of Hunyadi's army, the Ottomans renounced their initial plan and attacked. The great vizier Halil Pasha said with contempt that he owned more buffaloes in his herds than the soldiers he could see in front of him. It was a difficult situation for the Transylvanian voievod: he was confronting the fierce enemy far from home, in a mountainous, unfamiliar place, in cold, snowy weather. Before the battle, John Hunyadi might have ad-

[137]Vasile Grecu, the translator and editor of Chalkokondyles's work, *Expuneri istorice* (*Historical Chronicles*), affirms, based on the work of Akdes Himet, *Die türkische prosopographie bei Laonikos Chalkokondyles*, Hamburg, 1933, that "Izlati", identified with Zlatitsa, was near Niš; cf. Chalkokondyles, op. cit., pp. 184, note 1. The majority of the historians agree, however, that this place was east of Sofia. The Byzantine chronicler Ducas, in *Istoria turco-bizantină,* București, 1958, places "Izlati" halfway between Sofia and Philippopolis, cf. p. 272.

dressed his soldiers with these words: "Be brave! It is better to lose our lives than to lose the fight! Are you frightened by the number of the enemies? You have seen many times the strength of their morale: of those who so many times ran away from us... we can drive them away again!"[138] He told them that after crossing the mountains they would reach the plains of Thrace, where things would be easier than in the devastated places they would have left behind. Retreat would have meant losing everything they had accomplished until then, because the enemies would reconquer everything, and this at a time when Europe was almost completely free of them. Hunyadi led the battle himself. Encouraged by his words and his example, the soldiers fought fiercely and drove the Ottomans back to their fortified positions in the mountains.[139] In the following days, the army of Hunyadi tried to force their way across the mountains. The soldiers were cutting down trees to make their way ahead, while the Ottomans were covering them in arrows from their high positions. The cold and hunger were becoming stronger all the time. In the second half of the month, probably on 23 December, after an encounter with the sultan himself, the king gave orders to retreat. According to their plan, the Ottomans set out to pursue with an army led by the beys Kasâm and Turakhan. The sultan was coming fast behind them, only three march stages behind. John Hunyadi was again leading the section that was threatened the most: the rear guard. Thinking that the retreat from Zlatitsa meant the demoralization and rout of the enemy, Kasam and Turakhan did not wait for reinforcements and advanced imprudently and on 24 December they attacked the rear guard, somewhere near Melstitsa. But they did not

[138]Thuróczi, in *Scriptores*, I, p. 416. The authenticity of the speech is doubtful. It is a method transmitted from the ancient historians through which heroes found it difficult moments are attributed words that are in accordance with the situations described by the chronicles.

[139]According to the Turkish chronicler Orudj-bin-Adil, Kasâm-pasha was defeated there and Mahmud Çelebi, the brother of the Great Vizier Halil, was captured; cf. Guboglu-Mehmet, *op. cit.*, pp. 55. Another chronicler, Mehmed Neshri (*Ibidem*, p. 123), as well as the Byzantine chronicler Chalkokondyles affirm that the defeat of Kasâm-pasha took place later on, during the pursuit of John Hunyadi.

take into consideration the tenacity of the Transylvanian voievod. The Ottomans found themselves facing an army that was ready for battle instead of the scattered and discouraged one they were expecting to find. The two beys were defeated, the sultan decided not to attack, but limited himself to ordering a pursuit from a distance. Turakhan-bey was found responsible for the imprudence that had led to defeat. He was removed from command and imprisoned, in Asia Minor.[140] The army of John Hunyadi retreated further, beyond Sofia and Pirot, toward the northwest. They suffered a great deal. Most of their horses died, the cold was bitter, food could not be found in a region which had just been crossed by two armies only six weeks earlier.

Between Bela Palanka and Niš, near Kunovitsa, the troops of the Serbian despot were taken by surprise and scattered by an Ottoman attack. John Hunyadi and the bulk of his army hurried to help. On 2 January 1444, another defeat of Beylerbey Kasâm[141] showed the Ottomans that the retreating army was not defeated or disorganized, and that it had remained a powerful force. It was probably only then that Mahmud Çelebi, the brother of Great Vizier Halil and the brother-in-law of the sultan, was captured, because the chronicles say that following this episode the battles ceased. The sultan, persuaded by the tears of his sister, the wife of Mahmud Çelebi, offered peace to be able to redeem his brother-in-law. On the plain of Dobrogić, west of Niš, Ottoman messengers caught up with King Ladislas and offered peace in very advantageous conditions. They proposed the cessation of hostilities for twenty to thirty years, the retroceding of Serbia, of the fortresses of Semendria and Golubac, and the repatriation of the two blinded sons of Branković. The despot was insisting on the continuation of the war and offered 40,000 florins for this purpose. It appears that the king was tempted for a while to spend the winter in Serbia and to begin the war again in the spring. It was, however, an unrealistic plan to which John Hunyadi was opposed. The army had gone through too many se-

140 Chalkokondyles, *op. cit.*, p. 188.

141 Ibidem, pp. 187-188.

vere difficulties during the retreat. Their horses had died and almost all their wagons had had to be burned.

The Ottoman offer did not lead to direct peace negotiations, but the king did not remain in Serbia either. On 6 January 1444 Hunyadi was in Prokopje. The king was near Kruševac on 13 January, near Jagodina on 20 January, and entered Belgrade on 25 January. After 8 days, on 2 February 1444, Ladislas I, John Hunyadi, and the army were received festively in Buda. The crowd gathered on the streets, marveling at the trophies they were bringing: weapons, flags, and prisoners. Thirteen Ottoman commanders and four thousand prisoners were marching behind the army. A solemn service of gratitude was celebrated in the church of the fortress of Buda, during which the young king entered the church and walked barefoot to the altar, as a sign of humble gratitude for the victory that had been "granted" to him. Certain noblemen were generously rewarded by the king. Among those – with the exception of John Hunyadi, who in this campaign had all the merit of an army commander – no one had distinguished himself in an exceptional way. Nevertheless, it was ordered that the blazons of twelve higher noblemen who had participated in the battles be displayed, as a sign of appreciation, on the walls of the Church of Virgin Mary of the fortress of Buda. Among them there was the coat of arms of John Hunyadi and, next to it, that of Cardinal Cesarini. Even earlier, the news of the victories had spread throughout the West. In Rome, on 10 January 1444, a letter written by Cesarini was read during a meeting of the bishops, and on the following Sunday a religious service was celebrated in honor of the victory. A rumor circulated throughout Italy that Adrianople had been occupied and a son of the sultan had been captured. Delegates of the pope, of Philip, the duke of Burgundy, of Genoa and Venice, of the Byzantine Emperor John Palaiologus, soon arrived in Buda. They were bringing congratulations and praises for the victories that had been obtained, together with new plans for the continuation of the war. Some of them resumed the project of sending a fleet to the Straits to prevent the army of the sultan to cross from Asia into Europe. The Byzantines were promising to attack the Ottomans from behind, trapping them between themselves and the army of the king of Hungary, which was supposed to advance into Bulgaria again.

The campaign of the winter of 1443-1444 was called "the long campaign." The name was appropriate for that time, when feudal armies generally carried on very short campaigns, which lasted a month or two, after which they would return to their camps. This time, Hunyadi's army was in continuous action for more than six months, four months of which on foreign territory, fighting seven major, victorious battles, both during its advance, as well as while retreating. It penetrated into enemy territory more than 300 kilometers from the point where it had crossed the Danube, as far as Zlatitsa. The Ottomans suffered repeated defeats in the open field, had to withdraw from Serbia and the western part of Bulgaria, and had to fight, with all their might and means, to defend the roads to their capital. They had never before faced such a situation since their arrival in Europe. A Turkish chronicler observes that "never had the Muslims suffered so much from the cunning and malice of the *giaours*."[142]

The Ottoman world was terrified. In December 1443 news arrived in Venice that the Ottomans on the coasts neighboring the island of Corfu were panicked by the victories of the Christian army and were making haste to fortify Valona, Argyrokastron, and other fortresses in Albania and Epirus, which appears also to have been the consequence of the Albanian rebellion. From Jerusalem news came that the sultan of Egypt had ordered his fleet, found on the coasts of Syria, to set sail for Egypt to defend Cairo if they heard that John Hunyadi entered Asia Minor.

In Hungary, Transylvania, and Wallachia the victories against the Ottomans contributed to the strengthening of royal power. The prestige of John Hunyadi was increasing. All the forces interested in defending the country against the danger from the outside and in maintaining the peace within the country by annihilating the anarchic tendencies of the great barons gathered around him. At this time, a "party" of John Hun-

[142]Guboglu-Mehmet, *op. cit.*, p. 345.

yadi took shape, with a general "program" along the lines mentioned above. The ideas of this party were expressed by some younger representatives of the clergy, from the ranks of the lower and middle nobility who were exposed to classic literature which was being revived in Italy. Among them was John of Zredna, a personal friend of John Hunyadi. These first representatives, in Hungary, of the new "Humanist" culture would support the idea of a struggle against Ottoman occupation, connecting it to that of the necessity to defend the Christian religion, the common civilization, and cultural heritage of the European peoples.

CHAPTER VII

VARNA

In April 1444, the King Ladislas obtained a new prolongation of the armistice with Jan Jiskra. Temporarily, the rear of the Hungarian army was again protected in case war would begin again on the southern front. As an effect of the victories won during "the long campaign," the king of Bosnia, Stepan Tomas, signed a treaty with John Hunyadi, hoping to strengthen the possibilities to unify his country and to defend it against the Ottomans.

At the same time, when hopes of liberation for the peoples in the Balkans were being reborn, projects that had been abandoned in previous years were now resumed: those of a common anti-Ottoman campaign of the European peoples.

At the beginning of March, 1444, the sultan renewed his offers of peace, initiated in January. The Albanian rebellion, led by Scanderbeg, which proved extremely successful, was one of the important reasons for his insistence. This time the interventions were made by one of his wives, Mara, the daughter of George Branković.[143] They did not have an immediate result, but would not remain without effect on the complicated future evolution of diplomatic events.

In April, during a meeting of the Diet, they discussed the problem of resuming the war during 1444. The Polish entourage of the king was, partly, against this idea. The Polish noblemen were displeased

[143]Francisc Pall, *Ciriaco d'Ancona e la crociata contro I Turchi*, Vălenii de Munte, 1937, p. 19; idem, *Marino Barlezio, uno storico umanista*, Bucureşti, 1938, p. 89.

with the long absence of King Ladislas from Poland and with his more intense interest in Hungary. In Poland, internal revolts and Tartar invasions had occurred which required the presence of the king in the country. However, there was another opinion, held by those Polish noblemen who wanted to take advantage of the personal union between Hungary and Poland, with a view to a common expansion toward the Balkans, to thus ensure their domination over this geographic area. Of the same opinion were some of the Hungarian upper nobility, encouraged by the victories won in "the Long Campaign," as well as the lesser noblemen, who were concerned with the security of the kingdom and wished to distinguish themselves through merits won on the battlefield. The second opinion won out and the organization of a new campaign was decided. On 15 April 1444, Ladislas swore a solemn oath, in the presence of Cardinal Cesarini, that in that year he would set out with his army "toward Greece and Romania."

From then on, the diplomatic actions of the king followed a sinuous path, difficult to follow and to explain. On 24 April 1444, secretly and probably acceding to the insistences of Branković, to whom the sultan had promised to return his country, Ladislas entrusted his messenger Stoica Gizdavić with the mission to go to Adrianople to negotiate peace with the Ottomans. He was accompanied by a certain Vitislav, considered a messenger of John Hunyadi, and by two representatives of Branković, which points out the role of mediator played by the Serbian despot. Sometime around 4 June, the delegation arrived at Adrianople and on 12 June 1444 they signed a peace treaty with the sultan, which would afterwards be ratified by Ladislas. The treaty was signed for ten years, and included Serbia and Wallachia in its provisions, the latter being subject to a regime of vassalage divided between the Ottoman Empire and Hungary.

Under the influence of the contrary opinions among the upper nobility, and also because of the lack of scruples of the diplomacy of the time, the king did not halt his preparations to resume the war. Some saw in his behavior the spirit of duplicity characteristic of the diplomacy of the Renaissance, others saw the medieval tradition, servient to the religious mentality which tended to consider as invalid any agreements made with Muslim "infidels."

In any case, during the mission of Gizdavić, preparations for the campaign continued. An intense diplomatic activity took place in the spring and summer of 1444. Each of the Western powers was hoping to profit by the battle that was going to take place by offering small help, hoping to take hold of new possessions in the Balkans, while the Hungarians, Romanians, Serbians, Albanians, and Bulgarians would bear the brunt of the campaign.

Venice was hoping to conquer Thessalonika and the Gallipoli Peninsula, and also to take hold of Janina, Argyrokastron, and Valona, in northwestern Greece and southern Albania. Ragusa was also making calculations concerning the territorial annexations it could make. King Alphonse of Aragon was hoping to obtain Athens and Patras, and was even thinking of the Gallipoli Peninsula, which was demanded at the same time by Venice. All these plans were hidden behind the cover of the "help" offered by the Western states to Byzantium for the "rebuilding of the empire," for "driving out of infidels" and the "victory of the Christian religion."

The most important actual help that the Western states committed themselves to give was the equipping of a fleet that would be sent to the Straits and, if need be, all the way to the Danube. The promises were great. At the beginning of May, 1444, King Ladislas wrote to the great master of the Teutonic order that the pope would send thirty-eight galleys, Venice would send twelve, Aragon ten, Burgundy six, Milan eight, the great master of the Johannine monks on the island of Rhodes would send two galleys. The reality was much more modest, although the king had written, throughout the whole summer, to different European courts, requesting them to speed up and to increase their promised help. Cardinal Cesarini was also engaged in an active diplomatic correspondence, especially with Venice. The republic, as well as the pope, were delaying the preparations for various reasons. The Venetian Senate was asking for formal guarantees from the king of Hungary that he would advance toward Constantinople with a powerful terrestrial army. Under different conditions, it was not willing to engage its ships in the campaign. The papal delegate to Venice, Condulmer, was using the funds gathered from the tithes for the preparation of the papal ships for other purposes and was thus delaying the progress of the preparations. Eventually, about eight or ten Italian and four or five Burgundian galleys were gathered under the command of Walerand of Wavrin, to which two ships from Ragusa were added. The commander of the fleet was the Venetian Aloisio Loredano, and that of the papal galleys was Francesco Condulmer. At the end of June or the beginning of July the fleet set sail toward Constantinople.

During this time, preparations continued in Hungary as well. Cesarini, taking advantage of the relative normalization of the relations with Frederick III, following some negotiations that had taken place in May, was hoping for help from him as well. His hopes were shattered. The emperor and the imperial Diet that was held in Nuremberg refused to give any sort of help, committing themselves to neutrality at most.

In May, the plans for the future campaign were also studied in the king's council. Cesarini presented a plan through which he was trying to avoid some of the difficulties encountered during "the long campaign." He suggested that the army not cross the Danube too far west, and not even at Orşova, but to advance through Wallachia and cross the river at Nicopolis. For this purpose, they were to ask for the cooperation of the Italian and Burgundian fleets. From there they were to go south-east, toward the sea and, going around the Balkans on their east side, to advance toward Adrianople and Constantinople. This plan was intended to shorten the distance covered by the army on enemy territory, to thus protect themselves from prolonged harassments by the Ottomans and to avoid the passes in the mountains, which had proved difficult in the previous battles.

Apart from the fleet in the Straits, they counted on the help of George Branković, of Wallachia, on an attack from the west by Scanderbeg's Albanians, and on an effort by Byzantium to hamper the rear of the Ottoman front. The preparations had to be finished by July. Oradea was established as the gathering place for the army. On 20 July

1444, John Hunyadi asked the inhabitants of Braşov for reins with silver ornaments for the forthcoming campaign. At the beginning of July, Ladislas informed Florence of the forthcoming campaign, and on 24 July he informed he king of Bosnia of the same thing. The next day he left Buda, heading for Seghedin.[144]

During the spring and summer of the same year, one could notice a tendency toward the strengthening of relations among the Romanian lands, beginning with commercial ties. In May and August 1444, both Stephen II of Moldavia and Vlad Dracul of Wallachia regulated their commercial relations with Transylvania. Vlad Dracul confirmed, on 7 August 1444, the privilege granted to Braşov by John Hunyadi on 2 March 1443, which demonstrates the good relations between the voievods of Wallachia and Transylvania. Vlad Dracul was being asked insistently to participate in the campaign, but he hesitated. The Ottomans had recently returned his hostage sons for the precise purpose of winning him over. Reluctantly, he decided to offer a contingent of 4,000 men, which he wanted to place under the command of his eldest son Mircea.

Branković, however, opposed any collaboration. After "the Long Campaign" he recovered a large part of his country and was not bothered by the Ottomans any longer. He remained firm on respecting the secret negotiations at Adrianople. Now he found it convenient to rely on the Ottomans, for the purpose of taking back the fortress of Golubac from Hungary and a region near the Adriatic Sea from Venice. He strengthened his relations with the sultan, who was his son-in-law, and offered him an enormous tribute in exchange for his two blinded sons, and agreed to support the ratification of the peace between the Ottoman Empire and Hungary.

The procrastination and reduction of the help promised by the West, and the extremely favorable peace terms that Murad II had offered to Hungary, determined King Ladislas to ratify the treaty with the Ottomans. Messengers of the sultan arrived in Seghedin at the end of

---

[144] Francisc Pall, *Un moment décisif…*, pp. 111-112.

July and presented, in the presence of the king, the final clauses: the cessation of any reciprocal attacks for ten years, the evacuation by the Ottomans of the territories and fortresses in Serbia and northern Albania, the reciprocal returning of prisoners without any ransom payments, with the exception of the sultan's brother-in-law, Mahmud Çelebi, for whom Murad was offering an important sum of money. The Ottomans were also offering to pay a compensation of 100,000 gold *scuzi* and military assistance in case of war.

Ladislas, faced with such an advantageous proposal, signed the treaty. John Hunyadi was among the supporters of peace. His enemies insinuated that he was bought by Branković, who would have offered him the estates the despot owned in Hungary in exchange for his support of the peace treaty. It was true that in the spring of 1444, as compensation for what he had personally spent for the organization of the army for the campaign against the Ottomans, Branković had ceded to John Hunyadi the fortress of Şiria, which included over two hundred villages, in the area of Zarand and Arad.[145]

In fact, the Transylvanian voievod had not let himself be corrupted by anyone. He only realized how exhausted the country was, how much the last battles had cost it, and how difficult it was to make alliances and to obtain help from the outside.

After the peace treaty, written and sealed, had been concluded in Seghedin, Cesarini received news, on 30 or 31 July, which he had no longer expected, that the promised and long postponed fleet had left Venice toward the Straits. He immediately approached the king, urging him not to respect the treaty he had signed. He was also supported by part of the noblemen, reckless and adventurous, who were deceiving themselves into believing in an easy victory. Cesarini was trying to attract the king also with the news that the sultan had crossed with his army into Asia Minor, on 12 July, to suppress the revolts that had broken out in Carmania. If the fleet managed to block the Straits, it meant

[145]Fejér, *op. cit.*, pp. 74-75. Hunyadi was made owner of this estate on 20 March 1445; Teleki, *op. cit.*, X, pp. 159-164.

that the Ottomans would not be able to bring their army back to Europe and this would make it very easy to get to Constantinople. John Hunyadi, for the same reasons for which he had supported the signing of the peace treaty, showed reservation toward its violation, but he implied that he would submit to the king's decision. "I listen to the ruler, I do not rule," these were words attributed to him in relation to his attitude regarding the diplomatic intrigues of that summer.[146]

The cardinal objected to the remorse that the king invoked against breaking his promise – that of keeping peace – by saying that an oath made to the infidels had no validity. At the same time, letters of protest arrived from the Byzantine emperor, who was discontented with the signing of the peace treaty.

These insistences convinced the king to break the advantageous treaty and to choose instead the risk of a new war. On 4 August, he swore another oath in front of Cesarini, pledging himself to set for the Danube immediately. John Hunyadi, in accordance with the line of conduct he had undertaken, accepted the change in the situation, but we do not know with how much conviction. It is clear that he did not want to offend the king with too independent an attitude.

The breaking of the Seghedin Treaty was a mistake, given its advantageous conditions. Serbia chose neutrality, which in a few years would transform into an openly hostile policy. The Serbian despot signed a separate peace treaty with the Ottomans on 15 August, regaining the territories and fortresses he had lost in the previous years, and on 22 August he installed himself again in Semendria. The common fighting front of the peoples in southeastern Europe was thus weakening as a result of the mistake of the king of Hungary, of part of his entourage, and of the Pope's representative.

---

[146]Ducas, *op. cit.*, p. 273. With these words, according to the chronicler, John Hunyadi refused to fulfil the request of the Ottoman messengers to ratify himself, separately, the Treaty of Seghedin. This request indicates the great prestige that Hunyadi enjoyed, as well as, probably, the impression of independence that he gave to Ottomans due to his frequent presence in Transylvania and Wallachia.

The general state of mind in Hungary was less than enthusiastic. People were tired of the battles of the previous years. Because this was an offensive war, to be fought outside of the borders of the country, the noblemen would not participate. Only the bishop's troops and John Hunyadi's Transylvanian army joined the royal army.

The news of the Treaty of Seghedin caused confusion in the states that were directly interested in the project for a campaign against the Ottomans. On 8 September Venice sent instructions to the commander of the fleet, Loredano, to find out what the movements of the Hungarian army were and, if it was advancing in the Balkans, to support its action. Otherwise, the republic was not going to fight the war alone. In this case, Loredano would have to send a messenger to the sultan, assuring him of the peaceful intentions of the doge and the senate and blaming the pope for the initiative to go to war. He would have to ask, therefore, for the confirmation of the previous peace treaty, after which the fleet would return to Venice.

When Loredano received this order at the middle of October, it was already known on the ships that the king of Hungary had set out against the Ottomans. Cesarini had hurried to send three emissaries, dressed like Ottomans, who made their way into Constantinople, spreading the news of the denunciation of the Treaty of Seghedin and the resumption of the war by Hungary. Thus, the Western fleet began the blockade of Bosphorus and Hellespont (Dardanelles), although the Ottomans, entering in discussions with the commanders, tried to turn them back by showing them the sealed document of the peace of Seghedin.

After the decision was made to resume the war, John Hunyadi went, after 4 August, to Transylvania, to make final preparations. The king went to Oradea, together with Cesarini. The royal army left Oradea after 28 August. On 9 September, it was in Orşova, from where more letters and emissaries were sent to Italy requesting support for the campaign that had been initiated.

On 20 September 1444, John Hunyadi sent from Orşova a document of confirmation of the privileges of the Monastery of Tismana.

This fact proves, beyond doubt, the authority Hunyadi held in Wallachia, but it was not a novelty. Sigismund of Luxembourg had issued similar documents for monasteries in Wallachia in 1419 and 1428.[147]

On 20 September, and in the following days, the army crossed the Danube at Orşova, regrouping on the right bank. Afterwards, they aligned, marching along the river. The army was formed of soldiers from Hungary, and of royal and episcopal troops; there were many Romanians in the Transylvanian troops under the personal command of John Hunyadi. There were also Croatian troops, commanded by Ban Franko of Talovak. The army was advancing, in the manner of the Czech Hussites, followed by a long line of wagons, around 2,000, of which 800 were for transportation.[148]

On its way, the Hungarian army occupied Cladova. At the beginning of October[149] it arrived near Vidin, the strongest Ottoman fortress in those parts, which was the residence of a formidable bey by the name of Sinan. John Hunyadi did not have siege machines, nor did he want to waste time conquering every fortress. He only occupied the city, without attacking the fortress, and the Ottomans did not dare come out of it. Afterwards he passed through Rahova, toward Nicopolis, where the army, advancing along the right bank of the Danube, arrived on 16 October. This fortress was not occupied either.

There Hunyadi's army was joined by the army sent by Vlad Dracul, as well as by a new Transylvanian detachment which came directly through Wallachia. The Wallachian voievod personally came to Nicopolis, but he was rather distrustful. A day before, while passing through a village, an old Bulgarian fortune teller had told him that the king would not be successful in the fight. Seeing the Hungarian army worried him even more. He advised the king to return, telling him that "the Ottoman sultan, even when he goes hunting, brings along more

---

[147] *Documenta Romaniae Historica*, B. *Ţara Românească*, vol. I (1247-1500), pp. 92-93, 93-95, 118-122, and 168-171.

[148] Mihail Dan, *op. cit.*, p. 108.

[149] The Polish chronicler Długosz say that it was "the sixth day after they left Orşova."

soldiers than the ones gathered in the Christian army." The advice of the Romanian prince, who knew Ottoman power well, was ignored, just as the haughty Burgundian knights had ignored the advice that his father, Mircea the Old, had given them, in the same place, almost fifty years before.[150]

At Nicopolis, the army left the bank of the Danube and began a forced march toward the seashore. The soldiers encountered on their way stones with old Greek and Latin inscriptions. They occupied Razgrad and on a river, there they took by surprise and destroyed twenty-eight Ottoman ships which were supposed to go on the Danube and hinder the advance of the Hungarian army. On 24 October, the king sent a letter to the Ottoman commanders in Šumla, Matrovac, Petrets, Varna, Cavarna, and Galata,[151] summoning them to surrender. In the following days, they occupied the localities of Jeni-Bazar and Šumla, which was well fortified. From there, a detachment was sent to plunder, and they went all the way to Trnovo, on the Jantra River. Tass-Hissar and Pravadi were occupied next. Some Turkish chronicles mention that, on its way to Varna, the army of Hunyadi was attacked by the bey of Nicopolis.[152] From the fact that the advance continued, we deduce that the attack was repelled.

During the conquest of the fortress of Petrets, the Wallachian soldiers distinguished themselves. After having tried unsuccessfully to take the walls by assault by using ladders, they found out about the existence of an underground passage through which the Ottomans could secretly go into town. The army hurried in that direction and caught the Ottomans who were trying to escape.

In the first week of November, they conquered the fortress of "Mihelici," which could have been Mualici or Caliacra. The Greeks in

---

[150]It appears that the Wallachian prince did not participate personally in this campaign, but left his son Mircea in command of 4,000 soldiers.

[151]Localities in northeastern Bulgaria.

[152]Guboglu-Mehmet, *op. cit.*, p. 183.

those parts gave to the king of Hungary the keys to four neighboring fortresses.

The approach of the Hungarian army had caused panic among the Ottomans in Europe. The rich merchants in Adrianople and Gallipoli fled to Asia Minor, all the way to Brusa.

Hunyadi continued his advance toward Varna, where he arrived on 9 November. Shortly before his arrival, he received alarming news: the sultan, whom they thought to be in Asia Minor, prevented by the Italian and Burgundian fleet from entering Europe, had managed to cross the Straits and was approaching fast, with his entire army, being only a few days away.

How could this have happened, shattering all their hopes? The plan to block the Straits with a number of 14 to 16 galleys was, in fact, a naiveté. The Dardanelles and the Bosphorus had a total length of over 80 kilometers, and, at certain points, the Bosphorus had a width of only 550 meters, so that the cannons on the shore could keep the ships within their range. Thus, the number of galleys proved insufficient for blocking the Straits.

Sultan Murad II had hastily signed peace with the emir of Carmania,[153] returning to command the army on the Asian shore of Bosphorus. On 15 October, he sent the great vizier, Halil-pasha, to occupy the European shore of the Bosphorus, at the spot chosen for crossing, with an army of 7,000-8,000 men. Genoese merchants were constantly informing him about the movements of the Western fleet and they also promised him boats to enable the crossing of his army. The commander of the Burgundian galleys, Wavrin, and the commander of the papal fleet, Condulmer, asked the Byzantines to send urgently infantry troops to attack the great vizier. The Byzantines did not fulfil their request. They only sent two galleys to strengthen the fleet. Some of the Western ships had just left to bring provisions from the islands in the Aegean Archipelago. The Ottomans had begun to bombard the fleet from both the Asian and the European shores, from Anatoli Hissar. They

[153] Chalkokondyles, *op. cit.*, p. 194.

were also firing a big cannon which was throwing enormous boulders, but fortunately it broke at the third blow. On the evening of 26 October, a violent storm broke out and scattered the Western ships. When they regrouped, with difficulty, the bulk of the Turkish army was already getting into the boats and a powerful cannon fire stopped the galleys from intervening. In two days and two nights, on 27-28 October, the Ottoman army crossed over to the European shore. With all the justifications of the fleet commanders, who showed the difficulties they had encountered – the insufficiency of the means of battle and the unfortunate circumstances that prevented them from fulfilling their mission –, they were still suspected and even accused of having allowed themselves to be corrupted by the sultan.[154]

The Ottoman army headed directly toward Adrianople, where it arrived at the beginning of November. From there, in 6 days – according to the Turkish chronicles – it arrived at Varna. This means that the Ottomans took the shortest route to meet the enemy, through the Nadir Derbent Pass and through Pravadi, and from this last locality took the route covered by Hunyadi a day or two before.

On the night of 9-10 November one could see the fires of the Ottoman camp lighting up the western and southern horizon. King Ladislas held a council of war. He was in a difficult situation. His army was made up of 15,000-16,000 soldiers[155] and was facing the entire army of the *sul*tan. Cesarini thought that they should build a fortification with the wagons and try to resist inside of it. In the meantime, the Western galleys were going to arrive, which had no more use in the Straits. The fleet would disembark troops behind the Ottoman army, which, thus

[154]For instance, the accusation formulated by Aeneas Sylvius Piccolomini. Many chroniclers maintain that the crossing of the sultan's army was done at Gallipoli (Chalkokondyles, op. cit., p. 194), and also Andrea del Palatino and, after him, Długosz: "*quod classis maritima Apostolica prohibere nequiverit quin Turci furtive noctuque in parvis cymbis per inferiorem partem Phari Gallipoli trajecissent,*" a quotation from Bánlaky, op. cit., pp. 114-116, and notes 330-331. The crossing at Bosphorus is maintained by Ducas, *op. cit.*, pp. 276-277 and, much later, but based on Turkish sources, by Leunclavius.

[155]The highest numbers appreciated stop at 20,000.

caught between two fires, would be defeated. This plan was supported by the bishop of Eger and even by the experienced military man Franco of Talovak.

The voievod of Transylvania spoke next. First of all, he advised everyone to keep their cool. He showed that Cesarini's plan was unrealizable. They could not enclose themselves in a small fortress made out of wagons, in the way of the Hussites, because the Ottomans would have surrounded them and the army did not have enough food supplies for a long resistance. The terrain did not allow provisioning with water. Waiting for the arrival of the fleet which, in the Straits, had already proven its weakness and slowness meant putting their fate in the hands of a very doubtful expectation. Even if the fleet came to Varna, it would only be able to disembark a few soldiers who, besides, were not used to fighting on the ground, and thus they would not create any difficulties for the troops of the sultan.

John Hunyadi concluded that the plan of Cesarini would lead to certain defeat and showed there was only one solution for their situation: not to allow the enemy to realize the inferiority of the army they were facing, not to allow them to spread out their forces, but to attack them violently, to strike terror amidst them through the vigor and quickness of their movements and thus defeat them. Although later on chroniclers, especially the Polish ones, tried to condemn Hunyadi for having supported an open battle, the reality was as he saw it. In the case of a passive defense the only perspective was destruction. By risking battle, they had chances of victory, although – Hunyadi understood it well – the danger remained overwhelming.

On 10 November at dawn, both armies placed themselves in battle positions. The army of John Hunyadi did not arrange its wagons in three lines, as it was usually done; this was done to force all the soldiers to participate in the battle and to prevent them from running away and hiding behind the wagons. The battle line was shaped as an arch, and was about one thousand steps long, closing a valley which had Lake Devina on its left and a range of hills on the right. The left flank, near the lake, was commanded by Michael Szilágyi. It was formed of five big units, amounting to 5,000 soldiers. It contained, among others, the personal troops of Hunyadi, other Transylvanian units, Szecklers, and part of the troops of the Hungarian magnates. At the center, there were the royal troops, two nobiliary units, and a few Polish and mercenary detachments

The right flank was formed of the troops of the ban of Slavonia and those of the prelates. One could see there the flag of Cardinal Cesarini, of the bishops of Bosnia and Eger, and the one with the emblem of Saint Ladislas, which belonged to the bishop of Oradea, John of Dominis. At the back of the center were the Romanians: it was probably from there that John Hunyadi led the battle; the king might also have been there, with about 500 chosen soldiers.[156]

The Ottoman line had the sultan in the middle, with his troops of janissaries. The right flank was formed of the spahis from Rumelia and the left flank was made up of the spahis from Anatolia.[157] Before the front there were light troops, on camels. Historical sources estimate the total number of the Ottomans to have been between 80,000 and 120,000, which is certainly exaggerated.

Early in the morning, a powerful storm broke out in the west. It had hardly abated when, an hour after sunrise, the Ottomans attacked first, charging at the troops of the bishops of Eger and Oradea, of the right flank of the Christian army, along the close-by range of hills. The troops of the two bishops were scattered, ran away, and they were killed. The units of Cesarini and of the ban of Slavonia, Franko of

---

[156]The disposition is analyzed in detail by Bánlaky, *op. cit.*, pp. 139-140, and Mihail Dan, *op. cit.*, p. 102. Mihail Dan places Szilágyi on the right flank, which conflicts both with the disposition indicated by the rhyming chronicle of the contemporary Beheim, as well as by the Turkish chronicle of Orudj-bin-Adil, cf. Guboglu-Mehmet, *op. cit.*, p. 56. About John Hunyadi, the contemporary Andrea del Palatino says that he commanded "the army of the Romanians."

[157]Spahis = feudal Ottoman troops, usually fighting on horseback. In the Ottoman army, it was customary that the right flank be formed of the troops from that part of the empire (Rumelia or Anatolia) on the territory of which the battle was being fought. however, exceptions are known to have happened. Chalkokondyles, *op cit.*, p. 196, says that at Varna the Ottomans placed the Rumelians on the left flank. Leunclavius maintains the same thing.

Talovak, hastened to their aid. To support, indirectly, the right flank, John Hunyadi attacked with the left flank, along the shore of the lake. He managed to break the line of the Ottomans and to push them back about 4,000 steps. Only afterwards did he direct part of the troops that formed the center and the left flank toward the right flank, which was having serious difficulties. Hunyadi's counterattack required sacrifices. The experienced Ottoman mounted bowmen caused serious casualties; the camels scared the horses. They were wearing little sacks full of coins on their backs. When, in the turmoil, these heavier and clumsier animals tripped and fell, the coins in the sacks scattered on the ground. Those who were pursuing the Ottomans were attracted by their glitter, stopped to gather them, and in this way the Ottomans managed to escape. A lot of precious time was wasted by the greed for loot of the soldiers in the Christian army, which was slowing down the counterattack which John Hunyadi and King Ladislas had begun with the right flank as well, repelling the Ottomans and killing Karadja, the beylerbey of Anatolia. The Polish and Greek chronicles claim that Wallachian soldiers were also guilty of disorders.

One may consider that the first Ottoman attack did not achieve its aim and that until that moment the outcome of the battle was not decided. John Hunyadi advised the king to be cautious and wait first for the weakened and scattered lines to recover. But the king, young (he was only 20 years old) and vain, attacked the center of the Ottoman army with his units, composed of the choice troops of the janissaries, who had only participated in the battle in small numbers up to then. The rash attack of the royal troops was repulsed by the immovable wall of that fanatical and exceptionally well-trained infantry. King Ladislas lost his grip and fell off his horse. An Ottoman janissary, originally from Morea, by the name of Hamza (Chamnzes in the Greek sources),[158] cut off the king's head, which he placed, like a trophy, on the point of a spear, displaying it for the terrified eyes of the Christian soldiers. The Ottomans attacked again. The demoralization caused by

---

[158] According to another source, his name was Feriz.

Sixteenth Century Woodcut from a Polish Chronicle
Depicting the Battle of Varna, 1444

the death of the king quickly transformed into panic and general rout. John Hunyadi tried to hasten to the king's aid. He thought for a moment that he would be able to do the impossible. He rushed in front of those who were running, crying out to them: "we did not come here for the king, but for our faith!"[159] But everything proved to no avail. Hunyadi resigned himself to defeat and left the battle, heading north.

The Wallachian troops, who were more familiar with those places, retreated with him. They had suffered great losses as well. The Ottomans did not pursue the fugitives for long, they were content with taking over the battlefield. Under the dark sky of the autumn afternoon, Murad II, accompanied by the Ottoman commanders, rode across the battlefield. He was surprised to see that the fallen soldiers from the defeated army were all young men. A flattering answer for the victorious sultan came from someone near him: "Had there been just one man with a grey beard among them they would not have ventured into such a dangerous thing."

The numbers given by the historical sources regarding the casualties suffered by both sides are as varied as those regarding their initial manpower. The improbability of one of them results from the fact that, while it attributes to the defeated army from 3,000-12,000 casualties, it claims that the Ottomans lost between 30,000 and 80,000 men. Taking into consideration the probable manpower of John Hunyadi's army, namely 15,000-20,000 men, the relatively short duration of the battle, and the efficiency of the weapons of that time, the number of 3,000 casualties is already appreciable. Evidently, there must have been a great number of soldiers who were captured and made slaves, and since a lot of them never returned, they were considered dead. Ottoman casualties, even if we admit that they were bigger than Hunyadi's, could not have surpassed them by much.

John Hunyadi, having a few good guides, arrived in two days and two nights at the Danube, across from Cetatea de Floci, and crossed into Wallachia. There, not being recognized by the Wallachian sol-

[159]Gubolgu-Mehmet, *op. cit.*, pp. 183, 241, 347.

diers, he was caught and held under guard for a few days, until Vlad Dracul, finding out about his arrival, set him free, facilitating his journey to his country. Such an incident could have been the basis of the version circulated by the narrative sources, according to which Vlad held John as a prisoner for a while. Their relations in the following period do not justify this version.

The remainder of the army arrived at the Danube in four or five days. Cardinal Cesarini did not return from the battle. Various rumors circulated regarding his fate. Some claimed that they had recognized him, wounded by spears and arrows, agonizing in a swamp on the battlefield. According to other sources, he managed to run away and at a certain distance away from the place of the disaster, he stopped to rest on the bank of a river. A group of soldiers, fugitives like him, recognized him. In the fury and desperation of the moment, they held him responsible for what had happened and killed him. Another rumor was that he managed to arrive at the Danube. The ferryman, presuming, by the weight of the boat, that he had a lot of gold with him, killed him to rob him. This version is not well-founded. How could the cardinal, in his hasty flight, have carried so much gold for the ferryman to suspect something by the unusual weight of the boat?

The battle of Varna had a strong echo throughout the world. The sultan announced and celebrated his victory in the whole empire. The West refused to believe in the disaster for a long time. News arrived with great delay, On 1 January 1445, Pope Eugenius IV was still convinced that the fleet in the Straits had stopped the sultan from crossing from Asia Minor and was preparing to send reinforcements. In the second half of January, news came to Rome that the Ottoman army had crossed into Europe after all. Deeply concerned, the pope communicated the news to the doge of Venice, who had probably received it much earlier but had preferred to conceal it, given the suspicions of treason that were hanging over the commanders of the fleet. In February and March, the doge tried to justify in front of the pope the failure of the naval action in the Straits.

In May 1445, the Florentines wrote to King Ladislas (!), asking him if the bad news about his army was true. The news that confirmed the disaster were still coming one after the other and any doubt or hope soon disappeared. The European world was shaken and discouraged. An opinion circulated that the forces of Hungary were not sufficient for fighting against the Ottomans, and that the Western powers were not capable of uniting to offer more serious help.

The contemporaries of that period enveloped the defeat of Varna in empty words meant to conceal the real reasons for the defeat. They claimed that the disaster was a result of "divine punishment" for the violation of the promise of peace made to the Ottomans by Ladislas I. This again brought up the long and empty polemic which disputed whether a promise made to the pagans was valid or not and, consequently, whether breaking it could bring about divine punishment. In a letter to the pope, John Hunyadi complied with the conventions of the time, speaking about the defeat as "a punishment for his sins." However, he could not refrain from writing bitter words directed at those who had made great promises to him but did not keep them, forcing him to fight such an important battle with few resources, in unfavorable conditions, against an enemy whose number was overwhelming.[160] His justified reproaches were, once more, futile. Faced with the selfish hesitations by the Western courts, with the discouragement that had seized them, the peoples of Eastern Europe would remain for a long time at the mercy of fate. However, these people did not give up fighting for their freedom. It was in them that John Hunyadi found support. Despite all the unfavorable circumstances, he would not remain alone.

---

[160]Fejér, *op. cit.*, pp. 76-79. Mention should be made of the words of the chronicler Sphrantzes that reveal the position of the Byzantine emperor, who had sent him on a mission to the sultan, as well as to the king of Hungary and the commanders of the Western fleet: "...depending which side will have been successful;" cf. Georgios Sphrantzes, *Memorii, 1401-1477*, critical edition by Vasile Grecu, Bucureşti, pp. 68-69.

p̄meditat⁹e: paucos post dies mltis eū munerib⁹ (vt ipe sꝑabat) placatū regni hūgarie trāssiluanas traducere fecit in partes.
De electione dn̄i iohānis wayuode in gubernatorē: ⁊ de ta/lione per eundē a drakul wayuoda exacta.

Post hāc tādē belli tēpestatē: postq3 regis wladislai lu/gubrem interitū: ne quis in regno in alterius offensā moueretur: per dominos prelatos ⁊ barones regni in terdictum est. ⁊ nihilominus vt adueniente festo pē/

Depiction of John Hunyadi
from a Fifteenth Century Hungarian Chronicle

CHAPTER VIII

AT THE DANUBE BORDER

The defeat of Varna and the death of the king were especially detrimental to the internal situation of Hungary. The peace that the efforts of John Hunyadi and his party had managed to reestablish was again threatened. Ambitions hard to suppress were revived, the aspiration for power of the upper nobility was again growing, in detriment to the general interest of the country.

During those few months while it was believed that the king would be gone on the campaign, a regency was established in Hungary, composed of four higher noblemen. Among them were Dionysius Szécsi the archbishop of Strigoniu, and Lawrence Hédérváry, the palatine of the country. This temporary government was the first to endanger authority and order in the country. The four barons considered themselves entitled to keep the power in their hands. With that aim in view, and not to prevent demoralization in the country, they tried to conceal the death of the king for as long as possible. Their right to rule the kingdom was valid only as long as the king was alive. His death altered the legal situation and the regency would have been obligated to convoke the Diet and comply with its decisions regarding the succession to the throne or the next form of government. To prolong his mandate, maintaining the false impression that the king was alive and the campaign was continuing, Palatine Hédérváry resorted to forging a letter from John Hunyadi, dated 20 November 1444, from near Gallipoli (!).

Many barons were favorable to the tendencies of the small group that ruled the country. They believed that Hungary could be ruled very well without a king, keeping power directly in their hands. They were encouraged by the example of Poland, where a powerful nobility was restricting the rights of the king and moving the regime of their country toward a kind of "nobiliary republic." The scholar Aeneas Sylvius Piccolomini,[161] speaking of Hungary and the group of noblemen that was ruling it at that time, also used the term "republic" to characterize its political regime.

The attempt of some barons to remain masters of the situation was conflicting with the similar ambitions of others who, preserving the memory of the attacks launched by John Hunyadi during the civil war of 1440, were trying persistently to obtain foreign aid to seize power. The most dangerous group with such plans was the party that had supported Queen Elizabeth and King Ladislas Posthumous. These barons approached Frederick III of Hapsburg, the tutor of Ladislas, offering their cooperation to bring the child to the throne. Their arguments were very strong: had Ladislas I himself not recognized that, after his death, young Ladislas would be his successor? Ladislas was dead. Who and on what grounds could have opposed the ascension to the throne of the son of Elizabeth? The plans of the pro-Hapsburg party seemed as good as fulfilled. Ulrich of Cilli was again in good relations with Austria. Ladislas Garai lent large sums of money to the German sovereign. Another nobleman pledged to the duke of Austria some border fortresses, which would later enter into the possession of Frederick III. The feudal anarchy was taking serious forms again. Even a close relative of John Hunyadi, John Székely, was accused of taking over by force some villages in the county of Zagreb. A friend of the voievod, John of Zredna, wrote, on 24 April 1445 about the state of affairs in Hungary: "The truth is kept quiet, the barriers of common sense are broken, the reins of law have loosened... The iron, arbitrary, unrestrained violence de-

[161] He would later become pope, under the name of Pius II.

stroys and does not respect anyone's rights: hate, treason, and the most impudent oppression are free to rule...."[162]

Frederick III as tutor of the minor king, could already see himself as the new ruler of Hungary. He interfered in its internal affairs, gave orders to the city dwellers, among whom the people of Braşov. His chancellor announced with satisfaction to Palatine Hédérváry the certain news from Venice and Byzantium about the death of King Ladislas I, reminding him of the rights of Ladislas Posthumous and inviting the palatine to support them.

Other Hungarian barons put their hopes in the bringing to the throne of a foreign king: a rumor about the candidacy of a French or Burgundian prince began to circulate. Those interested would mention the names of Cilli or Branković.

There were also noblemen who were not as interested in the dynastic problem, but rather in defending their local interests. It was mostly the case of those in the border regions, such as the noblemen in Dalmatia, who orientated themselves toward closer relations with Venice and other Italian cities.

The reappearance of the hostilities and even of the civil war among the barons, under the pretext of a fight for the throne, the German domination over the country, the separation from Hungary of some border regions were only a few of the dangers that were threatening the kingdom when John Hunyadi, with his heart heavy after the defeat he had suffered, arrived in the country. Who better than him, who had seen once again the terrible force of the enemy threatening the borders, could understand better how prejudicial internal discord could be?

His first thought was to reorganize the army. We lack data regarding his activity in this respect during the winter of 1444-1445, but we know that in the spring of 1445, when the Ottomans were again attacking the borders, his army was ready to fight back.

---

[162]Schwandtner, *Scriptores*, II, p. 10.

Overwhelmed by his worries about the army and defense, he did not enter immediately into the political fight. He was being cautious. He could sense the hidden satisfaction with which the barons who, not long before, had trembled in front of him, were preparing to receive him, the defeated hero. He approached those noblemen from whom he could expect a more dignified attitude, and whose interests set them against the tendencies of Hapsburg domination and Ottoman expansion. He corresponded with Palatine Hédérváry, and with his friend and colleague Nicholas Ujlaki. His advice was always the same: that the discords should be brought to an end, that the foreign influence should be precluded by opposing its supporters, that they should keep in view, above all else, the cloudy southern horizon.

His opinions gradually began to win supporters. The defeat of Varna had demoralized some and frightened others. Fear had caused many to think more seriously about the possible ways to eliminate the danger, to see the prejudicial perspectives of the politics of the higher noblemen, to gather more closely around the man who had remained the most outstanding military personality of the time. The lesser nobility, especially, was on Hunyadi's side. It was numerous and widely represented in the Diet. Its attitude had a great chance of being supported by the townspeople and the peasants. The higher noblemen, with their quarrels and intrigues, saw themselves gradually becoming like islands in the middle of the waves of those determined to defend their peace and freedom.

The council that ruled the kingdom had to decide to convoke the Diet for April 1445. They were going to deliberate upon the succession to the throne and, in close relation to it, the cessation of the quarrels among the noblemen. The name of John Hunyadi already appeared among those of the great dignitaries who initiated the convocation of the diet. His influence was also felt in the measures for the consolidation of internal order, which the state council applied even before the meeting of the Diet. The country was temporarily divided into a few regions, each of them ruled by one to three "captains," having armed forces at their disposal and being commissioned with maintaining order. John Hunyadi, keeping his previous dignities as voievod of Transylvania and *comite* of Timişoara, became captain of the regions west of the Tisza.

However, this system did not produce the anticipated results. In some parts, they had to accept as captains old adversaries of central power, such as Jiskra in Slovakia, or turbulent noblemen like Pancraţiu of Szentmiklós, who would use the authority of their new dignity in their own interest, compromising order even more.[163] John Hunyadi, however, took his new position seriously. For the bishop's seat in Oradea, which has remained empty following the death, at Varna, of its occupant, Hunyadi recommended and obtained the approval of the pope for the naming of his friend, John of Zredna. He obligated the noblemen in that region, during a provincial assembly, to swear obedience to him and to support him in fight against those who trouble and plunder those parts. In Transylvania – according to historical sources –, after John Hunyadi was named captain, the disturbances ceased and people were leading a much more peaceful life than in other provinces.

His previous activity had prepared the way for the honor with which the voievod was received in the Diet in April and the success that he had there. The representatives of the party for order and consolidation of the state, whose views he represented, determined the Diet to take measures against internal wars and to try to bring about a reconciliation among the upper nobility. In a short time, the noblemen had to return the estates they had taken from each other by force and to demolish the fortresses and fortifications they had built on their estates, except for those which could be used as defense against the Ottomans.

The Diet forbade anyone from touching the royal estates; the revenues resulting from them were going to be used for the defense of the country and for the payment of mercenaries. If the sultan set out against Hungary, all nobleman and freemen were obligated to participate personally in the army, including the troops of the magnates and high prelates.

---

[163] Although the latter was in good relations with John Hunyadi.

A very important part in the decisions of the Diet of April 1445 were the measures that facilitated the customs system and commercial transportation. They also reaffirmed the right of a serf to move from one estate to another on the condition that they had previously paid his taxes on the land, the so-called *terragium,* and other legal obligations.

This decision shows, in a more systematic formulation, John Hunyadi's tendency to extend the social basis of his party, attracting the sympathy of the townspeople and gaining some popularity with the peasants.

His policy of consolidation of central power and elimination of outside influences is reflected in two other decisions of the Diet: one through which, in ecclesiastical cases, the rights of the courts in the country were expanded in comparison to those of the papal court; the other was the one through which the decision regarding the succession to the throne was postponed until after Pentecost. During this period of time, they had to make all possible efforts to find out news about Ladislas I. If nothing new was learned until then, his death being thus confirmed, Ladislas Posthumous would be recognized as king, on the condition that Frederick of Hapsburg would renounce his rights as tutor of the former and return the holy crown of Hungary which had been pawned to him. If he refused, the Diet would elect another sovereign, or would make any other decision it would deem appropriate.

In this way, John Hunyadi was fighting the pretensions of domination of the Hapsburgs, defeating them with their own weapons. If they really wanted to appear as disinterested defenders only of the rights to the throne of the child they had to give up their tutelage over him. Otherwise, they would reveal their intentions of seizing power in Hungary.

Not long after, the delegates returned with news that confirmed that Ladislas I had died. A delegation of the Hungarian nobility then left for Vienna to ask for Ladislas Posthumous. Frederick III would not give up any of his rights and offended the delegates through his behavior and they returned without success.[164] Some of the noblemen – among them Hédérváry and Ujlaki – began to believe that the Diet should elect a new king immediately. John Hunyadi was of a different opinion. He was concerned by the endless enmities that such an act would bring about, by the permanent deterioration of relations with the empire. That is why he considered that they should maintain the provisional state and continue negotiations with Vienna and, if it became necessary, take the minor king away by force from his tutor.

We cannot exclude the fact that John Hunyadi, pleading for this provisional state, was thinking that, until the king came of age (who at the time was only 5 years old), the perspective of ascension to the interim supreme authority in the kingdom was open to himself as well. Even so, his concern for internal peace was dictated first of all by the necessity to fight against the Ottomans. They had appeared at the end of the spring of 1445 around Belgrade with a small army. The army of the voievod of Transylvania went to halt their advance, on the opposite bank of the Sava River. Building camp fires, Hunyadi's soldiers kept the attention of the Ottomans directed to one point and, after dark, they crossed the river at a different spot, surrounded the enemy camp by surprise, and destroyed it. It was a local success, but not without importance, if we consider the losses suffered at Varna not long before that.

But John Hunyadi, as well as the Western fleet which continued to remain in the Straits at Constantinople, had bigger plans. In the spring of 1445, the galleys entered the Black Sea and attacked the Ottoman ships. They had orders to organize a strong operation to force the sultan to make peace. The crew of the fleet did not fully believe yet in the deaths of Cesarini and Ladislas I, although the Ottomans had shown the Burgundians, from the shore, across from the port of Gallipoli, a severed head with long, blond hair, which supposedly that of the king. Still the idea persisted that they should organize, in the area of the Danube, an expedition to search for Cesarini and the king.

---

[164] Teleki, *op. cit.*, X, pp. 173-179.

The circumstances within the Ottoman Empire also seemed favorable to the organization of a new campaign. Sultan Murad II, depressed by the death of one of his sons, Aladdin, had renounced the throne in favor of another son, Mehmed, and had retired somewhere in Asia Manor: where he wanted to lead a pious life. His successor took to a life of parties and hunting trips. Few could have seen in that pale young man with delicate features, with a frivolous nature, unrestrained in his fury, and an epileptic besides, the future Mehmed II, the conqueror of Constantinople, one of the most remarkable figures among the Ottoman sultans. Discontented with the indifference shown by the young sultan toward their war projects, the janissaries rebelled against him, disturbing the pious seclusion of Murad and compelling him to return to the throne.[165]

A few months passed during which negotiations were carried on for the preparation of an operation coordinated between the army of John Hunyadi and the Burgundian fleet. The commander of this fleet Walerand of Wavrin, had sent to Hungary a delegation composed of a Spanish knight, Pedro Vasque de Saavedra, and two Frenchmen, who arrived at Buda at the beginning of May, 1445, at the same time with many noblemen who had been taken prisoner at Varna and had freed themselves from Ottoman captivity. The delegation offered John Hunyadi six to eight ships on the Danube. According to the plan that resulted from the negotiations, in the middle of August, Wavrin would advance with eight galleys all the way to Nicopolis, where he would meet a Hungarian army of 8,000 to 10,000 men. Eventually, making several trips, the galleys would transport this army to Constantinople. From there, in cooperation with the Byzantines, they would continue the attempt to drive the Ottomans out of Europe. However, it does not seem likely that Hunyadi seriously considered such a difficult effort. His main intention was to secure the Danube border. After Varna, in

---

[165]Ducas maintains that the abdication of Murad took place before Varna, *op. cit.*, pp. 274-275. He might have manifested this intention, but he only put it into practice afterwards.

Hungary and the Romanian principalities, people were living in permanent fear of a mighty Ottoman attack.

The Hungarian noblemen requested two more things from the Burgundian messengers: upon their return, to try to convince Vlad Dracul to join this campaign, and, in Constantinople, to plead with the Byzantine emperor to allow the Ottoman pretender Saudji (Daud Çelebi) to leave for Hungary.

The Burgundian delegation fulfilled these missions. Upon their return, Pedro Vasque de Saavedra met with Vlad Dracul and convinced him to accept a meeting with Wavrin. At the end of July, the Wallachian voievod went to Isaceea, where Wavrin had already arrived with two galleys. Vlad committed himself to helping the campaign with soldiers, the necessary number of wagons, food, and forty or fifty boats.

Afterwards, the Spanish knight went to Constantinople, where he transmitted to the other ships the mission to set sail for Isaceea. The emperor granted him the request for Saudji and, together with him, he returned to the Danube, joining the crew of the fleet.

John Hunyadi, after the agreement with the Burgundian delegation, appealed again to the Western courts for assistance. He had high hopes in the pope and the king of France. On 11 May 1445, a canon of Oradea by the name of Blaziu left for Rome and a chancellor, Vincenţiu of Bala, knight of Bathia, left for France with Hunyadi's requests. The voievod delayed his departure on the campaign by a month, waiting for the results of his efforts. His waiting was in vain. The king of France answered him with praises and promises, apologizing that at the moment he was busy with the war with England.[166] The pope, instead of much-awaited financial support, had only words to offer as well. He sent a letter to the Western courts, asking them to help John Hunyadi and promising forgiveness of the sins of those who would engage in the campaign.

[166] Fejér, *op. cit.*, pp. 77-78.

In the first part of August, Francesco Condulmer arrived at Isaceea, at the command of three papal and three Burgundian galleys. These completed the number of ships promised by Wavrin. Vlad Dracul also arrived there, accompanied by his son Mircea, with 5,000-6,000 Wallachians, with two small cannons, and the promised boats. Meanwhile, news came that John Hunyadi would not be able to arrive at Nicopolis before 8 September. Therefore, the expedition stayed for a few more days in the vicinity of the Delta. In the middle of the month they set sail upstream on the Danube and on the 16th they passed through Brăila. The army of Wallachia was also advancing, along the left bank of the river.

They first tried to conquer the fortress of Dârstor (Silistra), but their spies found out that the Ottoman garrison there was very strong and, therefore, they stopped the siege and continued on their way. Turtucaia, having mostly wooden fortifications, was conquered and burned down.

For the prince of Wallachia, it was very important to reconquer the fortress of Giurgiu, from where it was easy for the Ottomans to get to Târgovişte, Câmpulung, and all the way to Braşov. Mainly at the insistence of Vlad Dracul, they began the siege of this fortress. He told the Burgundians how many blocks of salt it had cost his father, Mircea the Old, to build that fortress. He exaggerated a little when he added that, having the fortress of Giurgiu, the Wallachian women could conquer the Ottoman land... just with their spindles.

The fortress was built on an island, connected by a bridge to the Romanian bank. The Wallachian prince, who was very familiar with the area, gave the first instructions for the disposition of the soldiers and the ships. Some 300 Ottomans came out of the fortress and attacked the Wallachian camp, but they were pushed back inside the walls after a violent fight. Penetrating onto the island, the besiegers seized many wagons which they filled with wood, building a kind of moving shield, behind which they were advancing toward the walls, from where the Ottomans fired upon them.

The towers and walls of the fortress were strong. They had no openings, and the defenders were only firing from the merlons. The Burgundian commander ordered his soldiers to dig trenches behind the wagons and align the cannons in battle line. They began bombarding the walls. A large bombard was brought out of a ship and, during the night, they placed it in firing position. The next day it was put to use. With a great thunder, it was propelling hard Brabant boulders, which caused wide breaches at each blow, stirring up clouds of dust and fragments of stone. Hearing the noise, Vlad Dracul came by the large bombard. Wavrin left him in command of the fire during his absence. Out of his determination, the voievod did not allow the bombard to cool down between blows, and this is why two of its circles snapped, killing two men. The angry Wavrin calmed down when he learned that the bombard could be fixed. After this incident, Vlad went back to his two cannons, which were smaller and were firing often above the walls. Another attack of the Ottomans against the Wallachians was repelled.

The bombardment, no matter how powerful, did not help a great deal, especially after the large bombard broke down again and had to be taken back to the ship. The besiegers decided to take the fortress by fire and built big piles of wood near the walls. Foolishly, the Ottomans did not light the wood as it was being piled up, but waited too long. When they lit it, with the intention of thwarting the efforts of the assailants, the flames rose so high that they engulfed the wooden roofs of the towers, spreading inside the fortress.

The subashi,[167] who commanded the fortress, negotiated a surrender, on the condition that the garrison be set free and the bombardment cease to allow them to be able to put out the fire and thus leave the fortress in good condition. Their capitulation was accepted.

The Ottomans came out of the fortress, heading toward the Bulgarian bank. They were looking distrustfully at the galleys and were holding their bows stretched, ready for a desperate fight. They had rea-

[167] A military rank in the Ottoman army.

sons to be frightened, because bloody schemes were hanging over them. The commander of the garrison was the same subashi who, in 1441, had lured Vlad Dracul with promises to the court of the sultan, where the Wallachian prince was imprisoned for more than a year, having to leave two of his sons in dangerous captivity.

Now Vlad Dracul ordered his son to avenge him. The one commissioned with the cruel revenge was the future Vlad the Impaler. With 2,000 Wallachians, the son of the voievod crossed the Danube at some distance, took the garrison by surprise and massacred it, killing the subashi himself.

Wavrin listened in silence to the explanations for breaking the promise given to the garrison. The Frenchman probably realized that in a life-and-death struggle between the invaders and those endangered with occupation it is not always possible to apply the precepts of knightly conduct that were cultivated at the court of his masters, the dukes of Burgundy.

Vlad Dracul, happy with the conquest of Giurgiu, announced it to the people of Braşov, asking them for bows, arrows, and cannons, to be able to fortify the fortress again, "because it is your strength, our strength, and the strength of all Christians."[168]

The successes of the campaign upset the Ottoman world and gave new hope to the subjugated population of Bulgaria. The garrison at Rusciuc left the fortress without a fight. A few Bulgarians brought the Wallachian army the news that many of their countrymen, who had rebelled and run away, were being attacked by the Ottomans, not far from the Danube. Vlad Dracul swam across the Danube with 4,000 mounted soldiers and saved those Bulgarians. They asked for permission to cross into Wallachia. The voievod allowed them to do so because he considered them very brave people. He put the boats of his army at their disposal and for three days and three nights 12,000 Bul-

[168]I. Bogdan, *Documente privitoare la relaţiile Ţării Româneşti cu Braşovul şi cu Ţara Ungurească în sec. XV şi XVI*, Bucureşti, 1905, p. 80.

garians crossed the Danube with their families, the possessions that they were able to gather, and their cattle.

On 7 September, the fleet sailed further, toward its main objective, Nicopolis. It arrived there five days later. Before the eyes of the townspeople, the fleet was met with fire from the cannons which the Ottomans had placed on the bank, in a sandy place. Three ships were slightly hit. The fleet retaliated in passing with its cannons and then dropped anchor on the Wallachian bank, before a fortification – it was a big tower rather than a fortress. It was Little Nicopolis, today Turnu Măgurele.

From there, the commanders looked at the fortress on the other bank. The city of Nicopolis had an elongated, narrow shape; It was surrounded by a few hills, one of them guarded by a fortress. Two rows of walls, fortified with round towers, came down from the fortress to the river. Before the city, along the bank enclosed between the two walls to prevent the disembarking of the fleet's soldiers, the Ottomans had built a wooden parapet and sunk a few ships, whose sterns were showing above the water. While the commanders of the fleet were looking at this scene, an old Wallachian boyar, over 80 years old, approached them. He was the one who took care of the education of the son of Vlad Dracul. With a trembling hand, he showed Wavrin the place where, almost fifty years before, the great battle of Nicopolis had been fought, in which he had participated. He showed him where Duke John of Burgundy had stayed. Their conversation went on smoothly, as the old man spoke a little French and Italian. He had learned these languages from the Genoese, to whom the Ottomans had sold him as a slave after he had fallen prisoner in that battle.

Already on 13 September Vlad Dracul began to besiege Turnu, the fortress on the Wallachian bank. The Ottomans resisted. During the foggy night that followed, a ship brought them reinforcements from Nicopolis. On 14 September, the army of John Hunyadi arrived. The tireless soldier got on a boat and went aboard the ship where Wavrin was lying sick in his cabin to talk to him. He also met with Francesco Condulmer after which, returning to the bank, he had a talk with Vlad

Dracul. Following these discussions, they decided to continue the siege, hoping that in a day or two the Ottomans in the fortress would capitulate. But, even after a week, this did not happen. The walls resisted the bombardment, and the attempt to set the roofs on fire, as had been done at Giurgiu, failed. The Ottomans on the opposite bank always managed to secretly bring reinforcements.

Since the season was getting cold, they decided to end the siege. The plan of the campaign required, in fact, an attempt to cross the Danube, and not the conquering of all the fortresses on its bank. The crossing of the Danube at Nicopolis, as it had been planned initially, proved difficult, because a rather powerful Ottoman army had gathered in the meantime on the Bulgarian bank. That is why John Hunyadi chose a new crossing point at the mouth of the Jiu River, where he sent orders ahead for the building of a large number of rafts. The reunited armies left Turnu toward the west and the fleet set sail in the same direction.

Observing their maneuver, the Ottomans in Nicopolis began their own march toward the west, along the Bulgarian bank, watching day and night the movements of the galleys and the enemy army. From aboard the ships one could see every night the fires of the Ottoman camp. According to the information brought back by spies, the Ottomans were building more fires than they actually needed, to appear more numerous.

The Burgundian commander who was substituting for Wavrin, who was always ill, ordered several soldiers to embark on a boat one night, with a few small cannons, and to simulate a disembarking against the Ottomans, discharging a noisy bombardment from the galleys. The Ottomans were frightened and abandoned the camp and left those few Wallachian and Hungarian prisoners whom they were taking with them. The former prisoners swam across the river and said that, if only 2,000-3,000 men had really disembarked, they could have seized the camp where the Ottomans had now left all their supplies. The next afternoon, realizing that they had been deceived, the Ottomans appeared again on the bank and began to bombard the galleys, from where the enemy soldiers responded with mocking laughter.

On 28 September, they arrived at the mouth of the Jiu, across from which, on the Bulgarian bank, there rose the ruins the fortress of Rahova, which had been destroyed in the campaign of 1396. The fleet carried out a disembarking and the Burgundians fortified themselves among those ruins with bowmen and war machines. From there, they opposed the Ottomans who were attacking them. This way they gave time to the army of Hunyadi to cross the Danube. The Ottomans put up a weak resistance, but they carried out an orderly retreat toward the interior, destroying everything they could on their way. Hunyadi pursued them for a time, but returned unexpectedly and crossed onto the left bank again. The voievod explained to Wavrin that he did not wish to be drawn too far from the Danube where he would risk a defeat. Their provisions were scarce, enough for only a few days. The food promised by Vlad Dracul was taking a long time to arrive from Wallachia. The people in those areas were also impoverished. For three or four years the wars, with their pillages and the obligations of the people to supply the armies, had not ceased.

At the beginning of October there came such a frost that it was feared that the Danube could freeze over in a short time. The commanders of the fleet proposed that they spend the winter somewhere west of Rahova and resume their campaign the following year. John Hunyadi explained to them that beyond the Iron Gates there was no place of safety where the ships could stay protected from Ottoman attacks. He advised them, therefore, to sail downstream, toward the sea, before the waters of the river froze and trapped them, turning them into easy prey for the Ottomans.

This is how this campaign along the Danube ended. John Hunyadi and Vlad Dracul returned each to his own country, and the fleet sailed down the Danube. On 2 November 1445, it reached Constantinople, where the Westerners found out that the Byzantine emperor had signed a separate peace with the Ottomans. In a few days, the galleys left for Venice.

The most important result of this campaign was the consolidation of the alliance and military cooperation between John Hunyadi and Vlad Dracul. It also led to an important local success: the reconquering of the fortress of Giurgiu. This campaign kept alive in the Balkan peoples the sentiment that they had not been abandoned after the defeat of Varna which had shattered so many hopes.

The cooperation with the fleet helped preserve in the heart of the voievod of Transylvania the illusion of military support from the West. Already at the time of the battles of Nicopolis and Rahova he had drawn, together with Condulmer, a plan of action for the next campaign. To this, we must connect the intention, manifested at one point by the commanders of the fleet, to spend the winter on the Danube. The established plan is not known, but it was probably based on the one drawn up a year and a half earlier by Cardinal Cesarini, which established the crossing of the Danube as close as possible to its mouth, with the help of a fleet, and to advance toward Adrianople along the shortest route, going around the natural obstacle of the Balkans on the east side.

In the fall of 1445, immediately after his return from the Danube, John Hunyadi shared this plan with the pope and, in the winter, he again sent messengers to Rome and to the court of the duke of Burgundy. The answer was taking a long time to arrive. On 20 February 1446, Hunyadi, who was then in Debrecen, was insistently asking the pope for a definitive answer by the middle of April. A contemporary wrote that the messengers sent to Rome and Burgundy "brought back nothing but empty words."

An atmosphere of calmness now characterized the relations between the European states and the Ottomans. The Venetians concluded a peace treaty with Sultan Mehmed II in February 1446. The treaty was signed in September by the old sultan, Murad II, who, following the revolts of the janissaries, had come back to power. In the Balkans, the Serbian despot maintained good relations with the Ottoman Empire, relying on its support in his enmity with Venice, and Vlad Dracul continued to pay tribute to the Porte.

CHAPTER IX

AT THE HEIGHT OF GLORY

During this relative peace, John Hunyadi found the necessary time to dedicate his attention to improving the domestic situation and to solving the difficult problem of the state's leadership. The negotiations with the Hapsburgs for the effective return to the throne of the child king, Ladislas V, were unsuccessful, and the election of a new king would have caused too many animosities within the country and too many diplomatic complications outside of its borders.

The system of government through "captains," one of whom was John Hunyadi himself, proved inadequate for maintaining of peace and order. A strong need was felt for a single leader, with the prestige and necessary experience for imposing his authority over all categories of the nobility and for organizing the defense of the borders.

The Diet of the country was convoked on 1 June 1446 at Pest. After the opening ceremony, they moved onto the field of Rákos, near the capital. The Diet recognized, in principle, the rights to the crown of Ladislas V, but at the same time, considering that those rights could not be translated into fact and realizing the necessity for a centralized government, they proposed the election of a governor.

On 5 June 1446, they met for the election. The higher noblemen wanted to withdraw from the meeting, as usual, to consult on the person they were going to propose. The provincial noblemen, strongly represented in the Diet, did not allow them to leave and began to acclaim the name of John Hunyadi. The higher noblemen did not oppose them, and thus John Hunyadi was unanimously elected governor of Hungary. He was the only one who tried to object, maybe out of calculated modesty, to his election to such a high rank to which he did not aspire. The response he received was that everyone was obligated to submit to the decisions of the Diet. Convinced by this argument, he accepted and took the oath. Beginning on 13 June, official documents and laws were already being issued in his name.

The ascension of John Hunyadi to the leadership of the country was certainly due to the prestige he had gained during the campaigns he had led against the Ottomans, during which he had demonstrated so many qualities, both in victory as well as in defeat. But it was also a consequence of his personal power and the special place that he held among the noblemen. As a result of his political views, he was close to the lesser nobility and supported by it. But in actuality he had become one of the most prominent higher noblemen in Hungary. The barons considered him somewhat of an "upstart" and did not agree with some of his actions, but they could not disregard his power and the necessity to be in good relations with him.

As a result of the great and many services he had brought to the king under different forms, John Hunyadi was able to gather an immense fortune, especially after 1440. Around that year his estates comprised approximately 700,000 acres. As a reward for his victories in the following years, for the expenses that he personally supported in those campaigns, he was given many other estates. For instance, after "the Long Campaign" he received the great domains of the fortresses of Deva and Giurgiu.[169] In the summer of 1444 he received from George Branković the domain of Şiria, in the region of Arad. After the campaign of Varna, in reprisal for the attitude of reserve shown by the despot during the campaign and because of his ongoing relations with the Ottomans, all the estates that Branković owned in Hungary were confiscated. These were also transferred to Hunyadi's possession. In

[169]He came into effective possession of Deva in May 1447; cf. Teleki, *op. cit.*, X, pp. 197-199.

1446, when he was elected governor, the total area of his domains reached a few million acres.

The revenues from these estates constituted one of the bases of his rule and of the anti-Ottoman struggle. It is clear that he used the revenues from his estates for hiring mercenaries. For such purposes, John Hunyadi tried to strengthen this basis of his power, not only by extending his estates, but also by increasing their revenues, both through the usual increase in the taxes paid by the serfs, as well as by introducing certain more "rational" methods of working the land. On some of his estates, in the counties of Turda and Cluj, the usual lot given to the serfs to work was expanded. This land was worked by the serfs with their own tools, the harvest being divided, probably, in a proportion advantageous to the owner.

Hunyadi also tried to put to use new lands of his estate by colonizing them. It is claimed that the western part of the county of Békés began to be populated after it became his possession. He brought there especially Serbians and Bulgarians, who had run away from the Ottomans.

Another method of increasing the revenues from his estates was the proportional development of the different branches of agricultural economy. He encouraged the raising of cattle on his domains, in addition to the usual forms of working the land. Hunyadi used people with a certain degree of education as administrators of his estates, which is significant for his tendency to "rationalize" to some extent the management of his domains.

He tried, in general, to spare the serfs, understanding that without their work it would not be possible to maintain the class to which he belonged, nor his personal position, nor that of the entire state. He objected, whenever and as much as he could, to the abusive, anarchic forms of exploitation of the serfs, which were leading to the destruction of their households and to the disintegration of some villages. Several times, the decisions made under his influence by the Diet recommended respecting the right of serfs to move from one estate to another, under the usual conditions, namely the payment beforehand of the tax on land.

Also with a view to increasing his revenues, John Hunyadi gave his attention to the mines on his estates. On some of his lands, such as in Hunedoara and Zarand, there were places for washing gold. He encouraged the same occupation in the north of Transylvania as well, on some domains confiscated from Branković, supporting the development of the cities of Baia Mare and Baia Sprie.

Supporting the development of the cities was necessary as, until the middle of the fifteenth century, Hungary had not been so advanced economically for a real "domestic market" to be created, within which the cities would maintain permanent relations, throughout the entire country. Their interests were directed toward certain regions.

The cities in the south of Transylvania had close relations with Wallachia, and Bistriţa with Moldavia. The mining cities in Slovakia also represented a separate economic area. The cities in the west of Hungary, Pojon, Györ, and even Buda, were oriented toward Vienna. This characteristic of their development had determined them, during the civil wars of 1440-1442, to take the side of different parties, usually of the noblemen whose domains were in their vicinity. Those political animosities hindered even more the development of relations among them. For that very reason, after his election as governor, John Hunyadi was not able to rely on the cities, at least not on all of them, but only on the provincial nobility.

Because the provincial nobility was not strong enough on its own to support solving the domestic and foreign difficulties he confronted, proving itself more useful at a military level, Hunyadi tried to expand the basis of his government, attracting the cities on his side.

While he was voievod of Transylvania, in 1441 and 1443, he had helped Braşov and Sighişoara to establish a mint, opposing the right that Vlad Dracul had received from the king of Hungary to have a mint in Sighişoara.

Also as voievod of Transylvania, John Hunyadi manifested his intention of giving back to the city of Cluj the rights that had been taken from it as punishment for having taken the side of the insurgent peasants in 1437-1438.

Some of the cities on his estates received the right to be market towns, which was a right enjoyed by royal free cities. He authorized the fortification of the walls that surrounded Sibiu and Braşov. He constantly placed orders for weapons, cannons, and various kinds of equipment from some cities in Transylvania and Hungary, thus encouraging the craftsmen. He insisted on the participation of the representatives of the cities in the Diet. After the closing of the meeting of the Diet, he sometimes asked these representatives to remain for a few days to consult with them in matters that concerned them. Every time when he concluded a peace treaty with Austria or the Ottoman Empire, opening the possibility for an expansion of the commercial relations of Hungary, he would inform the cities that the way was open to Vienna or Wallachia. He gave orders that, on the occasion of the issuing of a new coin, trustworthy people from the cities be chosen to supervise the operation. Soon after he was elected governor, he went to Transylvania and gave notice to vice-voievod Nicholas of Ocna Sibiului to cooperate in the capture and punishment of those who, through plunder, were disturbing the commerce of the Saxon cities.[170]

The townspeople responded to these measures by repeatedly manifesting their faith and attachment toward the governor. The mayor of Buda gladly announced to his counterpart in Pojon the news that John Hunyadi had escaped the danger in which he had been during the battles with the Ottomans in the year 1448. In 1451, delegates of the city of Pojon were sent to Hunyadi five times over the course of four months, for different matters, having orders to find him "wherever he

---

[170]Teleki, *op. cit.*, X, p. 186. The document was issued from Apold, on 31 July 1446. On 4 November 1447, John Hunyadi sanctioned the right of the Saxon university not to be obligated to return serfs who run away from the noblemen's estates and taken refuge on its territory. *Ibidem,* pp. 224-225.

was."[171] In 1457, when the higher noblemen took revenge on his family, killing his oldest son, Ladislas, there appeared the fear of a revolt of the poor and the workers of Buda.

Besides his attitude toward the serfs, we should also mention his concern for the fate of the workers in the salt mines. He took measures, through the administrators of the salt mines, for the increase in the payment of the workers in Maramureş and Dej. Never, until the end of the fifteenth century, had the salt cutters been better paid than in the time of his government.

The free peasants and the lower noblemen received many estates as rewards for their military services. By doing this, Hunyadi contributed to the ascension of some families of *cnezi* in Hunedoara, Banat, and even Maramureş, some of whom eventually entered the class of the lower nobility. The motivation for the donations consisted, most frequently, in the military merits of the beneficiaries, gained in the campaigns on the Ialomiţa, in the Balkans, of Varna, Kosovo, and others. After Hunyadi's death, the families of those *cnezi* continued to be rewarded with donations, for the acts of bravery performed during his time.[172] Those were, therefore, the social elements on which John Hunyadi relied.

In general, it is considered that the period of his government, especially the years 1446-1448, from his election until the battle lost at Kosovo, represented an effort and a considerable success for the policy of centralization of the state. In general, it is a valid characterization, but to be accepted with certain precautions.

The tendency of John Hunyadi to support the provincial nobility, of a middle and inferior position, the *cnezi* and the townspeople, to put an end to the flagrant abuses in the relations between the noblemen and the peasants, or between the miners and the financial authorities, is an

[171]In 1447, Hunyadi sanctioned the privileges of that city; cf. Teleki, *op. cit.*, X, pp. 221-222. Subsequently, almost until his death (1456), a great number of documents prove the close relations that he had with the city of Pojon.

[172]Cf. Ştefan Pascu, *op. cit.*, p. 45 ff., p. 59 ff.

indisputable fact, if not absolute truth. It constituted an important element in the politics of centralization, having the role to oppose and to defeat the anarchic tendencies of the upper nobility.

Centralization in its typical form was realized precisely through the preponderant force of the diverse social elements mentioned above, united around the monarchy, representing the "order" favorable to the interests of these elements (and to the progress of society in general), against the "disorder" represented by the upper nobility, which inherited the typically feudal traditions of local sovereignty and state division. Everything was based on the development of the relations of production and trade, on the slow but steady process in economic relations through which domestic market was formed.

In the case of John Hunyadi, centralization – as much as this political principle had advanced – was not realized by putting the higher nobility in its place, which had an authority in the state capable of imposing itself by force and that of the social elements on which it relied, nor by undermining it, as an effect of an erosive, insidious action by the new elements of economic life.

The authority of John Hunyadi was derived from the Ottoman danger and his military prestige, and by the confusion and dismay caused by the death of Ladislas I at Varna – a dynastic crisis which could not be solved immediately, because of the dubious attitude, suspicious of intentions of interference by the "king of the Romans," Frederick III of Hapsburg, the tutor of the minor Ladislas V.

These special circumstances resulted in the necessity of a temporal political compromise, to be made by all the social classes, of greater or lesser status in the economic and political life of the country. The upper nobility, in a significant number, also participated in this political bloc.

The argument for the election of John Hunyadi as a result of the acclamations of the representatives of the provincial noblemen, to whom the barons were forced to yield, must be confronted with another, of much greater importance for defining the position of the governor and of the basis of the regime ruled by him: the conditions under which he committed himself to govern, which were stipulated by the magnates and contained in the document of his election.

A whole series of limitations of power were imposed on John Hunyadi at that point: he could not make permanent donations, except under special circumstances; he was obligated to consult the Diet in all cases of treason and proscription; he could not have at his disposal archbishoprics, bishoprics, and the bigger abbacies, except with the approval of his counselors; he would be able to use royal revenues only with the approval of the prelates and the barons; he was allowed to make donations out of the royal estates, but only from those with less than 32 lots, and only once to the same person; he could confiscate estates only according to the law and based on judiciary sentence; laic and clerical counselors would participate at his trials, and the decisions he might render in their absence could be amended by regular judges, etc.[173]

Those provisions did not remain simple declarations. The important documents issued by John Hunyadi as governor regularly carried the formula "with the agreement of the prelates and barons." More diets than usual were held, and the local assemblies, of the provincial nobility and the free cities, were also more numerous than in other periods. There are no indications that John Hunyadi might have violated the conditions he accepted with the occasion of his election, entering this way into an open conflict with the upper nobility. Vague accusations in this respect were brought to him after his death, in the climate of the passions released by the killing of Ulrich of Cilli by Ladislas, John Hunyadi's son, and by the resounding trial and the execution of the latter.

Undoubtedly, oscillating between the limits of his power, John Hunyadi crossed them sometimes, but within them he governed with authority and energy. The centralization process continued. But it was unstable, being based on a conjunction of circumstances rather than permanent and deeply-rooted factors. It was a conjunction that estab-

---

[173]Fejér, *op. cit.*, pp. 87-91.

lished a well-organized "nobiliary regime" rather than a true centralization.

It would be a mistake, however, to see John Hunyadi, as a result of the above-mentioned, as a simple instrument controlled by the nobility. He governed with strong authority, based on the temporary consensus of the upper and lower nobility, with the support of the cities and in an atmosphere of a relative leniency of the regime toward the peasants – especially the free ones – and the workers. Consequently, the phenomena of centralization present during his time should not be exaggerated, but established and viewed at its real dimensions. It represents a historical merit to the personality of John Hunyadi.

It is obvious that, after his election as governor, Hunyadi consolidated the position he held, using the key factors of state power. During the Diet held between 12 and 25 March 1447 he was empowered to use the royal revenues, in the interests of the country. These amounted, in theory, to approximately 200,000-250,000 gold florins annually.

A great part of this sum, however, could not he effectively collected, because many royal estates had been given as donations and pawns to barons and the Church. Also, the administration of the salt mines was very disorganized. Receiving the right to use these revenues, the governor concerned himself intensely with increasing them. He took strong measures to assert control over the salt funds and managed, in a few years, to increase the sums deposited in this treasury to up to 100,000 florins per year.

Also, in March 1447, a decision was adopted that stipulated that from then on, the Diet would be convoked annually and that all the noblemen who owned estates with at least twenty villages were obligated to attend, which meant that the middle nobility would have a stable representation.

The election of a new king could not be done without the knowledge and approval of the Diet. Anyone who did not comply with this decision was guilty of treason. These were measures that regulated the political balance between the governor, the Diet, and the upper and middle nobility, which resulted in the consolidation of that nobiliary regime of order and authority, as we characterized it earlier. Gradually, the noblemen saw themselves forced to solve their differences through the Diet. The higher nobility was limited in its possibility to use the connections it had abroad.

The consolidation of central power by John Hunyadi was more evident in his politics toward the Church. Taking advantage of the fact that, during the periods of anarchy, the estates of the Church were threatened by plunders and confiscations from the lay noblemen, the governor adopted an extremely significant position: he did not simply determine to solve these problems in favor of the Church, but he established, as criteria for the right to own estates, the loyalty of the respective proprietor toward the country and the payment of military service as contribution to its defense. He was therefore willing to protect the possessions of the Church, but he made it clear that those favors required obligations that had to be respected. Although the Church was not entirely contented with this point of view, which tended to subordinate it to the central power, it preferred the given situation in place of the violence to which some of the higher noblemen had subjected it.

Further aiming to subordinate the clergy to him to a certain extent, he tried, during meetings of the Diet, to limit the dependency of the Hungarian Church on the papal court in matters of appointments to ecclesiastical dignities, of taxes collected by the clergy, and of the competency of the ecclesiastical courts. Thus, he declared those clerics who received their positions directly from the pope, without the consent of the state power, as disloyal to their country, and he advocated the eradication of the abuses committed during the collection of church taxes.

Some sources claim that John Hunyadi ruled with an "iron hand." The phrase is true mostly at a military level. At a political level, the upper nobility was very attentive to any excess of authority. Hunyadi was confronted with a permanent opposition, which was not, however, manifested openly, but was transposed in the area of political combinations and intrigues, tied to the activity and decisions of the Diet. This represented, in its turn, a sign of modern mentality and political methods typical of the medieval era.

In September 1447, following the death of Palatine Hédervåry, the Diet entrusted the security of the fortress of Buda to Hunyadi, which had been the responsibility of the palatine. But at the same time, the Diet named as palatine one of the most inveterate enemies of the governor, Ladislas Garai. In the same year, the nobility restricted the military measures that Hunyadi would have liked to apply, preventing the governor one more time from proclaiming a general call to arms, except in extreme cases. But, even then, the troops of the nobility would not fight beyond the borders, thus preventing an offensive war against the Ottomans which Hunyadi was planning. In turn, he was given the right to proclaim a general call to arms in the case of internal revolts, even if they were started by noblemen.

This shows the limited character of the support offered to John Hunyadi by the nobility, even in matters of military defense. This determined him to increase efforts to strengthen his army of mercenaries. For this purpose, he managed to institute new taxes, like the one florin tax per five serf households, or per four noblemen who did not have serfs.[174] These taxes caused a certain discontentment, but, given the lack of understanding from the noblemen and the other countries, there was no other way of obtaining the means for the maintenance of the army, at the level required by the circumstances. In 1447, with the agreement of the Diet, a new and unique coin was issued, with the specification that no other coin except the new florin would have power of circulation.

The work of consolidation of internal peace and the authority of the governor became complicated again, in the years 1446-1447, due to the older conflict with the Hapsburgs and their powerful partisans: Cilli, in the west, and Jiskra, in Slovakia.

Already in March, 1446, Hunyadi had been commissioned by the Diet to gather an army and put an end to the disturbances caused in

[174]Fejér, *op. cit.*, pp. 95-97.

Croatia by the Cilli family. In April, he had entered unexpectedly on the domains of this family in Slovenia, defeated Vitovec, the commander of the army of Ulrich de Cilli, and forced the disobedient duke to make peace, in the terms of the agreement that he had accepted once before, in 1441, toward King Ladislas. He had to promise under oath that he would remain loyal to the government of Hungary, that he would submit to its orders regarding the estates he owned throughout the country, and that he would never initiate any action tied to the interests of Hungary without the consent of the same government. The defeat of Cilli intimidated the upper noblemen opposed to Hunyadi and his party.

As a result of the same event, relations with Frederick III became increasingly tense. He refused with obstinacy to return Ladislas Posthumous and the royal crown to Hungary. He had occupied and refused to return the border fortresses which Queen Elizabeth had pawned to him long before. The important city of Győr was among them.

When he was elected governor on 5 June 1446 John Hunyadi was again authorized to use, when necessary, the force of arms to end the conflict with the Hapsburgs, which had been lasting for so long, interrupted only by unreliable armistices. For the time being, the governor wanted to avoid an armed conflict, and on 11 June he wrote in this sense to the "king of the Romans." His precaution was due to the attitude of Pope Eugenius IV, who was interested in maintaining good relations with Frederick III; consequently, he would have been upset if Hungary attacked Frederick. For his part, John Hunyadi did not want to cause the deterioration of his relations with the pope. But, all the negotiations with the Hapsburgs having failed, the state assembly finally decided to declare war. In a letter to the pope, dated 18 October 1446, Hunyadi justified the step they had taken, closing with these words: "That is why we are forced to begin this just war, because not even the pagans have caused us so much trouble as this Christian prince."[175]

---

[175]Fejér, *op. cit.*, pp. 97-98.

In the middle of November, 1446, hostilities began. The Hungarian army entered the south of Austria, Stiria, Carintia, and Carniolia, which it devastated rather cruelly. Hunyadi did not command the army in this campaign. Vienna, which had been warned through letters to remain neutral, was spared. In December, the army returned to Hungary. The governor had received unsettling news from the Danube border and had begun to prepare for an expedition to that area. For the moment, he received the messengers sent by Frederick III to negotiate peace. He imposed the preliminary condition of returning the fortress of Győr, which the delegates of the Hapsburgs did not accept, avoiding a decided answer. In fact, this was only a maneuver of Frederick III meant to give him time to prepare his army. While he initiated these negotiations, only for the sake of appearances, he was at the same time sending letters to the cities of Hungary, urging them to revolt against their governor.

On 23 February 1447, Pope Eugenius IV died. His successor, Nicholas V, did not have as many obligations toward the "king of the Romans." For that reason, and maybe for others also, he was able to treat more freely the problem of reconciliation between Frederick III and Hungary. In April, 1447, the new pope wrote to the king of the Romans, advising him in this sense. He also sent a letter to John Hunyadi in the same spirit.[176] As he did not receive any answer from Frederick III, the pope repeated his advice, offering a mediator in the person of Cardinal Carvajal.[177] The latter actually began his activity only after the two sides had agreed on a new armistice for two years, concluded on 1 June 1447, whose main result was Frederick III's acceptance to return the fortress of Győr. He would keep the other cities until the conclusion of definitive peace, in view of which his representative and those of Hungary were going to meet on 11 November in Vienna with the papal legate. If they would not reach an agreement

---

[176]Teleki, *op. cit.*, X, pp. 200-201.

[177]Ibidem, pp. 201-202.

during that future meeting, the question would be subjected to arbitration by the pope and the College of Cardinals.

This time, Frederick III respected the armistice and returned the fortress of Györ, at the end of June. The settling of the conflict in the west entailed reconciliation with Jan Jiskra as well, against whom they had just fought in the spring. This reconciliation took place on 21 July 1447, through the peace of Rimaszombat,[178] which stipulated in essence the right of Jiskra to rule in Slovakia for three more years, at the end of which he was to return everything to Hungary. He also committed himself to aid the governor against any domestic enemy.

This pacification, be it only temporary, of the western and northern parts, showed that John Hunyadi was, at that time, powerful enough to impose a peace, but not strong enough so to impose peace as he would have liked it. The results of his political efforts during the years 1446 and 1447, however, remain of considerable importance. Hungary was at that moment stronger and more united than it had been under any sovereign in the last sixty to seventy years. The rear of its front was secured by the Hapsburgs, for which it also had the diplomatic assistance of the pope, through the legate Carvajal. The relations of Hungary with Serbia remained uncertain, but those with the Romanian principalities would be consolidated and Hunyadi would be able to count on them for military assistance with about 10,000 men. The subjugated peoples in the Balkans were waiting for him to fulfill their hopes of freedom. Through his fight and activity carried on after his election as governor, he prepared a more solid base for a new attempt to fulfill the hopes set upon him.

[178] Today's Rimavska Sobota, in Slovakia.

CHAPTER X

JOHN HUNYADI AND THE ROMANIAN PRINCIPALITIES

The historical circumstances and his own exceptional merits raised John Hunyadi to the head of a powerful and vast feudal state. The same circumstances also engaged him, a few years earlier, in what we could call "the great politics" of the European world of that time. One of its essential problems was the confrontation of forces in the southeast of the continent with the Ottoman Empire. In this context, John Hunyadi, the central figure in the anti-Ottoman struggle, was in permanent relations with the pope and with the main European powers, being a prominent figure in the diplomacy of the time.

The vast horizon of his political actions did lead him to neglect the immediate picture, or the concrete, traditional basis that his actions were founded on. Hunyadi always showed a special attachment to Transylvania. He owned numerous estates there and the majority of the soldiers under his personal command were originally from there. The family ties, the important dignities that he held there beginning in 1438, the Ottoman threat to the Carpathians and the Danube, also demanded his attention continue to be directed toward his native land.

For its defense, Hunyadi initiated several military and political actions, whose purpose and result was a stronger alliance among the three Romanian lands. Its beginning was represented by the campaign of 1442, and its highest point was around the years 1447-1448.

The relations that were established then among Transylvania, Wallachia, and Moldavia led to the appreciation that John Hunyadi tended toward a political centralization of the three principalities.[179] Evidently, we are not dealing with a centralization in the proper sense of the word. It was a beginning, based first of all on the necessities of the common defensive struggle, realizing a more profound system of alliances than before, but still keeping the aspect of "some agglomerations of sovereign feudal estates, tending to integrate into a larger agglomeration."[180]

Was the intention of personal domination part of his politics? His enemies accused him, after his death, that he had removed some princes of Wallachia and Moldavia, even when they were his allies, and replaced them with others, who would thus be indebted to him personally.

The relations among the three Romanian principalities, under the aegis of John Hunyadi, were part, in all appearances, of his politics of consolidation of the anti-Ottoman front. During the years 1447-1448, they were under the sign of the preparation for a new offensive campaign in the Balkans, which required the political and military security of John Hunyadi all the way to the Danube.

The creation of a common political and military system, imposed by force and comprising all three Romanian principalities, was realized through direct interventions of John Hunyadi, first in Wallachia, and, shortly afterwards, in Moldavia as well. The moment of their occurrence was determined by several immediate causes.

---

[179] Barbu T. Câmpina, "Dezvoltarea economiei feudale şi începuturile luptei pentru centralizarea statului în a doua jumătate a secolului al XV-lea în Moldova şi Ţara Românească," in *Lucrările sesiunii generale ştiinţifice a Academiei*, 2-12 June 1950, Bucureşti, 1951, pp. 1602-1638. The author, a representative of the Marxist historiography in Romania at that time, tried to apply an "official" interpretative model.

[180] Barbu T. Câmpina, op. cit., pp. 1610, 1614. A subtler and more pertinent judgement than the previous one.

After the Burgundian campaign on the Danube, Vlad Dracul signed peace with the Ottomans in the summer of 1447.[181] It appears that, among other conditions of the peace, he returned to them the few thousand Bulgarians who had taken refuge in Wallachia after the reconquest of Giurgiu. John Hunyadi would not accept that Wallachia would become again an insecure territory for him. The more so as in the first stage of the preparations of a new campaign in the Balkans he continued to study the possibility of using the attack plan of Cesarini, in which Wallachia was going to be the main base of operations against the Ottoman Empire.

The Polish chronicler records the information that, in July 1447, Vlad Dracul intervened in Moldavia in favor of his brother-in-law, Roman II.[182] If this date is correct, which is not certain, the action of the Wallachian prince, disliked by Hunyadi, could be connected to the change in his politics. In the same month, Vladislav, a pretender to the throne and called a "relative" by Hunyadi, took refuge from Wallachia in Braşov, the governor recommending the city to receive him well.[183]

These facts numbered themselves among the immediate reasons that determined the governor to strengthen his influence in the Romanian principalities.

The circumstances in which the campaign took place remain a rather obscure chapter in the history of Wallachia. A relatively recent study appears to have elucidated the question of the date which it took placc.

On 6 November 1447, in the treaty with Alphonso V, the king of Aragon and Naples, John Hunyadi expressed his conviction that he would be able to obtain, without expenses, 10,000 soldiers from Wal-

[181]Francisc Pall, "Intervenţia lui Iancu de Hunedoara în Ţara Românească şi Moldova, în anii 1447-1448," in *Studii*, XVI (1963), no. 5, p. 1054.

[182]Cf. I. Minea, "Din trecutul stăpânirii româneşti asupra Ardealului. Pierderea Amlaşului şi a Făgăraşului," Bucureşti, 1914, pp. 25-26 and note 48.

[183]Ibidem, p. 27.

lachia. This could be an indication regarding the campaign that he was preparing.

In the second half of November, John Hunyadi was in Braşov, where he issued documents. After 23 November, he entered Wallachia. He was bringing with him a pretender, a certain Dan, possibly a son of Basarab II, the one who had an ephemeral reign in the spring of 1442. Vlad Dracul was caught unprepared and fled from Târgovişte. But he was caught and killed, together with his son, Mircea, at the orders of Dan. His other two sons, Vlad and Radu, escaped to the Ottomans. On 4 December 1447, Hunyadi issued from Târgovişte, "our fortress," a document in which, to his usual title, he added that of "voievod of the Transalpine land." On 16 December, he was again in Braşov, where he remained until the last days of the year.[184] A letter by John of Zredna, bishop of Oradea, dated 15 January 1448, confirmed the end, crowned by such a rapid success, of this expedition, saying that Wallachia was reduced to submission.

On 1 February 1448, a document from Bistriţa mentions "the unfaithful Vladislav (namely Vlad), who was not alive any longer. In the last day of the same month, Hunyadi, who was in Timişoara, wrote to the city of Braşov and he gave orders that its money circulate in the Transalpine area also, inviting it, together with Sibiu, to consult with "the prominent figures of Wallachia."[185] The fact that Hunyadi did not mention any voievod, but only the boyars, indicates that the situation in Wallachia was uncertain at that moment and that Dan, the initial replacement of Vlad Dracul, was not able to maintain the throne, probably because of internal struggles among the parties, in which the Ottomans might have intervened as well. "Through the foreign chronicles," says Nicolae Iorga, "whose information is valid for that time, passes the wretched and unintelligible phantom of a Dan or Danciul,

---

[184]D. Csánki, *Magyarország történelmi földrajza a Hunyadiak korában*, V, p. 212; Francisc Pall, op. cit., pp. 1052-1053.

[185]Francisc Pall, *op. cit.*, p. 1060.

who is said to have been blinded for his ambition to become prince...."[186]

These are conflicting pieces of information, which complicate the picture even more. According to Długosz, Hunyadi wanted at first to bring as prince of Wallachia, in the place of Vlad Dracul, a certain Stanciul (=Stanciul, Danciul?), but he changed his mind, meaning that he withdrew his support. Stanciul was blinded, and Hunyadi intended to keep the throne of Wallachia for himself. A letter from Constantinople, dated 7 December 1448, says approximately the same thing, except that the respective pretender – whom it does not name – had Ottoman support and was defeated by John Hunyadi. Besides, the letter places the event in November 1448, which is certainly mistaken, as Hunyadi was somewhere else at the time, and the situation of the reign of Wallachia had been clarified to a certain extent.[187]

This information seems to be the echo of an internal struggle that took place in Wallachia,[188] involving two figures: Dan, the direct protégé of Hunyadi, an ephemeral presence on the throne, but whom we shall find again, with the conferred title of prince of Wallachia, during the next campaign of Hunyadi against the Ottomans. This indicates that he might have maintained his authority, possibly in the west of the country. The second figure, Vladislav, also an initial protégé of Hunyadi, appears as prince, but as an exponent of a line of compromise: good relations with both Hungary and the Ottomans. We find him as a refugee in Braşov, under the protection of John Hunyadi, who referred to him as his relative in one of his letters; on 7 August 1448 he occupied the throne of Wallachia, after carrying out negotiations with Hun-

[186]Nicolae Iorga, *Istoria românilor,* vol. IV, pp. 89-90.

[187]I. Minea, *Vlad Dracul şi vremea sa*, p. 215 and note 3.

[188]Without any intention to make a connection, because the uncertainties of the text do not allow it, we are reminded, however, that the humanist Nicolaus Olahus speaks of his uncle, Stanciu, enemy of Vlad Dracul and relative of Hunyadi, who, "captured with cunningness, was given to the axe." Leaving aside the vague character of the entire passage, it seems more plausible, chronologically, to refer to the reign of Vlad the Impaler.

yadi.[189] Without documentary proof, we can assume, based on this contradictory and confusing data, that, faced with the anarchy following the death of Vlad Dracul and with Ottoman interference, John Hunyadi had to resort to a person who would also enjoy Ottoman consent and this is how Vladislav II came to the throne, where he would remain until 1456. During the campaign of the autumn of 1448, John Hunyadi had Dan next to him, to whom he entrusted the command of an important detachment of his army. Either his recent short reign, or the maintenance of his authority in the western regions, toward Severin, could explain the title of prince of Wallachia that was still being attributed to him, but which did not reflect, at that moment, the real situation. In the fall of 1448, the prince of Wallachia was indisputably Vladislav, who was in good relations with Hungary, as well as with the Ottoman commander at Nicopolis. Therefore, including Wallachia in the common front of the anti-Ottoman struggle, following the campaign of the winter of 1447-1448, and the violent death of Vlad Dracul, succeeded only partially.

John Hunyadi made a similar attempt in Moldavia. He had been in good relations with Stephen II, the son of Alexander the Good. He had ruled in Moldavia since 1432, together with his brother Iliaş, whom he had removed in 1444, remaining the only prince until July, 1447, when he was killed by Roman II, the son of Iliaş.[190]

Determined to consolidate the system of alliances, directed by him, to thus ensure the military cooperation of the three principalities, John Hunyadi intervened in Moldavia as well. Chronologically, this action took place immediately after the removal of Vlad Dracul, which indicates its integration in a unitary and deliberate plan. The expedition took place in February, 1448. It was not personally led by Hunyadi. The possible presence at the command of the army of a nobleman by the name of Csupor and his stay in Moldavia for a short time would

[189]Francisc Pall, *op. cit.*, p. 1060.

[190]*Cronicile slavo-române din sec. XV-XVI*, published by Ion Bogdan. Edition revised and completed by P.P. Panaitescu, Bucureşti, Editura Academiei, 1959, p. 15; *Istoria României*, vol. II, p. 421.

explain the recording by some Moldavian chronicles of the two-month reign of a "Ciubăr-Vodă."[191] In reality, Hunyadi only enthroned the pretender Peter II, the brother of Stephen and another relative of his.

The Transylvanian army accomplished its mission between 18 February, when Roman II was still in Suceava, and 23 February, when he was a refugee in Colomeea.[192] Peter II recognized Hunyadi's sovereignty and ceded Chilia to him, also promising to contribute 3,000 soldiers to the next campaign against the Ottomans. Hunyadi installed at Chilia – an important defensive point on the Lower Danube – a garrison, which was commanded for a time by Stoica Gizdavić, who had been entrusted with the negotiations at Adrianople in June, 1444.[193]

Just as in Wallachia, the strengthening of the influence of Hunyadi was opposed by Ottoman interference, leading to the solution of a somewhat neutral prince, of whom both parts approved – Vladislav II – , in the same way the integration of Moldavia into the political system that Hunyadi was hoping for came up against Polish interference. To reach a *modus vivendi*, Hunyadi wrote on 1 August 1448 to the king of Poland, Casimir IV, in favor of Peter II, asking him to accept his presence on the throne of Moldavia. The success of his measure was partial. Poland gave its consent, on 22 August 1448, but only with the condition of the obedience of Peter II. In the document signed on this occasion, the prince committed himself to try to recover what he had estranged from Moldavia. The allusion is clearly made to Chilia and it indicates a certain alienation of Peter from his protector. This justifies the supposition that, at the end of 1448, after the conclusion of the new campaign in the Balkans, John Hunyadi recognized Peter II's rights as

---

[191]This might also refer to the probable presence of a Transylvanian army in Moldavia before 5 April 1445, during a short sharing of the reign between Stephen II and his brother, Peter II; cf. *Istoria României*, vol. II, p. 421.

[192]Francisc Pall, *op. cit.*, p. 1063.

[193]Idem, "Stăpînirea lui Iancu de Hunedoara asupra Chiliei şi problema ajutorării Bizanţului," in *Studii*, XVIII (1965), no. 3, pp. 620-621.

ruler of Moldavia and Chilia, where he maintained, however, an administration, probably until his death.[194]

Although John Hunyadi's attempt to integrate the Romanian principalities into a system of close alliances, under his aegis, was not successful, he would continue this policy. We shall find attempts at this politics after 1448 as well, which indicates not only his constant interest in this problem, but also a certain favorable climate that, in the interest of a common defense, he was enjoying with part of the upper nobility and with the middle and lesser nobilities in the three principalities.

[194]Francisc Pall, "Stăpînirea lui Iancu de Hunedoara asupra Chiliei...," in *Studii*, XVII (1965), no. 3, pp. 621, 630.

CHAPTER XI

BESIDE THE GRAVE OF MURAD I

John Hunyadi was contemplating a new offensive campaign to drive the Ottomans out of Europe already in the year 1447. After the election of Nicholas V as pope, he sent to Rome Nicholas Laszocki, archdeacon of Cracow, a Pole who had arrived in the country with Ladislas I. On his way to Rome, he made a stop in Venice as well. Count Stephen of Segno[195] was sent with a similar mission to Naples, by Alphonso V, the king of Aragon. He sent letters with requests for assistance to Duke Philip of Burgundy and to the king of France, Carol VII. The ban of Croatia, Franko of Talovak, went to Ragusa.

The messengers returned from Rome and Naples only about a year later, without any results. Only Ragusa promised financial aid. On 1 April 1447, Hunyadi received a letter from Ragusa saying that, despite all the difficulties they were having, they would, by all means, send 2,000 florins during that summer, on the day when he crossed the Danube with his army. It is evident here that the campaign was planned for the summer of 1447. The promises of assistance being so poor, Hunyadi had to postpone the campaign by a year. He was determined to do this also by the hope of a definitive conclusion of peace with the Hapsburgs, which was expected in the fall. Once it was obvious that such a peace could not be realized, only the armistice remaining valid until 1449, before it expired the governor had decided to take

[195] Today's Senj, in Croatia.

action during the year 1448.[196] He resumed, therefore, in 1448, with more persistence, the diplomatic efforts that he had initiated a year earlier. The European countries could help him in different ways: with regular weapons, with troops of voluntary "crusaders," with a fleet, and with sums of money.

John Hunyadi did not ask for any assistance from Frederick III. He was content only with the thought that he would not be attacked by the Hapsburgs during the campaign; he did not expect anything else from them. In turn, he wrote to the king of Poland, who, apologizing that the continuous Tartar invasions forced him to keep his army on the eastern border, sent him only a small detachment of 1,000 mounted soldiers.[197]

The governor insisted more in Italy, from where he was hoping to receive money and a fleet that would operate in the Straits again. The negotiations advanced further with Alphonso, the king of Aragon, by whom Count Stephen of Segno continued to stay, as delegate. A messenger of Alphonso, Bernardo Lopez (or Lepiz), came in April 1448 from Naples to Buda bringing gifts and some hopes that his master would be in favor of an alliance against the Ottomans. The Aragonese message seemed insufficient to Hunyadi and, on 28 April, he wrote again to Alphonso, in a tone that denotes irritation, soliciting concrete aid, and not gifts and promises. After two days, he sent a letter to the pope, with the same content and in about the same tone.[198] In June, Stephen of Segno returned to Buda, with the formulation of the points of the treaty of alliance with Aragon. On 24 June 1448, Hunyadi informed the king that he accepted the treaty, that he was preparing for the campaign and would send him the action plan. What were the points of this convention? Its details are not clear. It is almost certain that it stipulated the naval cooperation of Aragon, for a repetition of

[196]Lajos Kiss, "A rgómezei hadjárat," in *Hadtörténelmi Közlemények,* 1895, pp. 17-18.

[197]Ibidem, p. 34.

[198]Fejér, *op. cit.*, pp. 108-111; in Pray, *Annales Regum Hungariae*, part III, Vienna, 1766, pp. 62-63, the letter to Alphonso is dated 23 May.

the attempt of 1444 to block the Straits. Mention should be made that, for the realization of such a plan, the naval forces of Aragon were insufficient. The naval participation of Venice, as well as the financial cooperation of the pope, were necessary.[199]

These two conditions could not be met. The trips that Nicholas Laszocki made to Rome brought the governor, from the pope, the title and emblem of duke; as for any financial or military assistance, he only received promises which would never be kept. The few attempts that the pope made to collect some money were initiated so late that the planned campaign could no longer use it. Only on 28 August the pope asked the great master of the Teutonic order to send to Rome a third of the sums collected for the conversion of the Ruthenians and of other "infidels," to be given as aid to Hungary against the Ottomans. Hunyadi benefitted nothing from the tithe collections or other papal revenues either.[200]

The military assistance from Venice was completely compromised by the events that were taking place in Italy. In 1447, Filippo Visconti, the duke of Milan, died without leaving any heirs. The only one who could claim certain legal rights to succession was Alphonso V of Aragon. Taking advantage of the situation created in Milan (the city would have preferred to form an independent republic), Venice occupied the localities of Lodi and Piacenza, which caused the war between it and Milan. Venice sent a fleet toward west, on the Pad River, but Francesco Sforza, the commander of Milan's troops, destroyed it, just as he defeated Venice's infantry in September 1448. Alphonse V began war against Venice. The latter destroyed his fleet in the naval battles of Messina and Siracuza, on the coasts of Sicily. Aragon and Venice made peace only in 1449. Thus, the conflicts among the Italian states prevented the application of the treaty of alliance between Hungary and Aragon, and shattered any hopes of assistance from Venice. Impressed by the events and seeing them as a timely pretext for ex-

---

[199]Kiss, *op. cit.*, pp. 37-38.

[200]Kiss, *op. cit.*, pp. 38-39.

plaining his failure to cooperate, Pope Nicholas V advised John Hunyadi to postpone the campaign for another year, when the circumstances would allow him to offer him more assistance.[201] It was the confirmation of another dissolution of any hopes for a European alliance.

On 8 September 1448, the governor answered the pope with a dignified letter in which he made efforts to hold back his reproaches to preserve the respectful manner in which he was supposed to address the supreme pontiff: "We have addressed Your Holiness with complete faith, with the conviction that we shall obtain not only promises, but real help. Your Holiness, however, encouraging us rather than giving us support, wishes the postponement of the campaign and anticipates a delay in the assistance. But when our old enemy has gained new powers as a result of its latest victories over Christianity and is gathering great forces at our borders, it is useful for us to take up arms, so that an attack does not find us unprepared... The news came too late. The war has been decided, the army has been gathered, the orders have been given. *Power is always greater when used in attack rather than in defense,* and the outcome of the war smiles more favorably upon the one who pursues the enemy in its own land. Besides, it is not certain that next year we shall be able to gather the same army and that it will be as enthusiastic. We are prepared to do everything to defend our country from the impending danger. Our descendants will glorify our victory, as well as our death in battle. We and our brave comrades have endangered our lives for the well-being of Christianity, and it would be appropriate for the Holy Father to offer financial help for the gathering of a supporting army."[202]

The letter points out, in a rhetoric that reveals the style of a humanist, the political and military conceptions of John Hunyadi. Without waiting for the outcome of the negotiations with the West, he was making preparations. With expressions of the same eloquence, he also

---

[201]Ibidem, p. 39.

[202]Fejér, *op. cit.*, pp. 116-119. The same ideas are also found in the letter dated 17 September 1448, also addressed to the pope. Pray, *op. cit.*, pp. 64-66.

announced his departure on campaign to the doge of Venice, Francesco Foscari. He was counting on the help of the countries that were directly threatened by the Ottomans, but especially on the domestic forces that were at his disposal.

The historical sources mention a contingent of 8,000 Wallachian mounted soldiers, under the command of Dan, "the prince of Wallachia."[203] They also mention a Wallachian attempt to cross the Danube at Nicopolis, rejected by the Ottomans. In October, 1448, the prince of Wallachia was, as we have shown, Vladislav II, who was in good relations with the Ottoman commander in Nicopolis, but still worried about an Ottoman attack. There appears again the difficulty to establish the truth regarding the situation in Wallachia in 1448 and the Wallachian assistance given to this second campaign of John Hunyadi in the Balkans. We have made a supposition earlier that Dan and Vladislav shared, for a short time, the reign in Wallachia, the first ruling west and the second east of the Olt River. Dan presumably participated in the campaign (and maybe that is why he lost the throne definitively), and Vladislav did not. In this case, though, Dan would not have been able to offer such a considerable military contingent from Wallachia, the 8,000 soldiers mentioned by the sources. On the other hand, this would explain to some extent why Vladislav II, although in good relations with the Ottomans, was still worried about an attack from their part; he could, eventually, be suspected of secret complicity with the other prince. This Wallachian cooperation in the battles of 1448 is still an obscure question. In any case, even if we admitted it, we believe that the number of 8,000 soldiers is exaggerated. Another hypothesis might be that Dan, retired in Transylvania after his short-lived reign south of the Carpathians, participated in the campaign commanding Transylvanian troops, and the title of prince was still attributed to him out of esteem, or due to a mistake of the chroniclers.

The cooperation of Despot Branković could not be obtained in any way. The campaign was going to take place on Serbian territory,

[203]Chalkokondyles, *op. cit.*, pp. 209-210.

and, under these circumstances, the provisioning, the transportation of the army, and, to a great extent, the success of the expedition depended on Serbia. John Hunyadi solicited an alliance in advance, but Branković, consistent with his policy of good relations with the Ottomans, adopted after the peace of Seghedin, rejected it.

After 1443, the relations of George Branković with Hungary deteriorated. Eventually, the estates that the despot owned in the country were confiscated. Ever since 1446, Branković had felt offended that he had not been elected governor of Hungary and now, in the campaign organized by Hunyadi, he, a sovereign, could not accept to be subordinated to the governor.

The reasons invoked by Branković for rejecting the alliance with Hungary were the deplorable situation of Serbia and the week chances of success of the campaign, given the cold season. In reality, there were many deeper reasons for controversy between the two countries than personal discontentments or the invoked pretexts. Branković, a man over 80 years old, had come to fear the force of the Ottomans too much to be able to believe in the power of the Hungarian army. He did not fully trust Hunyadi's intentions either. He was afraid that, under the cover of the liberation struggle, the Hungarian governor was hiding the intention to subjugate the peoples of the Balkans to Hungary. This fear was also nourished by the difference in religion. After the council held in Florence in 1439, when the papacy had manifested so clearly its intention to take advantage of the hardships of the peoples in the East to bring them back to Catholicism, the Serbians – an Orthodox people –saw in the help offered by a Catholic country a hidden attempt at conversion to Catholicism. Even the traditional Serbian songs about John Hunyadi – whom they called Jank Sibinianin[204] – sometimes present him as a fanatical crusader who aimed to forcibly convert to Catholicism the peoples liberated by his army.

Another reason that prevented Serbia from engaging in the campaign of 1448 was the conflict between Branković and Bosnia over the

[204]The Transylvanian.

region of Srebrenica, on the left bank of the Drina River. In September, when John Hunyadi was preparing to begin the advance, battles were being fought between the Serbians and the Bosnians.

However, all these facts do not justify the attitude of Branković, who could have at least kept a correct, if not benevolent neutrality. He adopted a hostile attitude, doing everything he dared and could to hinder the provisioning of Hunyadi's army, constantly informing the Ottomans about its movements.

In turn, an effective cooperation was possible between Hungary and Albania. The close relations between the two countries began in 1446 at the initiative of Scanderbeg and with the help of Ragusa. During the preparations for the campaign of 1448, John Hunyadi sent messengers to Scanderbeg and to his father in law George Arianiti, asking for their assistance. It appears that on this occasion they concluded an alliance[205] whose existence is confirmed by the movements of the Albanian army in the fall of that year, meant to join forces with Hunyadi's troops in Macedonia.

The campaign of 1448 assisted the struggle of the Albanian people, even if we do not assume the existence of a formal alliance. Toward the end of the spring of 1448, the sultan, determined to end the Albanian "rebellion," attacked Scanderbeg with an army of about one hundred thousand men. He conquered a few localities, and besieged Croya, the main center of resistance, but was not able to conquer it. The news of Hunyadi's preparations and possibly other reasons also determined the sultan to raise the siege of Croya and retreat from Albania during the month of August.[206] Once more, Scanderbeg could not be defeated, due to the indirect help of Hunyadi, although his enemy, Venice, in cooperation with the Ottomans, was plotting his destruction. The war with Venice, which ended only on 4 October 1448, prevented

---

[205]Francisc Pall, "Les relations entre la Hongrie et Scanderbeg," in *Revue historique du Sud-Est européen*, X (1933), nos. 4-6, pp. 127-128 and note 5.

[206]Francisc Pall, *op. cit.*, p. 128; idem, *Marino Barlezio…*, p. 73.

Scanderbeg, to a great extent, from advancing into Macedonia to join forces with Hunyadi.

The diplomatic preparations of the campaign required less time than the practical preparations: gathering weapons, equipment, provisions, and soldiers. The failure of the negotiations with other states in view of obtaining assistance demonstrated that the campaign would have to rely mostly on its domestic forces.

The regions where Hunyadi traveled most for the purpose of obtaining help were mainly in east of the country, where he owned many estates and had more personal connections. Transylvania and the Banat were almost entirely under his authority; in 1448, he was still holding the title of voievod of Transylvania, *comite* of the Szecklers, *comite* of Timişoara and Solnoc.

From October 1447 to March 1448, the governor traveled throughout Transylvania, taking different administrative measures. We find him in Caransebeş, Aiud, Braşov, Odorhei, Bistriţa, Sebeş, Sighişoara, Turda, and Timişoara.[207] In the spring of 1448, he went back to Hungary, and in May he participated in the Diet at Buda. During this meeting, the Diet gave its approval for the campaign against the Ottomans and the expenses required by it. At the same meeting, the Diet named Emeric Pelsöczi Bebek, Hunyadi's trusted associate, as the second voievod of Transylvania, and Nicholas Ujlaki as the surrogate for the governor when he was not in the country.

After the Diet, John Hunyadi intensified his preparations. In July, he went to Transylvania again. He gave orders that soldiers be paid their remaining pay. On 1 August, from Mediaş, he announced to the king of Poland, Casimir IV, of his approaching departure on the campaign, adding among the reasons, as befitted the occasion, that of vengeance for the violent death of his predecessor, Ladislas III, at Varna. After a few days, he left for Timişoara. He returned to Transylvania, where he ordered his treasurer, the Italian Odoardo Manini, to col-

[207]During this time, he also organized the campaigns in Wallachia and Moldavia, the first of which he commanded himself.

lect the money for the salt[208] mines from certain noblemen who had committed themselves to this contribution. He also ordered him to have 1,000 horseshoes and other equipment sent from Dej for the needs of the army.[209] At the end of August Hunyadi was in Caransebeş, and then at the Danube, in the camp at Kubin, where he remained to take measures for the beginning of the offensive.

What military forces did Hungary and Transylvania have at their disposal at that time and what could have been the outcome of the zealous activity of organization that the governor was carrying on?

Hungary, within its medieval borders, was, at the middle of the fifteenth century, an important military power among the European countries. It had at its disposal more soldiers than, for example, England, France, or Poland. It is considered to have been able to gather around 80,000 soldiers for a defensive war and about half of this number for a campaign outside its borders. However, just as within the Holy Roman Empire, numerous refusals by the noblemen prevented the full mobilization of these forces. In comparison with the Ottoman Empire, which could gather, even for an offensive war, 150,000 to 170,000 soldiers (counting auxiliary troops), the military power of Hungary appears rather reduced.

For the campaign of 1448, John Hunyadi was able to gather, in total, approximately 22,000 to 24,000 soldiers,[210] most of whom were mercenaries. Royal troops constituted the nucleus of the army, comprised of mercenaries paid out of royal revenues, which John Hunyadi, as governor, had received the right to use for such purposes. These units were formed mainly of heavy cavalry. The same army included the 1,000 Poles sent by King Casimir IV.

---

208 "*Pro pretio salium.*"

209 Fejér, *op. cit.*, p. 116.

210 These are numbers given by Bonfinius and Thuróczi; the number given by Długosz is approximately 30,000; according to Chalkokondyles, it was 47,000 to 51,000, and according to Aeneas Sylvius Piccolomini it was 70,000, which is much exaggerated.

The troops of the noblemen consisted in their majority of lightly-equipped mounted soldiers. This time, John Hunyadi was able to give more importance to the infantry, especially to its transportation by wagons in the Hussite manner. This was the campaign in which he tried to apply to a large extent this system of transportation and battle. His army included about 4,000 infantrymen, mercenaries of different nationalities, but especially Germans and Czechs.

Regarding the armament, besides the usual weapons – the bow and arrow, the sword, and the spear, special attention was given to firearms, which, at that time, represented the latest technology. In many cities of Hungary, in the first half of the fifteenth century, many cannon foundries and gunpowder workshops opened. John Hunyadi made numerous orders to such foundries and workshops, especially to those in Bardiov (Bártfa) and Pojon. They manufactured both large cannons for sieges, as well as smaller cannons, for battle, placed on four wheels. The cannon balls were usually made of stone, but also of lead or copper.

The historical sources agree that John Hunyadi had many cannons in the campaign of 1448. They say that his army had brought along about 2,000 wagons, of which many were pulling cannons. A special model is mentioned among these, called *zarobotana,* a transformed Italian word *(cerboccana)* which meant a cannon that fired at a greater distance, because it had a barrel longer than was common at that time.[211]

The wagons that transported the infantry were loaded with the necessary provisions and weapons. Two soldiers were riding in each wagon, one of them carrying a rifle, the other one carrying usual armaments and a shield.[212] The rifles were very difficult to handle and could only be used for defense, in places chosen beforehand, because they had to be rested on a support stuck in the ground.

---

[211]Lajos Kropf, "Zarobotana," in *Hadtörténelmi Közlemények*, 1914, pp. 471-473.

[212]Chalkokondyles, *op. cit.*, p. 209.

These preparations were taking place in a rather difficult atmosphere for John Hunyadi. The higher noblemen would only give him limited support. Some of them, upset by his energetic rule, were secretly hoping that he would be defeated and not return or have his prestige weakened to such an extent that he could be removed from power. The noblemen were not obligated, according to the laws of the country, to participate in campaigns across the border. Knowing what he could expect from some of them and being limited by legal provisions, John Hunyadi did not declare a general mobilization and did not oblige the high prelates and the higher noblemen to participate with their troops.

He was followed only by those who had kinship, friendship, or direct vassalage ties to him. The chronicles mention the presence in the army of the following: the other voievod of Transylvania, Emeric Pelsöczi Bebek, together with his brother Ladislas; John Székely, the ban of Slovenia, a nephew, or more likely the brother-in-law of the governor;[213] the great *uşier* Emeric Marczali; Michael Szilágyi, another brother-in-law of Hunyadi; Franko of Talovak, the ban of Dalmatia and Croatia; a few less important magnates and noblemen. They also mention the presence of the Ottoman pretender Saudji (Daud Çelebi), who had come to Hungary during the Burgundian campaign on the Danube.

The goal that John Hunyadi pursued in this campaign was to some extent different from that of the previous one. Consequently, his attack plan was different also. Although in a letter to the pope, dated 17 September 1448, he declared that his intention was to advance into enemy territory, "not only to fight the war, but *to end it*,"[214] it is very unlikely for such an experienced military man to have entertained the hope to accomplish such a goal with the limited resources that he had. Not even cooperation with Scanderbeg would have justified his belief that, during that year, he would be able to drive the Ottomans out of Europe.

[213]"*Corvini e sorore frater*," Bonfinius, III, 7, p. 341.

[214]Pray, *op. cit.*, p. 65.

He was hoping, however, to win a victory against the Ottomans that would open the opportunity for him to continue the campaign in the following year, all the way to the shores of the Bosphorus. This explains why, at the end of September, when there were only a few days before he gave the signal to begin the advance, he was still sending messengers to Rome and Venice to present his plans and solicit assistance.

John Hunyadi was, therefore, planning to drive the Ottomans out of Europe in different stages. The first step, which was going to be accomplished in the fall of 1448, with the help of Scanderbeg, was going to be the conquest of Macedonia and the port of Thessalonika. Advancing through southern Serbia and joining forces with the Albanian army, he would have split the European part of the Ottoman Empire in half.

By conquering Macedonia, Albania was protected from new Ottoman attacks. Thessalonika could become a base for the Venetian and Aragonese fleets, in view of blocking the Straits, and a starting point, on land, for a decisive attack in the direction of Adrianople.

In his camp on the Danube, during the month of September, 1448, John Hunyadi was finalizing the last details of this plan. On 28 September,[215] he began his advance south, from the spot where the Morava River flows into the Danube. Another section of the army crossed the big river by the fortress of Severin. It was probably that part of the army which, Wallachian or not, was under the command of Voievod Dan. It advanced through the valley of Timoc,[216] and, when there were three or four days of marching to Niš, it met with the main group that was coming along the right bank of the Morava.

---

[215]"*Pridie penultimam Septembris ab Danubio... castra mota fuere.*" Fejér, *op. cit.*, p. 126.

[216]This probably is the source of information in Turkish chronicles that, during the preparations made by the sultan, an army from Wallachia crossed the Danube "at Nicopolis" (which is wrong), being rejected by the beys at the borders. The fact that part of the army crossed at Severin explains the error made by Thuróczi, part IV, chapter 46, p. 426, who claims that Hunyadi crossed the Danube there, since a series of incontestable documents certify that he was at Kubin from 6 to 28 September.

The entire army arrived at Niš, from where it headed southwest toward Prokuplje; from there it followed the Toplica River, all the way to Kursumlija; then it turned even more toward the south, crossing over part of the Kopaonik Mountains, south of the pass called Jankova Klissura in traditional Serbian songs.[217] Then it descended into the valley of the Lab River, and in not more than two days it arrived at the Field of the Blackbirds. This was on 14 or 15 October 1448.

A mistake that John Hunyadi made during this advance of over 300 kilometers into enemy territory – despite his vast experience – was the poor organization of intelligence concerning Ottoman movements. His spies brought him little information, mostly inaccurate, convincing him that the sultan was in Adrianople or Philippopolis, east of Bulgaria, when, in fact, the Ottoman army was gathering at Sofia. Not even when he crossed through Niš, which was 3 or 4 days away from the Ottomans, did John Hunyadi know these details; the appearance of the Ottoman army at the Field of the Blackbirds and the direction from which it was coming were a surprise to him.

On the other hand, Murad was extremely well-informed about the movements of the Hungarian army, both through the information sent by Branković, as well as by his own spies.

Another mistake was that of confusing, while crossing through Serbia, the feelings of the Serbian people with the attitude of the despot. Branković's refusal to assist him was hastily interpreted by Hunyadi as hostility from the Serbian population as well. Thus, according to some sources, he allowed his army to plunder the regions it was marching through.

Where were the Ottomans at this time and how were they preparing to confront the most dreaded enemy they had encountered in Europe until then?

In the summer of that year, the sultan was in Albania, where he besieged Croya. That was where he received the news from Branković

[217]But it is not certain that its name came from that of John Hunyadi. Legends and traditional songs made this association.

about the forthcoming attack from Hungary. At the beginning or middle of August, he left Albania and headed for Sofia. He was expecting to be attacked by greater forces than those he had fought at Varna, and so, from Sofia, he took serious measures of defense. Messengers traveled throughout the entire empire, all the way to Asia Minor, announcing, in the name of the sultan, a holy war and general mobilization. The usual troops gathered in the camp at Sofia: the janissaries, the spahis from Rumelia and Anatolia, and a great number of auxiliary troops. Even the remote emirate of Carmania, which had often rebelled against Ottoman domination, sent a detachment. The historical sources give immense numbers regarding the army gathered by the Ottomans on this occasion. The exaggerations of some of them reach as high as 150,000 and even up to 400,000 soldiers.[218] The oldest and most reliable Turkish chronicles speak, however, of 50,000-60,000 soldiers,[219] to which a number of auxiliary troops was probably added.

The sultan took a few new measures regarding the training and equipping of his army. Part of the janissaries were armed with firearms. The army included a mobile artillery, although weaker than the Hungarian one. It was well-equipped with supplemental weapons, which was going to be obvious during the battle, when Murad would be able to give weapons, against custom, to auxiliary personnel: wagon drivers, servants, etc.

The Ottoman army left Sofia after John Hunyadi had crossed through Niš and headed southwest. The Ottomans advanced through Pirot, by Niš, arriving at Kursunlu-Kilisse (The Lead Church), which was, in all probability, today's Kuršumlija. From there they followed the Hungarian army, taking the same route that it had taken two or three days earlier.

---

[218]Chalkokondyles, *op. cit.*, p. 210, and a French letter from Constantinople; cf. Kiss, *op. cit.*, pp. 169-170.

[219]The Turkish anonymous chronicle from 1486. More recent research demonstrates that, in the fifteenth century, the difficulties of provisioning it with food, fodder, and water made it impossible for any army to exceed these numbers.

John Hunyadi was supposed to meet Scanderbeg before the passes that led into the valley of the Vardar, toward Macedonia. He stopped to rest his army for a few days, north of the Field of the Blackbirds, near Pristina, an old residence of the Serbian *cnezi* from the twelfth century.

The Field of the Blackbirds is the name of the region in the superior valley of the Sitnica river, which flows from north to northwest. It is a region with rolling hills, about 500-600 meters high. It is about 40 kilometers long, from north to south, and 14-17 kilometers broad, from east to west. Around it there are mountains, between 1,000-1,300 meters high. The Sitnica and Lab rivers, which join on the northern border of the region, allowed the army to provide itself with water during its stops.

In the offing, among the soft hills that surrounded it, at a certain distance from the junction of the two rivers, toward the south, loomed the outline of a tall, somber, stone pyramid, which was guarding the area, like a bad omen. It was the tomb of Murad I, whose life had ended there, sixty years before, by the dagger of a Serbian hero named Milos Obilić.

While the army of John Hunyadi was waiting for the arrival of Scanderbeg from the south, on the morning of 17 October, a Thursday, Ottoman detachments appeared unexpectedly from the opposite direction. It was the vanguard of the sultan's army. Later in the day, his entire army appeared in endless lines, positioning itself in the valley of the Lab River, on its southern bank, having the Sitnica River to the west and the hills that bordered the Field of the Blackbirds to the east.

John Hunyadi, faced with the unexpected appearance of the Ottomans, had two choices: either to retreat toward the south, to thus hasten the joining of forces with Scanderbeg, or to resist on the spot, waiting for the Albanians, who could not be far behind. The governor renounced the idea of a retreat to the south. It would have been demoralizing for the soldiers to find themselves being pursued during a march through an unknown territory and in a direction leading them farther away from their home country. At the same time, it would have been difficult to avoid an Ottoman attack on the army aligned in marching position, a situation in which they would be risking certain defeat. On the other hand, in the place where it was at the time, Hunyadi's army was in a favorable position for battle, which he did not know if he would again find.

Those were the reasons that determined him to fight on this spot. He immediately sent the cavalry to block the way to Pristina against the Ottomans, which it succeeded in doing, at the cost of some rather bloody clashes, throughout the entire day of 17 October. Only toward evening did the Ottoman vanguard retreat toward the Lab River where the sultan had established his camp.

At the same time, John Hunyadi's soldiers were putting together a makeshift fortification made of wagons around their camp. The position occupied by them was more advantageous than that of the Ottomans. They were situated on a hill, from where their cannons dominated the valley, toward the north. The position of the Ottomans had one main disadvantage: in case of a retreat, their army would have immediately been split in two. One side would have been pushed toward the valley of Sitnica, and the other upstream on the Lab. That would have happened because, behind their camp, at the junction of the two rivers, there were hills that would have prevented a retreat. On the other hand, the Ottoman army was not in danger of running out of water, while Hunyadi's army was at quite a distance from the river. The distance separating the two camps was about 4-5 kilometers.

Hunyadi deployed his army in two main sections: the cavalry and the infantry. He placed the latter inside the fortification of wagons, where he also placed his reserves.[220] The cannons were aimed toward the field in front of them, crowded with the white multitude of the Ottomans. Some of them were placed on wagons, others were placed directly on the ground. The plan of the governor was to fight the main battle with the help of his cavalry. After it had been repulsed, the in-

---

[220]Michel de Montaigne, in his famous *Essais*, book III, chapter 6, describes the utilization of wagons by the Hungarian army, "*du temps de nos péres... contre les Turcs.*" Montaigne had read the chronicle of Chalkokondyles; cf. Kropf, "A régi magyár szekérvár," in *Hartörténelmi Közlemények*, 1914, pp. 297-299.

fantrymen from inside the camp would hold the enemy back, while the cavalry would gather its strength to be able to fight again. This plan, which took into consideration the necessity of cooperation between the cavalry and the infantry, combining of attack with the defensive, as well as the extensive utilization of firearms – cannons, guns – made the second confrontation on the Field of the Blackbirds, in 1448, one of the first battles using modern military concepts.

At the break of dawn on Friday, 18 October, the army prepared for battle. The thirty-eight flags[221] of the cavalry were disposed into two lines. In the middle of the first line was the heavy cavalry from Croatia, Slovenia, and Transylvania, under the command of John Székely, next to whom was the Croatian Ban Franko of Talovak, a veteran of many difficult battles in the previous years. At the center, but in the second line, John Hunyadi himself was commanding the royal troops[222] and other units of mercenaries, as well as troops from Transylvania. Eastward, on the right flank, there were the troops of the magnates, commanded by Benedict Losonczi, having the light cavalry in the first line and the heavy cavalry in the second line. The left flank was arranged in the same way, the flag of Voievod Dan waving in front of it, and that of the nobleman Stephen Banffy at its back. The third line of the army was formed of the infantry and the cannons inside the fortification of wagons.

In front of the Hungarian army, along the entire width of 10-11 kilometers of the valley, from the Sitnica River toward the east, the Ottoman army took up positions. On the northern bank of the Lab River, at the foot of the Gredec Hills, there were the tents and wagons, guarded by troops of sorts, in large numbers. By way of exception, the-

[221]Military units.

[222]Chalkokondyles says that under the command of Hunyadi there were some soldiers that he calls "*bitezides, bitaxides,*" a term that was connected to the Hungarian word *vitéz*, meaning, probably, heavily-equipped mounted soldiers. This is also the opinion of Mihail Dan, op. cit., p. 82. Hammer, the well-known author of a great Ottoman history, assumed that it referred to *pixides = Büchsenträger*, meaning riflemen, infantrymen; cf. Teleki, *A Hunyadiak kora Magyarországon*, vol. II, Pesta, 1852, p. 86, note 4.

se soldiers, who usually did not participate in the battle – servants, wagon drivers – were also provided with weapons and placed under the command of Bey Sinan, ready, if necessary, to enter the battle. To enhance the courage and discipline of these men, who were not used to weapons, the sultan left among them a few detachments of regular troops, cavalry, and infantrymen. The sultan gave weapons to the auxiliary elements for the defense of the camp, considering that in this way he would have more freedom in using the janissaries in his attack.

South of the Lab, there was the army proper, disposed in two lines, like the Hungarian army, in a slanting position, its eastern end being in front and its western farther back, by the Sitnica. The imposing tent of Sultan Murad II rose in the middle, surrounded by others, belonging to the Ottoman commanders. The heir of the sultan, the future Murad III, was also there. During the previous afternoon and evening they had dug a trench around the tents, behind which they had piled the dugout earth, thus building a slope, interrupted from place to place by recesses, which displayed threatening cannon barrels. In front of the tents, there stood the tight lines of the janissaries. On the shoulders of some of them glittered the steel of rifles. Beyond the trench, on three sides, there were the *asapi* – the non-regular infantry.

Toward the Sitnica River, on the right flank of the Ottoman army, the Anatolian troops had been arranged, commanded by their new beylerbey, Skuras-pasha (Sguro), of Albanian origin. In the second line, there were the *spahis*, in front there were the *asapi* and the *akingi.*[223] It is notable that, against their custom, in this battle, even though it was being fought in Europe, the Ottomans placed the troops from Asia on their right flank.

On the other side, the troops from Rumelia, arranged in the same manner as the right flank, placed closer to the Hungarian front, were

[223]Non-regular, mounted troops.

standing ready to launch the first attack, under the command of Bey Karadja.[224]

Some sources claim that the commanders of both armies held a speech before the beginning of the battle. John Hunyadi is said to have reminded his troops of the defeat of Varna and the death of the king, asking them to avenge these facts. He would have told them that, without victory, no retreat was impossible. "If we win," he would have concluded, "we shall win a good and secure life for our country, forever, and an immortal name for ourselves. If we are defeated, we shall die with glory and eternal life is waiting for us on the other side....[225]"

In the center of his camp, the sultan, facing Mecca, is said to have dismounted and pressed his face against the ground for a while; afterwards, he raised his arms toward the sky and prayed aloud to Allah: "Almighty Lord! Do not destroy us in front of the infidels, for the multitude of my sins, these faithful servants of yours, but help them and grant them victory!" He would have also told his soldiers that he, the sultan, was forced to fight this battle, meaning that he was the victim of an unprovoked aggression. He urged his soldiers to battle, saying that he was confident in their victory, both because of their previous victories, as well as their numerical superiority.

Both speeches, as they are presented, reveal the influence of humanist rhetoric and are, evidently, formulated in detail, in the classic manner. We do not exclude, however, the possibility that the two commanders held speeches consisting of these ideas, but which would have been much shorter and less elegant in their style.

At the beginning of the battle, a soldier from Hunyadi's army stepped out of the line and challenged anyone in the Ottoman army to fight him. The son of a janissary from Anatolia immediately answered

[224]Chalkokondyles, *op. cit.*, p. 210; Kiss, *op, cit.*, claims that the left flank was commanded by Great Vizier Halil.

[225]Aeneas Sylvius, in his letter to Pope Nicholas V, sent from Wiener Neustadt, on 25 November 1448. Apud Fejér, op. cit., pp. 130-131. Bonfinius also attributes such a speech to Hunyadi; cf. IIIrd decade, book 7, pp. 339-340.

the provocation. The two soldiers fought fiercely, their spears broke, and the Hungarian fell to the ground, together with his horse.

The Ottoman, who had broken his weapons and his saddle girths, could hardly stay mounted and therefore returned to his camp without attacking the fallen adversary. The sultan immediately gave orders that he be rewarded with rich gifts.[226]

The Ottomans were the first to attack, with their left flank, formed of the troops from Rumelia. At the first clash, the first line of the Hungarian right flank, formed of light cavalry, retreated, without dispersing its lines, and made room for the heavy cavalry. The latter entered the battle and a fierce fight began on the entire eastern part of the field. The fight also began on the flank by the Sitnica River, developing in the same manner. John Hunyadi weakened his center, to some extent, sending troops to aid the flanks. Part of the heavy cavalry, which he directed toward the eastern flank, was under his personal command. Observing the maneuver of the governor, Murad II sent his first line against the center of the Hungarian army; the *asapi* managed to penetrate deeply, but the intense fire of the cannons and of the rifles in the wagons stopped them, and the Hungarian infantry, counterattacking, drove them back to where they had come from.

On the western side of their front, the Ottomans were also being held in place. On the right flank, which was the central point of the battle, they retreated toward their camp. Hungarian cavalry pursued them as far as the bank of a brook, called Brnjica, where they stopped to water their horses. Evening fell upon the battlefield and both armies retreated to their camps.

In the Christian camp, the general opinion was that the day represented a victory. The Ottomans had been repelled and suffered great casualties; they were talking about 15,000-16,000 Ottomans that had remained on the battlefield. They believed, remembering previous battles, that the next day the Ottomans would retreat without a fight. Never, in the previous years, had a battle lasted longer than a day. The

---

[226]Chalkokondyles, *op. cit.*, pp. 210-211.

truth was that the Ottomans had not been weakened nearly as much as the Hungarians believed. The janissaries and part of the Asian spahis had not yet participated in the battle. Also, the auxiliary troops had not yet moved. Greater losses had only been suffered by the Ottoman left flank. A great part of it had dispersed into the surrounding mountains, where the Serbians, driven out of their villages, began to harass the isolated groups of Ottoman fugitives. On the whole, the outcome of the first day was undecided.

The night did not bring the usual calm. The Ottoman *asapi* and *akingi* harassed the Hungarian camp even after dark. John Hunyadi held a war council. They listened to the opinion of the Ottoman pretender Daud Çelebi, who proposed a surprise attack, at night, against the sultan's camp. He maintained that the Ottomans would not expect such an attack and that this was a decisive way to claim victory for their side. The plan was agreed to and, after midnight, part of the army set out to make the attack. The Ottoman camp, however, was well guarded. The Hungarian attempt was discovered in time and they sounded the alarm. The janissaries remained at their posts and repulsed the attack.[227]

At the break of dawn, on 19 October, before resuming the fight, the sultan removed the cavalry from Thessaly from his left flank, placing it under the command of Turakhan, the beylerbey of Rumelia, and giving it a special mission: to outflank the left flank of the Hungarian army. This powerful detachment took a roundabout route, remaining for a time away from the battle.

On that day, the Ottomans attacked with their troops from Anatolia, which had suffered far fewer losses the previous day. Therefore, this time the battle had its central point on the right bank of the Sitnica

---

[227]Chalkokondyles, op. cit., p. 213; John Hunyadi, in a letter to Nicholas, the dean of Cracow, dated 30 December 1448, as well as Aeneas Sylvius, in the quoted letter, speak only of a continuous exchange of cannon fire. The same Aeneas Sylvius claims that during the night part of Hunyadi's army deserted: "*Non parva Hungarorum manus per tenebras elapsaest, quae secuturae lucis noluit experiri fortunam*;" Fejér, *op. cit.*, p. 131.

River. Hunyadi had learned something about the intentions of the Ottomans, and therefore he had strengthened his western flank overnight and placed it under the command of John Székely.[228]

The first wave of the Ottoman light troops was repelled. The Anatolian spahis attacked, being met by the heavy cavalry of Hunyadi. His flanks held, and the center, under his personal command, made a breach in the lines of the janissaries. John Hunyadi concentrated his cannon fire on the Ottoman center and began to attack, using his infantry and mobile cannons. The janissaries resisted obstinately in front of their camp. The attack gradually weakened. Unexpectedly, there appeared the Ottoman reserves, the auxiliary troops commanded by Sinan-bey, which the sultan had brought south of the Lab River. Although these troops were not very valuable, at least in terms of their numbers, they facilitated the mission of the janissaries and caused casualties among Hunyadi's lines. The Hungarians began to retreat. John Hunyadi's life was endangered: he fell off his horse and was saved by a soldier from Hunedoara, Teodor Cnezul, who gave him his horse. Later on, the governor would reward him with estates.[229]

The right flank fought a difficult battle, and Benedict Losonczi, who was commanding it, could not send any help to the center. Disaster struck on the left flank. The troops of Turakhan-bey appeared behind it. Caught between two fires, the army of Voievod Dan was massacred and forced to capitulate. John Székely was killed. Losing the battle on the left flank had immediate consequences on the entire battlefield. The remaining elements of Hunyadi's army were forced to retreat inside the wagon fortification. During the night, before 20 October, the Ottomans continued to attack the Hungarian camp, watched by the sultan, who stayed awake the whole night amidst the janissaries.

---

[228]Bonfinius is the only one who reports this change of command.

[229]Some authors believe that this incident took place on the first day. But the mention in the document: "helping him escape from the hands of the enemies," although it could be gratuitous, meant to underline the merits of the beneficiary of the reward, makes us believe, however, that the incident happened on 19 October.

A quick inspection of his camp convinced Hunyadi of the gravity of his defeat. He had lost about 17,000 soldiers.[230] Among those who fell in battle were: John Székely, the ban of Slavonia, Franko of Talovak, the ban of Croatia, the great *uşier* Emeric Marczali, Benedict Losonczi, who had commanded the right flank, Stephen Bánffy, George Csáky, the *comite* of Sătmar; there were rumors of the death of the papal legate Bartolomeu, bishop of "Corona;"[231] Emeric Pelsöczi Bebek, the second voievod of Transylvania, was also seriously injured.

The only thing Hunyadi could do was to save, before the break of dawn, at least part of his army. Around 3 or 4 o'clock in the morning, a detachment led by Michael Szilágyi feigned an exit, attracting the attention of the Ottomans in his direction. John Hunyadi, with part of his army, exited the camp in a different place. He went around the Ottoman lines and escaped toward Serbia. On the morning of 20 October, the Ottomans took the camp by assault, conquering it in a few hours. They found there mostly infantry and auxiliary troops, among whom were Wallachian wagon drivers. They killed many of them in the fury of the first moments. They took the remainder as slaves. Among them was Michael Szilágy, the brother-in-law of John Hunyadi, who had covered his retreat.

Among the fugitives, those who escaped toward the south were luckier. After about two days, somewhere near today's Dulje, they met

[230]The Ottoman causalities are evaluated by the majority of sources at 30,000-34,000 soldiers. Aeneas Sylvius, in the above-mentioned letter to Pope Nicholas V, speaks of 90,000 Ottomans killed, but he is not very convinced either: "*sed hoc mihi videtur victis unicum solamen, ne satis victoriam hostibus dimisisse credantur*," Fejér, op. cit., p. 132. Chalkokondyles, on the contrary, maintains that the Ottomans lost 4,000 soldiers. Even if this number was reduced, it seems closer to the truth than the first ones; cf. also Teleki. *A Hunyadiak kora*, II, p. 100, note 6.

[231]The information in the historical sources that the papal legate died at Kosovo is not true. It is possible that he did not even participate in the battle, or, if he did, he managed to escape. This character can be identified with Bartolomeo Rimbertini, bishop of Cortona, in Italy, transferred later on, in 1499, as bishop of Coron, in Morea, where we find him until 1457; he died in 1466; cf. Gams, *Series episcoporum*, pp. 431 and 743; Eubel. *Hierarchia Catholica Medii Aevi*, vol. II, p. 138.

with the army of Scanderbeg. At the news of the disaster, he returned to Albania.

Others arrived, exhausted, as far away as Ragusa, from where, having recovered, they returned to Hungary. Those who were taken prisoner had their own odyssey. Some managed to escape along the way, arriving at Constantinople. From there, boarding Venetian vessels, they traveled toward the ports of Dalmatia. Another nobleman managed to escape from captivity as far away as Brusa, in Asia Minor, where he had been taken. The sultan set Michael Szilágyi free shortly after his capture.[232]

Where was John Hunyadi at this time? Serbian tradition says that, accompanied by 12 men, he fled north, through the valley of the Ibar River, in which Sitnica flows. After one day, he arrived at the fortress of Zvecan, where he rested and from where he went on alone, so as not to attract the attention of the Ottoman detachments sent to pursue the fugitives and which, at one point, almost captured him.[233] Three days later, on 24 October, encountering a Serbian shepherd and asking him for something to eat, the man invited him into his poor cabin and offered him bread, onions, and water. Later on, Serbian tradition says, he often said that no other meal had ever tasted so good to him. The shepherd guided him toward Semendria, where the governor intended to cross the Danube, to get to Timişoara.

He went to see George Branković who put him in prison. The despot probably wanted to eliminate any suspicions that the Ottomans might have had regarding his complicity with Hungary. But, most of all, he was upset with Hunyadi for having confiscated his estates in Hungary and taken possession of them. Branković had connections with the Hungarian upper noblemen, adversaries of Hunyadi, and he probably wanted to help them get rid of a "troublemaker."

---

[232]The mysterious Wallachian Voievod Dan is mentioned as a prisoner by some chroniclers, among whom Chalkokondyles, but the information is very uncertain. In any case, after this date, there is no information about him.

[233]Pray, *op. cit.*, p. 68 and note 2.

In Hungary, news about the defeat arrived two or three weeks later. At first no one knew anything about John Hunyadi's fate. Vladislav, the prince of Wallachia, had found out about the disaster already on 28 October from the Ottomans in Nicopolis. On 17 November news arrived at Buda that the governor had escaped and was in Semendria, where he was being "treated with honors" by Branković.[234] But when they found out that, in fact, the despot was holding the governor prisoner, Nicholas Ujlaki, the governor's surrogate, convoked the state assembly at Seghedin on December 6 and sent an energetic protest to Branković, demanding the immediate release of John Hunyadi. The despot was forced to give in, especially since a group of Serbian noblemen of anti-Ottoman orientation had rebelled, headed by George Marnavić.[235]

Branković did, however, set certain conditions that he insisted that they promise to respect: the return of his estates in Hungary; the reconciliation of John Hunyadi with the Cilli family, consolidated by the engagement of the younger son of the governor, Matthias, to the daughter of Ulrich Cilli, Elizabeth, who was Branković's granddaughter; the leaving as a hostage at Semendria of his older son, Ladislas. Hunyadi only carried out this last condition. He was absolved from all the others by the pope, as he had given his word under duress.

On 24 December 1448, John Hunyadi arrived at Seghedin, where the state assembly met him with displays of support and without reproaching him for the disaster. This was the attitude of a limited group of noblemen, connected to the party and politics of the governor. The defeat did not take long, however, to reveal its detrimental consequences. Other higher noblemen propagated mistrust in him, considering that the time had come for them to undermine his prestige and seize power from him. A new period began, of internal crisis and struggle between royal power and that of the noblemen. This time,

---

[234]The letter sent by the vice-governor and palatine of Buda to the city of Pojon, published by Házi Jenö, in *Hadörténelmi Közlemények*, 1913, pp. 631-633.

[235]Fejér, *op. cit.*, pp. 135-136.

Hunyadi lacked the necessary support to emerge victorious. A great part of the results of his domestic policies were now lost.

In the history of anti-Ottoman battles, the defeat at the Field of the Blackbirds in 1448 marked the end of offensives by the European peoples. After the resounding victories of the previous years, there followed a new, not less glorious, defensive stage. Despite all the defeats, hardships, and deceptions of the period that followed, John Hunyadi would leave to his descendants new examples of how the energy and ability of one man can mark a stage of history.

CHAPTER XII

ANXIETIES AND DISAPPOINTMENTS

The defeat on the Field of the Blackbirds meant the gradual decline of John Hunyadi's power. The feudal oligarchy asserted itself again. The party of the governor and his policies had received a serious blow. The army he had tried to put together for two years had been destroyed. Many of his most important partisans were dead or captives. The provincial noblemen were becoming more and more hesitant, afraid to support Hunyadi. The cities remained faithful to him, but they did not have the necessary force to ensure the stability of his regime.

As a consequence of this state of affairs, John Hunyadi could not act with the same energy against the feudal leagues. His regime was weakening, the relative political equilibrium among the noble classes, on the basis of which the compromise of 1446 and the election of Hunyadi as governor had been realized, was slowly dissolving. The great leader was forced into political concessions, desperately trying to save as much as possible of what he had accomplished between 1446 and 1448.

The years after 1448 reveal a side of his qualities that had been less obvious up to that moment: his ability as a politician. At the time of his ascension, he knew how to be determined, going straight on the path he had chosen, being merciless to his enemies. Now, when the circumstances no longer allowed him to do this, he did not lose sight of his aims, but he proved capable of changing his methods with malleability. His purpose was to strengthen central power and to force the higher noblemen to respect it, obliging them to resolve their litigations, not personally, but through the Diet and the law, under the authority of the governor. He had been fighting until then to end to the formation of "leagues" of the magnates and political alliances fighting for group interests that had cultivated, unavoidably, the tendency toward domestic upheaval. The policies of John Hunyadi, although limited by the circumstances of the epoch, reveal his idea of diminishing the party spirit and subordinating it to the superior interests of the state.

After the tragic autumn of 1448, seeing that he no longer had sufficient resources to maintain openly and on a large scale this policy, he adopted the tactic of allying with some of the barons against others, entering into a certain league of his own. This did not mean a renunciation of the idea of consolidation of central power, but only a new means to achieving it.[236]

During the first months of 1449, one could notice a strengthening of the league of noblemen led by the Cilli and Garai families, together with Branković. The latter recovered part of his estates in Hungary. The Palatine Garai, under different pretexts, tried some of the noblemen who had opposed Frederick III, once again asserting his pro-Hapsburg orientation. The death of Michael Székely and Franko of Talovac made the strengthening of the Cilli family in Slovenia and Croatia possible again. Transylvania alone remained strongly subject to the influence of the governor, although here also there were examples of noble families strengthening their power, such as the Rozgonyi family.

Conflicts and struggles among the higher noblemen began again over the ownership of certain estates and fortresses. Even a close friend of John Hunyadi, John of Zredna, lost his faith in him and entered into an alliance, in May 1449, with the magnate Albert Losonczi.

At the beginning of June, the governor convoked the Diet, trying, through its decisions, to counteract the phenomena of disobedience, even anarchy, that were beginning to appear in Hungary again. It is not

---

[236]Elekes, *op. cit.*, pp. 384-386.

certain what the Diet decided, but, judging from the events that followed, we may conclude that the lesser nobility did not offer Hunyadi enough support. Especially with regard to Hunyadi's main goal, that of continuing the war against the Ottomans, the Diet showed reservations. It would not give him its consent, except on the condition of foreign assistance; the prospects for which were more reduced than ever.

The position of the governor had also been weakened in foreign affairs. In Moldavia, his protégé, Peter II, had been removed by the pro-Polish party of Alexăndrel-vodă. A period of confusing struggles among the boyars rendered unlikely, for the moment, the efforts of John Hunyadi to turn that country into the eastern base of his front for a defense against the Ottoman Empire.

The initiative in foreign policy slipped into the hands of the higher noblemen. In May, 1449, through the good offices of Garai and Ujlaki, they entrusted Branković with the mission of mediating a peace with the Ottomans, under conditions which John Hunyadi would never have accepted if he had not realized the instability of his regime. The higher noblemen renounced the idea of any offensive action and accepted the vassalage of the neighboring countries to the Ottomans. It is possible that, already at that time, Vladislav II, the prince of Wallachia, intervened as a mediator. The conditions that the Serbian despot was authorized to offer the Ottomans were the following: Wallachia and Serbia would pay only half of the tribute. The Ottomans would not prevent the inhabitants of these countries from going north of the Carpathians and the Danube for their commerce. The merchants of the Ottoman Empire would only be allowed to travel as far as Severin, Kubin, and Caransebeş. They would also establish how far the Christian merchants would be able to go in Turkey. Legal matters that would arise regarding these merchants would be tried by judges from both sides.

If the Ottomans did not accept these conditions, Branković was authorized to offer even more onerous terms such as those contained in the peace signed by Sigismund of Luxembourg in 1429, which stipulated the payment of the entire tribute by Wallachia, Serbia, and Bosnia.[237]

For the moment, peace had not yet been concluded; at most, they reached a tacit armistice. In any case, the negotiations continued, which was probably the reason why there was a relative peace on the Ottoman front during 1449 and 1450.

The pope himself advised Hunyadi to limit himself from then on to defending his borders. The governor answered him on June 24, stating that, through his previous campaigns, he never aimed at anything else but at defending his borders, at ensuring peace by driving the threatening enemy as far away as possible. "To remain now within our kingdom... what else could it mean but to bring this enemy, which is already too close to us, even closer?"[238] It was only the circumstances he now faced that determined him to accept the momentary cessation of hostilities.

Great internal difficulties drew his attention in a different direction, thus leaving the negotiations with the Ottomans to be carried on. There appeared again the constant conflict with the Hapsburgs and with their man Jiskra. The armistices previously concluded had expired or had been violated. From the end of July until December 1449, Hunyadi fought with Jiskra, in Slovakia. He was forced to give up the siege of the fortress of Kremnica, an important mining center, and, on 30 November 1449, he concluded an armistice through his intermediaries, among whom was Jan Długosz, a canon of Cracow, the famous Polish chronicler. But hostilities began again after a short time and were interrupted on 28 March 1450 by a new armistice,[239] the durability of which, given previous events, no one believed in.

The situation of the governor during this period was considered serious, even by his friend and partisan, John of Zredna, who, on 20

---

[237]Teleki, *op. cit.*, X, pp. 243-244. The document is dated 24 May 1449.

[238]Pray, *op. cit.*, p. 74.

[239]Confirmed on 31 March by the representatives of the cities of Slovakia; cf. Teleki, *op. cit.*, X, pp. 256-258.

October 1449, wrote to Pope Nicholas V with much concern about the increasing danger of internal anarchy, combined with the always present peril of conflict with the Ottomans.[240]

Confrontations with Cilli took place on the western border of Hungary until August 1450. To prevent a unitary action of the army of Jiskra and that of the Hapsburgs against him, Hunyadi strengthened his relations with the city of Pojon, taking control of its fortifications himself. This city represented an obstacle between Austria and Slovakia.

Also, to isolate Jiskra and to prevent an understanding between him and the higher noblemen, the governor began negotiations with some of the latter. He especially supported the noblemen in the territories recently taken from Jiskra. Under the pretext of a common plan to bring King Ladislas Posthumous back into the country, he formed a league with Nicholas Ujlaki and Ladislas Garai.[241]

This was a difficult struggle, through which he tried, by force when he could, by diplomatic means in other cases – unfortunately more and more frequent – to control the rising wave of anarchy fueled by support from outside the country.

Hunyadi also obtained a few successes in this period. He managed to convince the noblemen in the state assembly to adopt an energetic attitude toward the disloyalty that Branković had shown in 1448. In March 1450, they decided to confiscate again his estates in Hungary. Immediately afterwards, Hunyadi attacked and devastated the Serbian regions neighboring Hungary. However, the higher noblemen put pressure on him, convincing him to retreat. Intimidated, the despot returned to Hunyadi his son, Ladislas, who had remained hostage at Semendria since 1448.

In Moldavia, a friend of Hungary came to the throne: Bogdan II, the father of Stephen the Great. John Hunyadi signed two treaties with him, on 11 February and 5 July 1450, with almost identical content, through which the prince of Moldavia committed himself not to at-

---

[240]Fejér, *op. cit.*, pp. 139-140.

[241]Teleki, *op. cit.*, X, pp. 262-265.

tempt to take back Chilia except with the permission of the governor. This also implied an eventual military assistance from Moldavia against the Ottomans in the Lower Danube.

The treaties stipulated the right of John Hunyadi to receive, in case of need, friendly asylum in Moldavia, which proves that at that time he was concerned about the final outcome of his conflicts with the Hungarian feudal oligarchy. Perhaps it was precisely the given situation that determined Hunyadi to rebuild close relations between Transylvania and the other Romanian principalities, within a system similar to the one of 1448. In the contents of the treaty, Bogdan II says, defining the future relations between Moldavia and Transylvania: "the country of My Majesty and the country of Your Majesty shall be one and the same."[242] In terms as explicit as these, John Hunyadi also signed a treaty with Alexăndrel-vodă on 16 February 1453, which recognized his protectorate over Moldavia.[243]

Relations with Wallachia and Vladislav II remained the same. A treaty later signed with the Ottomans recognized "the services, obedience, and subjection of the Wallachian prince" to John Hunyadi.

After John Hunyadi had solicited, in June, with the consent of the Diet, the cooperation of Pope Nicholas V to bring Ladislas V back to the throne, on 22 October 1450 the much-postponed peace with Frederick III of Hapsburg was finally concluded. The peace was not as Hunyadi would have liked it, but rather a compromise he was forced to make to convince the "king of the Romans" not to support the noble factions in Hungary.

The governor ceded the fortresses on the border with the Hapsburgs, among them Sopron, and obtained in return something from which he could benefit later: "the king of the Romans" promised that, upon the coming of age of King Ladislas Posthumous, when he would renounce his right of tutelage over him and agree that he occupy his

---

[242]M. Costăchescu, *Documente moldoveneşti înainte de Ştefan cel Mare*, vol. II, Iaşi, 1932, pp. 749-752 and 755-758; cf. also Barbu T. Câmpina, *op. cit.*, p. 1609.

[243]M. Costăchescu, *op. cit.*, II, pp. 762-764.

throne effectively, he would first confer with John Hunyadi. The young king would thus be under the influence of the governor and not under that of Cilli or the rest of the clique of higher noblemen. On the whole, however, the peace remained a concession made to Frederick, dictated by the necessity to normalize relations with the empire.

After settling the old conflict with the Hapsburgs, the most direct and aggressive enemy remained Jiskra. To permanently isolate him, John Hunyadi signed peace with the Cilli-Branković league, at Semendria, on 7 August 1451. He renewed his promise to marry his son Matthias to Elizabeth of Cilli. He also confirmed Ulrich of Cilli in the office of ban of Slovenia. Ladislas Garai received fortresses and certain rights of authority in Dalmatia.[244]

By realizing this reconciliation, also as a temporary solution, he tried to bring Jiskra again into submission. He launched a campaign against him on 10 August 1451, accompanied by a few noblemen. He warned the cities of Slovakia in advance not to aid Jiskra. But the cities were very favorable to him. Hunyadi was also betrayed by part of the noblemen who had accompanied him, and, therefore, he was defeated in September when he besieged a fortress near Lucenec and was then forced to retreat from Slovakia. With much difficulty, he was able to repel Jiskra who had advanced as far as Agria (Eger) in Hungary. He had to content himself again with a compromise peace.

The unsuccessful fight against Slovakia, a region rich in mining localities and of great importance to the Hungarian kingdom, shows that the noblemen were afraid of new victories, which would have consolidated the position of Hunyadi; they were ready to oppose him, to keep him in the difficult situation in which he had been since his defeat on the Field of the Blackbirds.

But this was not the first time he had been unsuccessful against Jiskra. Not even when Hunyadi was at the height of his power did he manage to reduce this enemy to silence. How can one explain the fact that the man who obtained glorious victories against the Ottomans and

---

[244]Fejér, *op. cit.*, pp. 149-157.

against some united armies of noblemen failed with regularity in his encounters with Jiskra? The desertion of some noblemen that occurred during this last encounter, or the support received by Jiskra from the Hapsburgs, are not sufficient to explain the entire decade of struggles that took place on the border of Slovakia.

We must also consider the problem, not yet studied enough, of the politics of Jiskra in Slovakia, of the socio-political relations in this region, of the interests that connected the social classes of Slovakia to the turbulent imperial representative. It is certain that the mining towns in Slovakia favored, from the beginning of his rule, the man who embodied many of the socio-political ideals of the Hussites. These towns remained faithful to him.

From the viewpoint of the Hungarian feudal regime, of the centralization of the state as it was intended by the party of John Hunyadi, of the struggle using all their forces against the Ottomans, the presence of Jiskra in Slovakia and his disobedience toward Hungary were evidently detrimental. But the population there, certainly for socio-economic reasons, preferred this state of affairs to domination by the Hungarian noblemen in any political form that it might have manifested itself. We must also remember that Hussitism also represented the awakening of the national conscience of the Czech people, even if not in the total, modern sense of the term. It is not unlikely for the irradiation of this current to have caused such sparks to occur in Slovakia as well. It is probably in these areas that one should look for the key to the continued successes of Jiskra. His rule seems to have been, to some extent, more favorable to the interests of the townspeople, the miners, and the masses in general, than Hungarian domination. It was on this larger social basis that the power of his rule might have originated.

During the years 1449 and 1450, John Hunyadi no longer had enough support from the social classes upon which he had relied until then to further consolidate central authority. The middle and lesser noblemen became increasingly passive. Part of them had perished in battle, the remaining ones were tired of military service, and had either received high dignities or had considerably increased their wealth and now began to orientate themselves toward the interests of the higher noblemen.

The efforts of the governor to keep the neighboring countries in close relations with Hungary became increasingly difficult. In Moldavia, his ally, Bogdan II, was killed. The throne became the object of new internal struggles, occupied either by Alexăndrel, supported by the Poles, despite his temporary homage to Hunyadi, or by Petru Aron, a representative of the boyars who capitulated to the Ottomans.

The relations with Branković remained cold; in Bosnia, the pro-Ottoman current became stronger; even the more remote but quite loyal Ragusa made some moves that denoted a weakening of its confidence in Hungary.[245]

In this situation, it is understandable why Hunyadi made efforts to reach a temporary normalization of relations with the Ottoman Empire. As a result of long negotiations, mediated by Branković and, to some extent, by Vladislav II, the prince of Wallachia, a three-year armistice was concluded on 20 November 1451.

The conditions of the armistice were not very favorable. The situation in the Balkans remained, in the best case, similar to the one that Hunyadi had found at the time when he had begun his great campaigns.

The Ottomans promised Hungary, Serbia, and Ragusa peace for the period agreed upon. Wallachia entered into a double dependence, expressed through the payment of tribute and military services to the Ottomans and through the honoring of the old ties of vassalage to Hungary. The usual tribute remained in force for Serbia and Bosnia. The two sides promised each other not to build new fortifications along the border, which meant, first of all, on either bank of the Danube.

The armistice, despite its compromising character, which implied the recognition of the failure, be it only partial, of the long struggle led by John Hunyadi, was not a defeat. In his turn, the sultan was confined

[245]Elekes, *op. cit.*, p. 406.

to his old positions. The new treaty was signed by Mehmed II because his father, Murad II, had died in February 1451.[246]

The events of this year determined John Hunyadi to make a new effort to reestablish internal peace and especially to remove Jiskra from Slovakia: this included bringing Ladislas Posthumous back to the throne. Hunyadi understood, undoubtedly, the danger that, once installed on the throne, the young king might fall under the influence of the upper nobility. He understood very well that he would have lost his prerogatives as governor and that the loss of power presented serious risks for his party. On the other hand, he also saw certain advantages. He was hoping that the reestablishing of a legal, normal state of affairs would take away from the noblemen the pretext and possibility to create disorder. He even believed that his gesture would lead to a more durable reconciliation with the magnates.

Hunyadi had one main goal: to bring Slovakia back under Hungarian domination, which would have increased considerably the revenues of the state. Jiskra had been entrusted with the ruling of Slovakia by the former Queen Elizabeth, the mother of Ladislas Posthumous, under the pretext of protecting the latter's rights during the time that the Hungarian throne was occupied by Ladislas I, an "usurper" from the point of view of the party of Elizabeth. By the full reinstatement of Ladislas Posthumous into his royal rights, the mission of Jiskra in Slovakia lost any justification.

There was another reason that determined the governor to bring the king back to the throne of Hungary. Through his dynastic ties, Ladislas Posthumous was not only the king of Hungary, but had rights over the thrones of the Czech state and Austria. John Hunyadi envisioned, therefore, the future formation of a dynastic union among these states, which would have concentrated their forces and represented a larger base for resuming the struggle against the Ottomans. Now, when

[246]It is possible that they agreed on the conditions already in the spring, and that at this date the armistice was confirmed; cf. Moravcsik Gyula, "Ungarisch-bysantinische Beziejungen zur Zeit de Falled von Byzanz," in *Acta Antiqua Academiae Scientiarum Hungaricae*, volume II, fascicles 3-4, 1954, p. 353.

he realized that the internal social forces of Hungary and the neighboring countries, to the south and the east, were not enough to support him to finish the work of political centralization he had begun in 1446-1448, Hunyadi modified his methods and tactics, without losing sight of, but precisely to fulfill the same great goals: the assurance of domestic tranquility and the defense of the borders.

Hunyadi's plan was favored this time by the internal difficulties confronted by Frederick III, difficulties which made him more willing to negotiate regarding his renunciation of tutelage over Ladislas Posthumous.

In Austria there had appeared discontentments against him, which led to a revolt of the noble council against the regency left by Frederick in the fall of 1451, when he went to Italy for the last imperial coronation that the German sovereigns performed in Rome.[247]

In February 1452, the Hungarian Diet decided to take new steps to bring Ladislas V back to the throne. A large delegation left for Vienna, at the beginning of March, coming into contact with Ulrich of Cilli, and with the noble councils of Austria, Bohemia, and Moravia. Another delegation went to Rome.[248]

The emperor again refused the request to return the child king. The rebellion in Austria having aggravated after his return from Italy, Hungary which was on the point of taking up arms against him, supported by the Czech state. The refusal of the princes of the empire to offer him assistance, all forced the emperor to concede and, at the beginning of September 1452, he entrusted Ladislas Posthumous to the protection of Ulrich of Cilli. The emperor was thus disregarding the convention of October 1450, through which he pledged himself to consult John Hunyadi before renouncing his rights of tutelage. Monarchy was restored in Hungary, but as an instrument of the power of the higher noblemen, headed by the Cilli family.

---

[247]On 19 March 1452.

[248]Fejér, *op. cit.*, pp. 167-174; Teleki, *op. cit.*, X, pp. 326-330.

In December 1452, John Hunyadi went to Vienna, where the king was, and resigned from his position of governor in the first days of the following year. He received instead the title of supreme captain of Hungary. The group of noblemen around the king, already constituting his court and suggesting to him the first actions of his reign, did not yet dare to reveal their plans to overthrow John Hunyadi. They spared him for the time being, granting him this title and naming his older son, Ladislas, in the dignity of ban of Dalmatia and Croatia, which he shared with Cilli. John of Zredna became chancellor of the king's court.

In February 1453, the Diet, gathered at Pojon confirmed the restoration of royal power in Hungary and other measures taken as a consequence of this fact. At Pojon, where he appeared in front of the Diet, the king issued, on 30 January and 1 February 1453, several documents, through which he added to the coat of arms of the Hunyadi family – a raven with a ring – a purple lion, on a white background, holding a crown in one of its front paws, as if offering it to someone. This symbol is very transparent.

He also enumerated all the merits of John Hunyadi, presenting his entire military activity, named him permanent and hereditary *comite* of Bistriţa, and donated to him the fortresses of Giurgiu and Deva, as well as several Romanian districts in the county of Timiş.[249] On the surface, the power of Hunyadi and his party remained considerable, especially since Jiskra's mandate, on the basis of which he ruled in Slovakia, had been withdrawn.

In the course of the year 1453, however, the plans of the court to remove John Hunyadi from any important role in the political life of the country became very clear. The higher noblemen monopolized all the high dignities, trying to weaken his position in Transylvania and fueling discontentment in the Saxon cities. Bistriţa, for instance, as an old free city, had reason to be concerned about its being placed under the direct authority of John Hunyadi. The latter was forced to confirm

---

[249] Fejér, *op. cit.*, pp. 177-189; Teleki, *op. cit.*, X, pp. 347-363, 365-368.

its privileges (on 22 July 1453), but, at the same time, he began the construction of a new fortress, not far from the city, thus worrying the inhabitants.[250]

His enemies tried to set various traps to eliminate him. They invited him to a conference in Vienna, then to a Diet in Pojon. Hunyadi, warned about the dishonest plans of the court, did not go. He accepted, on the other hand, a personal meeting with Ulrich of Cilli, to which both came accompanied by powerful armed retinues.

Suspicious of the hidden intentions of the duke, Hunyadi did not consider sufficient the guarantees that the former gave him concerning a discussion in a restricted circle. Fearing an assassination plot, he returned without having discussed anything with Cilli. Ostensibly, the higher noblemen – Garai, Ujlaki, and others – headed by the bishop of Strigoniu formed, on 13 September 1453, a new league, which took upon itself in writing the obligation to defend the king and Ulrich Cilli against anyone, against any hostile action.[251] Trying to appease his discontentment and to eliminate the tension among the parties, the king gave Hunyadi a document that confirmed his ownership over all his estates.

At the time of these domestic intrigues, an event occurred that shook all of Europe: on 29 May 1453, the Ottomans conquered Constantinople. After they had resumed hostilities against Byzantium already in the winter of 1451-1452, surrounding and blocking the capital, in the spring of 1453 they began to besiege it on 6 April. From the sea, the Ottoman fleet formed of 300 larger and smaller vessels, blocked the city, while all the infantry forces of Sultan Mehmed II surrounded its walls.

The Ottoman cannons fired at the walls for weeks in a row. Among these cannons there was an immense one, manufactured by a craftsman named Urban, probably of Hungarian origin. This cannon

---

[250]Fejér, *op. cit.*, pp. 196-199; Teleki, *op. cit.,* II, p. 286.

[251]The league of Colli, Garai, and Ujlaki would be renewed on 7 April 1455; Teleki, *op. cit.*, X. pp. 437-438.

was pulled by about thirty pair of oxen. Two hundred soldiers guarded it, and three hundred and fifty other soldiers had the sole mission to build bridges and roads for its transportation.

Byzantium had very limited resources for defense: only a few vessels and around 7,000 soldiers, the majority of whom were mercenaries. None of the European states responded to the desperate calls for help of Emperor Constantine XII, except for Genoa, which sent 700 soldiers.

In the fall of 1452 messengers of John Hunyadi sailed to Constantinople offering the Byzantines to send troops to their aid, on the condition they be allowed to use either the port of Selimvria[252] or the port of Mesembria.

For the moment, the Byzantines rejected his offer, but when the Ottoman attack became imminent – toward the spring of 1453 – the emperor ceded Mesembria to Hunyadi. The concluding of this alliance led to no practical result. Hunyadi no longer had time to organize the promised help, especially since, during those weeks, he was absorbed in domestic political intrigues.

All that Hunyadi did was to send a delegation to the sultan, at the beginning of April 1453, asking him to stop the attack. But Mehmed II paid no attention to his appeals, nor to the possible denunciation of the armistice of 1451 by Hungary, which was not even carried out.[253]

During the decisive stage of the siege, Mehmed II executed a daring maneuver. He organized the bringing to shore of some of the war vessels over the small peninsula between the Bosphorus and the Golden Horn, thus avoiding the obstacles that the Byzantines had placed at the entrance to the famous gulf. The Ottoman vessels arrived in this way directly in front of Constantinople. "He transformed the land into sea and took his vessels over the tops of the mountains, as if they were

---

[252]Today's Silivri, in European Turkey, and Nesebar, in Bulgaria.

[253]Georgios Sphrantzes, *Memorii, 1401-1477*, București, 1966, pp. 102-105; Moravcsik, *op. cit.*, pp. 355-359; Francisc Pall, "Stăpânirea lui Iancu de Hunedoara asupra Chiliei…," pp. 623-633.

the waves of the sea," wrote the Byzantine chronicler Ducas about Mehmed II.[254]

On 29 May 1453, the Ottomans, in a general attack, climbed over the walls and, after a fierce battle of a few hours, annihilated the last resisting elements they encountered. Constantine XII lost his life, defending with his sword the last remainder of his formerly glorious empire.

Mehmed II moved his residence to his new conquest. In Europe, the amazement and consternation caused by the news of the fall of Byzantium was followed by a terror that paralyzed any initiative. Plans were made for a new crusade, for the reconquest of Constantinople, but their realization proved illusory. On the contrary, Venice did not hesitate to congratulate the victorious sultan, entering into negotiations with the Ottomans for the purpose of ensuring for itself advantageous conditions of commerce through the Straits and the possession of some former Byzantine islands in the Greek Archipelago.[255] On 1 August 1453, the messengers of Branković were also preparing to visit the feared victor in his new capital, bringing him an increased tribute.

The conquest of Constantinople brought once again to the forefront the specter of the Ottoman danger. It was clear that the Ottomans could no longer be driven from Europe. On the contrary, new and powerful attacks from them were to be expected. The Hungarian noblemen, who neither wanted to defend their country, nor to lose it completely, ceased their open actions against John Hunyadi, realizing that they would need him again. In the fall of 1453, Cilli began to withdraw into the shadows, his influence at the court weakened, as a direct consequence of a new *"pronunciamento"* of the noble councils in Austria, this time directed at him. Hunyadi's title as supreme captain of the kingdom renewed.

---

[254]Ducas, *op. cit.*, pp. 338-339.

[255]The Ottoman-Venetian treaty was concluded on 23 April 1454, in conditions less advantageous than Venice had hoped; cf. Nicolae Iorga, *Geschichte des Osmanischen Reiches*, vol. II, pp. 45-46.

At the end of October, he went to Prague, where he participated in the coronation of Ladislas Posthumous as king of the Czech state. There he signed an alliance with Jirzi Podebrad, the most powerful and influential Czech nobleman, and carried on negotiations with the representatives of the ruling class in Moravia and Austria for military assistance against the Ottomans, which he received, at least from the Czech state, in the battles of the following year.[256] In January 1454, John Hunyadi returned to Hungary and participated to the debates of the Diet in Buda which dealt with the problem of defense against the Ottomans. Its decisions show a new increase in his influence. He was named commander, for one year, of the new army that would be organized. They took measures to control the way in which the royal revenues would be used for military purposes. The prelates and the noblemen were obligated to gather their troops, without being allowed to pay compensation in money for not participating. High penalties and threats of confiscation of their estates were the measures taken for guaranteeing their fulfilment of this obligation.

Besides the regular feudal armies, troops were going to be gathered through a kind of general conscription – accepting no exemption – through which the noblemen were obligated to give four cavalrymen and two lightly armed infantrymen for each one hundred serf plots they owned. There is no proof that this last part of the decision of the Diet was actually implemented.

Extensive plans for a "crusade" were also discussed in the imperial Diet held in April 1454 in Regensburg. Many resounding phrases were used, the author of some of them being Aeneas Sylvius Piccolomini, but their echo faded, without any practical result.

In Hungary, John Hunyadi began to apply with all energy the decisions of the Diet of January. His severity raised complaints from some of the noblemen who were unhappy because they were obligated to participate in the army. The royal court behaved with duplicity: they allowed Hunyadi to expend all of his efforts in the organization of the

---

[256] Elekes, *op. cit.*, p. 422.

resistance, but they did everything they could to prevent him from thus strengthening his political power. In another Diet, which assembled sometime in March or April 1454, convoked without inviting Hunyadi, it was decided to create a council of eighteen prelates and noblemen which would be allowed to use the royal revenues.

This was a serious offense brought to the supreme captain. The hesitation of the noblemen to comply with their military obligations made necessary, as in the not very distant past, the hiring of mercenaries. The revenues that could have been used to pay them were now given to others, when it would have been normal that Hunyadi, who was responsible for the organization of the army, have control over the matter.

Offended, Hunyadi asked the court for an explanation. Ladislas answered him, denying that the formation of this council had been done with his knowledge.[257] The duplicity of the royal party, hidden behind the apparent benevolence of a new act of confirmation of Hunyadi's estates, is evident also in the fact that at the same time Jiskra was returned to the fortresses in Slovakia, which he had just given up after years of struggle and negotiation. Chancellor John of Zredna appears to have been aware of the true sentiments of the court toward his friend, but he did not warn him, as he began to yield to the influence of the clique surrounding the king.

In this network of hostile intrigues, which was taking away from him with one hand what they pretended to offer with the other, Hunyadi was forced to find the necessary means to organize the army. For lack of money, he made contacts with certain Florentine bankers and with some wealthy townspeople in Slovakia. He also contributed again large sums of his own money.

In the summer of 1454, Sultan Mehmed II violated the three-year armistice of November 1451. He appeared in Serbia with a powerful

---

[257]We should keep in mind that the ones Hunyadi talked to were in fact magnates, counselors of the king; the latter was only thirteen at the time and was not capable of having such a dialog.

army, which he had been preparing in Adrianople already since early spring. Penetrating in southern Serbia, the Ottomans conquered the important mining city Novobrdo, about which a French traveler had said, twenty years before, that it was bringing the Serbian despot an annual revenue of over two hundred thousand ducats and that, had he lost it, Branković would immediately be thrown out of his country.[258]

Afterwards, the Ottoman army headed north and besieged Semendria. John Hunyadi arrived at the Danube in the first half of August. The sultan was informed ahead of time by his spies about the approach of the Hungarian troops; as he did not have sufficient forces, he ordered retreat, leaving behind a powerful enough rear guard, under the command of Feriz-bey. John crossed the Danube and ambushed this army, near Kruševac, destroying it completely, almost without a fight. Only one week later did the army of Branković and the one sent by Ulrich of Cilli catch up with him. The army of Hunyadi advanced as far as Pirot. At the news of the approach of superior Ottoman forces, he retreated toward Vidin, devastating its surroundings. Afterwards, Hunyadi went to Belgrade, where he remained until winter, fearing a new attack.[259] Branković implored the sultan to make peace, offering to increase the tribute.

The campaign of 1454 gave new hopes to the peoples of the Balkans. However, John Hunyadi was not powerful enough to confront the entire army of the sultan and to force him to make peace. His victory remained without any consequences, despite all the plans for assistance being promised by the West, especially by the Holy Roman Empire.

---

[258]Elekes, *op. cit.*, p. 310, note 43.

[259]The exact date of this campaign is not indicated in any source. It took place between August, when Hunyadi was in Belgrade, and November, when Ragusa received news of the victory. It most likely took place in September-October; cf. Nicolae Iorga, *op. cit.*, II, p. 62. The information given by Ducas, *op. cit.*, p. 396, about the Hungarians crossing the Danube and devastating the regions around Trnovo, seems unlikely. The relations with Vladislav II, the prince of Wallachia, were not at that time of a nature that would justify us to presume a cooperation. Besides, on 19 December, John Hunyadi was in Petrovaradin; cf. Fejér, *op. cit.*, pp. 210-211.

After a promising beginning, made during the Diet gathered in Frankfurt, in September 1454, when the emperor seemed almost determined to set out against the Ottomans, he changed his attitude and renounced the campaign planned for 1455, to which it was hoped that the empire would contribute 10,000 cavalrymen and 20,000 infantrymen.[260] In February 1455, a conference was held in Austria, at Neustadt, which was attended by Polish, Aragonese, and Burgundian delegates, as well as by John Hunyadi, heading the Hungarian delegation. The emperor listened without blinking to the indignant reproaches of the Hungarian messengers; "enough words, show us facts if you are a true a Christian and a true emperor!" In April 1455, he made the definitive declaration that all the preparations had to be postponed until the next year, using as a pretext this time the death of Pope Nicholas V.[261] In fact, what held Frederick back were his conflicts with the princes of the empire and his lack of authority, which did not allow him to rely on a substantial mobilization of military forces in Germany.[262]

The new pope, Callixtus III, called loudly for the "liberation of Constantinople," but with the same results as the comedy of war played by the emperor. The Franciscan monk John of Capistrano took upon himself the mission of preaching this crusade in Hungary and Poland.

Although in the spring and summer of 1455 the Ottomans made another incursion into Serbia, John Hunyadi was not able to do anything, as he was detained by more intrigue among the oligarchy. The league created by Cilli, Ladislas Garai, and Nicholas Ujlaki rose against him, reproaching him for the severity of his rule, the way he administrated the revenues that were put at his disposal by the king, and accusing him that he was using the army in his own interests. Tak-

---

[260]Holub József, "Adatok a török ellen tervezet 1455-iki hadjárat-hoz," in Hadjárat-hoz," in *Hadtörténelmi Közlemények*, 1911, p. 149.

[261]On 24 March 1455.

[262]Nicolae Iorga, *Geschichte des Osmanischen*, Reiches, II, Gotha, 1909, pp. 63-64.

ing into consideration the imminence of the Ottoman danger, John Hunyadi did not take up arms to liquidate his adversaries and thus unleash a civil war; on the contrary, he was very conciliatory, renouncing any personal ambitions.

In front of a hostile audience, in the Diet assembled at Győr, in June 1455, he offered at his own expense a number of 10,000 cavalrymen in preparation for the confrontation with the Ottomans. He reminded those present in vain about the promises received from the West – the pope, Burgundy, the Italian cities, Aragon –, of the support offered again by Branković, gravely betrayed in his political alliances with the sultan. He predicted that they would be able to drive the Ottomans out of Europe in three months, and even to advance to Jerusalem, if they had sufficient forces.[263] The noblemen did not let themselves be persuaded. They were afraid of the Ottomans, but they were also worried about the power and prestige that Hunyadi would have gained back, being at the command of a campaign of European proportions, especially if it was victorious.[264]

Tired of the hostility with which any of his actions were received, in July or August John Hunyadi renounced his title of supreme captain of the kingdom, keeping only his mission to defend the regions in the south and the dignity of *comite* of Bistrişa. He gave up several important fortresses, which were under his direct authority, among them Buda. His older son, Ladislas, ceded to Cilli the entire banat of Dalmatia and Croatia, and his second son, Matthias, was sent as a kind of guarantee to the royal court. With the price of these concessions, which meant the loss of his political power, John Hunyadi assured the realization of a new internal peace with the higher noblemen in the court, strengthened through the plans of marriage between his sons, Ladislas and Matthias, with the daughters of Garai and Cilli.

---

[263]Fejér, *op. cit.*, pp. 216-218.

[264]A tactless intervention was made by Capistrano, who proposed to Branković to convert to Catholicism. Offended, the old despot left the Diet and began negotiations with the sultan; cf. Teleki, *op. cit.*, pp. 378-379.

This gesture of a profound political significance disproves the accusations of his enemies that he had aspired to the throne, that he was an ambitious man who aimed, through the energy of his policies, only at the ascension of his own family. It cannot be disputed, however, at the end of so many sinuous acts, the appearance of a certain spirit of opportunism in his relations with the oligarchy.

Even after the displays of enmity that he had received, being left without the dignities to which he had ascended on his own merits, John Hunyadi did his duty with perseverance. Another, offended as he was, would have taken no further interest in his remaining mission, to defend the southern borders. But, beginning in August 1455, we find him in Transylvania, in the middle of his people where, among other things, he took measures for the fortification of the border cities and for the maintenance of good relations with Wallachia. His preparations determined the Ottomans to regroup their forces in the Balkans, evacuating some of the regions in southwestern Serbia. The townspeople of Ragusa expressed very well the role that he continued to play in the lives of the peoples subjugated by the Ottomans: "it is evident how useful he was to us: when he set out with his army to the defense of Wallachia, he eliminated the danger that was threatening us as well…."[265]

The insidious maneuvers of his adversaries in Hungary took away from him his titles, but they could not take away his military merits, which kept the eyes of the world on him. In the difficult moments that were near, all those who loved freedom and wanted to defend their Christian faith would gather once more around John Hunyadi.

[265]According to Elekes, *op. cit.*, p. 437.

Sixteenth Century Ottoman Miniature
Depicting the Seige of Belgrade, 1456

CHAPTER XIII

DEFENDER OF CHRISTENDOM

In September 1455, unsettling news reached Ragusa from Greece that the Ottomans were preparing a war fleet on the Danube. In the first months of the following year news of serious Ottoman preparations came more and more frequently. The king of Bosnia informed the Hungarian ban of Macva[266] that the sultan intended, as early as March, to set against Semendria and Belgrade.[267] Spies were dispatched to the Balkans to find out to how much of this information was true.

In March, they sent the first news, saying that in Üsküb (today's Skoplje), in Macedonia, the Ottomans had established workshops where they were hastening to manufacture weapons. From Constantinople and other places they brought the necessary materials to cast cannons. Other war machines were discovered on the Danubian fleet of the Ottomans, which began to assemble at Vidin.[268] In April, the sultan was in Adrianople; the city was swarming with Ottoman army. In the same month, a Venetian bail,[269] who was coming from Constantinople, told the people of Ragusa that it was certain that the Ottoman army

---

[266]A region in the south of Hungary of that time (today it is in Serbia), west of Belgrade.

[267]According to György Balanyi, "Nándorfejérvar ostroma és felmentése," in *Hadtörténelmi Közlemények*, 1911, pp. 171-172.

[268]Ibidem, p. 180; Guboglu-Mehmet, *op. cit.*, p. 41.

[269]A permanent commercial representative of Venice abroad.

would soon set out against the fortresses along the Danube and in Hungary.[270]

Mehmed II, the conqueror of Constantinople, wanted to crown his glory, recently gained, by subjugating the peoples that had been holding back the Ottoman Empire for years along the Danube and in the Balkans.

John Hunyadi had expected this decisive attack for a long time. He had warned the noblemen many rimes about the difficult times that lay ahead, in view of which he had asked them to set aside their personal interests and petty quarrels and put all their efforts into preparing the country for defense. But even now, when the first signs of the avalanche that was rushing toward the center of Europe began to appear, his voice was not heeded enough. At the end of 1455, John Hunyadi informed the papal legate, Cardinal Carvajal, that he was ready to contribute, through his efforts and at his own expense, 7,000 soldiers for future battles with the Ottomans. In return, he asked for serious military assistance. In January 1456, Carvajal answered him with flattering but equivocal words, implying a small chance for such assistance: "We have faith in God that those 7,000 men, even if they do not have the assistance of other soldiers, will be victorious, under the command of the governor, the Maccanaeus of our time."[271] For Carvajal, who was not exactly ignorant in the matter (for years he hold worked in Hungary on different diplomatic missions and knew the strength of the Ottomans), it was impossible not to see that it was completely absurd to advise Hunyadi to fight only with 7,000 soldiers that he hoped to gather by himself.

That is why the cardinal thought that he should plead again with Pope Callixtus III in favor of a new crusade against the Ottomans. In fact, the new pope had shown himself, right after his election, very zealous on this matter. The method of preaching a crusade did not create any difficulties and no special obligations for the Church. On the

---

[270]Nicolae Iorga, *op. cit.*, II, p. 74.

[271]Fejér, *op. cit.*, pp. 219-221.

contrary, it gained prestige in front of the world, showing that it was concerned with the defense of Europe. The money that the believers used to offer in such circumstances for support was never lost, no matter if the project was carried out or abandoned.

The Italian John of Capistrano sent to Hungary as an inquisitor to weed out heretics, was the first who took up the cross, on 14 February 1456, beginning to preach for a new crusade. At first, he did not obtain great successes, because he did not know the language of the population among which he was carrying out his zealous preaching and he did not have good translators. Quite a large number of middle and lesser noblemen enrolled, but only a few of them actually went, the rest being held back by their ties of vassalage with the higher noblemen, hostile to adhering to the crusade.[272] The common people looked distrustfully at the bigoted monk who, in his capacity of inquisitor, was persecuting the "heretics" and all those who were of any other faith but Catholicism. In Transylvania, Capistrano carried out brutal measures against Orthodox believers. At his urging, John of Caffa, a *vlădică* who functioned in the regions of Hunedoara and Alba, probably an Orthodox believer, was captured and imprisoned. Many Orthodox priests in the same regions met a similar fate. John Hunyadi supported Capistrano in his actions to some extent, but did not consider it at all appropriate, at that moment, to conduct religious violence against a peaceful population; he did not wish to estrange the common people from the idea of fighting against the Ottomans because of such persecutions. The support Hunyadi gave to Capistrano was determined only by the hope that the latter's influence at the papal court would contribute to his obtaining military or financial support from the West. Capistrano even complained about the difficulties that Hunyadi created for him, through the "slowness" with which he applied the measures advocated by him against the heretics.[273]

---

[272]Balanyi, *op. cit.*, pp. 177-178 and note 2.

[273]I. Minea, *Din trecutul stăpânirii româneşti asupra Ardealului...*, pp. 5 ff.; Elekes, *op. cit.*, pp. 447-448; I. Lupaş, "Voievodul transilvan Ioan Huniade – 'fortissimus athlete Christi'," in *Studii, conferinţe şi comunicări istorice*, vol. II, Cluj, 1940, pp. 70-71.

At that time, Hunyadi had more serious concerns. He was taking measures for the fortification of the Danube. He took advantage of the fact that the king and the noblemen, ever since they had received the news of the imminent Ottoman attack, had panicked. A Diet was convoked urgently, in April 1456, for the purpose of taking exceptional measures for defense. They decreed general mobilization. The primate archbishop of Hungary, the bishop of Oradea, and John Hunyadi immediately asked the papal legate to write to Pope Callixtus III about the gravity of the situation and to ask him to send urgently a fleet to the Straits to hinder the movements of the Ottomans. For years, the noblemen had prevented Hunyadi from organizing the defense of the country as he saw fit: now they recognized that Hungary would not be able to resist alone and were asking for help from abroad, saying that the fate of all of Christianity was at risk and that a delay of one day or even a few hours could be fatal.[274] Theirs was a shaky and inconsistent zeal. The king and his court gave further proof of their irresponsibility. In April, Ladislas V asked John Hunyadi for a loan of 8,000 florins, added to another 12,000 received earlier, giving him as guarantee the revenues of the county of Timişoara.[275] Why did the king need this money? To pay his personal debts to Ulrich of Cilli, to whom he owed the enormous sum of almost 53,000 silver *livre*. He paid half of this sum to the duke, and he pledged himself in writing to pay him the rest, before any other debts, until the end of May, from various royal revenues.[276] And this at a time when every ducat was precious for the equipping of his army. The king left Buda afterwards, under the pretext of a hunting trip, from which he did not return.... He simply ran to Vienna and stayed there until the Ottoman danger passed.[277]

John Hunyadi maintained the calm necessary in such situations. He reinforced the garrisons of the fortresses that were threatened more

---

[274]Balanyi, *op. cit.*, pp. 173-174.

[275]Teleki, *op. cit.*, X, pp. 497-498.

[276]Ibidem, II, p. 408, note 4 and X, pp. 522-523.

[277]"*Rex ivit venatum, neque amplius est reversus*" – Carvajal wrote to Capistrano with dismay; cf. Fejér, *op. cit.*, p. 222; see also Elekes, *op. cit.*, p. 442.

directly. He sent 5,000 mercenaries to Belgrade – Hungarians, Czechs, and Poles –, putting them at the disposal of the commander of the fortress, Michael Szilágyi. He ordered the latter to use any means to fortify the fortress. The inhabitants of the city answered the appeal to help with the transportation of the war machines. The changes in relations with Wallachia in the spring of 1456 must be related to the measures for the defense of Belgrade. In the last years, relations between John Hunyadi and Vladislav II had been rocky. The Wallachian prince had contributed to the mediation of the peace of 1451.[278] It appears, however, that he entered into close relations with the Ottomans because, after 23 April 1452, or in the first half of the following year, Hunyadi confiscated his possessions in Transylvania – Amlaş and possibly Făgăraş as well –, attracting Vladislav's protests and even attempts at revenge through incursions into the Saxon regions of southern Transylvania.[279] The conflict ended before 24 September 1453, but without totally clarifying the reasons for it.

At the end of 1455, relations between Hunyadi and Vladislav worsened again. A Wallachian incursion, assisted by the Ottomans, attacked the fortress of Saan (on the Ada-Kaleh Island). Vladislav himself plundered southern Transylvania, causing losses, especially to the Saxons, who had given shelter to the pretender to the throne Vlad, the son of Vlad Dracul. Estates of John Hunyadi were pillaged. Some Ottoman detachments were given permission to enter Transylvania. In the fall of the same year, in November, Hunyadi, who had gone to Braşov, tried to reach dome sort of reconciliation; he hoped to obtain the assistance of Vladislav II against the Ottomans.[280] His attempts had no lasting consequences. Before 7 April 1456 Hunyadi was faced with a re-

---

[278]Hurmuzaki, XV. 1, p. 36.

[279]Not long before that, on 6 February 1452, John Hunyadi informed the city of Braşov about the peace with the Ottomans, which included Vladislav, warning them to stop any hostile action against him by Vlad, the son of Vlad Dracul; cf. Teleki, *op. cit.*, pp. 322-323. On 30 March 1452, John informed the city of Braşov that this Vlad, the future Vlad the Impaler, had left for Moldavia (Ibidem, p. 333).

[280]Teleki, *op. cit.*, X, pp. 487-488, 489-490.

bellion of the Romanians of Făgăraş supported, in all probability, by the Wallachian prince. Under these circumstances, Hunyadi helped the pretender Vlad, who would later be called the Impaler, to enter Wallachia and to overthrow Vladislav II. Vlad also had the support of part of the boyars. This event took place sometime between 15 April and 26 June 1456.

Vladislav was killed in circumstances that are not clear – possibly in a fight – and Vlad ascended to the Wallachian throne.[281] This way, Hunyadi secured himself better against an Ottoman attack through Wallachia and was able to concentrate his forces on the main front at Belgrade. He was also hoping for the cooperation of the undefeated Scanderbeg and his Albanians. Scanderbeg actually intended to send an army into Serbia, but his action was prevented by an Ottoman attack, a second one, launched at about the same time as the advance of the Ottomans army toward Belgrade.[282]

John Hunyadi was left, therefore, only with Hungarian military forces, and those in relatively small number. Despite the obligatory general participation in the army, the higher noblemen and prelates did not move. A good pretext for them was the attitude of the king himself.[283]

Thus, in the camp of Seghedin only the armies of some lesser noblemen and of those who, having dignities or estates in the south of Hungary, close to Serbia, had a direct interest to defend them, gathered. They were joined by the Transylvanian troops, always loyal to Hunyadi, and his mercenary troops. Their army numbered about 20,000 soldiers in all, counting the part sent ahead to reinforce the garrison of Belgrade. It was a small army compared to the Ottoman tor-

---

[281]I. Minea, *op. cit.*, pp. 3, 37-39, 42-47; Nicolae Iorga, *op. cit.*, II, p. 74 and note 2, 75; idem, *Istoria românilor*, IV, pp. 106-110; I. Lupaş, *op. cit.*, pp. 95-96.

[282]Elekes, *op. cit.*, p. 439, note 7. The Ottomans had begun a new campaign against Scanderbeg already in the previous year; cf. Nicolae Iorga, *Geschichte des Osmanischen Reiches,* II, p. 83.

[283]Which must not be exaggerated, as some sources do. Could one really expect a fifteen year old boy to command an army?

rent – the rumor was that they had 100,000-200,000 men – which was heading toward Belgrade. But Hunyadi received unexpected help from those on whom the noblemen had never wanted to rely, but in whom Hunyadi had always had more confidence: the common people who rose to fight.

The news about the terrible danger of the Ottoman invasion vanquished the reservations with which the common people had received at first the crusade preaching of Capistrano and awoke their courage to fight to the surprise even of Capistrano and the clergy, the common people no longer contented themselves with putting their contribution in the hands held out by the monks, but this time they took up arms and were ready to confront the invaders. The poor of the cities and villages did not take into consideration any interdiction by the noblemen, who were unhappy about so many men leaving. They gathered in different spots in numbers that were ever increasing, asking for weapons, leaders, and guides, to be ready to leave for the theater of war. This happened not only in Hungary, but in other countries as well, especially in the empire. Poorly armed, few of them having spears and horses, but overcoming every obstacle with their enthusiasm, these men set out for Belgrade. There were many craftsmen, peasants, and poor priests. They crossed through towns singing, carrying on their shoulders the weapons they were able to gather. Many of them had only clubs and slings. Some of them, overcome by the difficulties of the journey, did not even reach the destination, or arrived after the battles had ceased.[284]

Thus, many such crusaders also gathered in the camp of Seghedin, coming from everywhere. The sources say that there were about 60,000 men. A collaborator of Capistrano, Giovanni Tagliacozzo, writing from Belgrade, speaks of only about 27,000-28,000, which is probably closer to their true number.

No matter how many they were, the example of the common people gave a lesson to the monarchs and noblemen. In some notes from

---

[284]On 3 August 1456, such a detachment was crossing through Vienna; cf. Nicolae Iorga, *Notes et extraits*, IV, p. 142.

that time, this sentiment is clearly expressed: "Where is the Roman Empire[285] which has always fought the barbarians?... Where is the French king, who wants to call himself the Christian king?[286] Where are the kings of England, Denmark, Norway, Sweden, Poland...? Unarmed peasants, blacksmiths, tailors, tradesmen are walking in front of the armies; it seems that they alone have been granted by God faith in great deeds!"

While the people rushed to join Hunyadi's banners, the Ottoman army was approaching Belgrade. It crossed through Sofia and then advanced toward the Danube, through the valley of Moravia. News was received in Venice according to which a Serbian army, of about 9,000 men, tried to oppose the Ottomans in those parts, but was destroyed on 18 June. Branković did not mention this episode in his letters, perhaps so as not to discourage the West. He only spoke of the sultan's passing under the walls of Semendria, toward Belgrade, and assured the papal legate that he was making his utmost effort in view of defense.[287] In the last days of June, the Ottomans began to appear within sight of Belgrade. They surrounded the city, spreading around it a vast sea of white tents. They placed their cannons in firing position, about twelve of which were 32 cubits long, and began bombarding the walls on 4 July 1456.

On the Danube, further upstream from Belgrade, there was the Ottoman fleet. It consisted of around 60 galleys and about 150 smaller vessels. Their mission was to prevent the provisioning of the city by water. Belgrade was a very strong fortress. It had confronted another Ottoman siege in 1440. It was located on a hill, at the junction of the Danube and the Sava rivers, being thus protected from three sides by the natural obstacle of the rivers. To the south, it had a double row of trenches and earth fortifications. Massive walls protected it from all

---

[285]It refers to the German Empire, whose official name was the Holy Roman Empire.

[286]This is how the king of France called himself (*le roi trés-chrétien*). The text is quoted from Elekes, *op. cit.*, p. 444.

[287]Balanyi, *op. cit.*, pp. 180-181.

sides, but especially its southeastern side, within the angle formed by the two rivers. The main fortress was built on a hill, in the immediate proximity of the river.

In turn, the Ottoman army proved to be weaker than rumors had described it. Its numbered not even close to 100,000 soldiers. Among them there were many renegade Christians. The Ottomans had brought them because they were good at siege battles. But their hearts were not on the side of the Ottomans: almost half of them deserted.

Also in June, the army of John Hunyadi set out toward the mouth of the Moravia River. On June 22, they passed through Timişoara, and in a few days, they arrived in Kubin, on the northern bank of the Danube, where Hunyadi repeated, for the third time in three weeks, his request to the Saxons of Transylvania to send him an army urgently, assuring them that Vlad would watch over their territory. The battles had already begun along the big river. The Ottoman fleet had not yet arrived, and so Hunyadi crossed the Danube and began a battle, harassing the Ottomans while retreating toward Belgrade.

On July 2, Capistrano arrived at the fortress, with five big vessels carrying the first detachments of crusaders. Immediately after his arrival he set out on the Danube, with three ships, to join Hunyadi, who was fighting the Ottoman vanguard not far east of Belgrade. But a powerful storm broke out and he was no longer able to sail down river. He was forced to take his ships to the bank and return to Belgrade by land. Had he advanced a bit further, he would have reached the banks already occupied by the Ottomans and would have fallen into their hands.

The day after this attempt, Capistrano wrote from Belgrade that the Ottomans would begin the siege at any moment, asking insistently for assistance from the king of Hungary, and of the prelates and noblemen. John Hunyadi ceased the harassing battles with the Ottoman vanguard and retreated northwest of the city, placing his camp near the fortress of Zemun.[288] In the direction of this fortress, on the Danube, were the numerous masts of the Ottoman fleet, which completely surrounded Belgrade.

The first thing that Hunyadi needed to do was to open the passage on the river, through which he could reinforce and provision the besieged garrison. The repulsion of the fleet was easier to attempt than a blockade on land. Hunyadi gave orders that all ships that could be gathered quickly meet on the Danube, at Slankamen, at the junction of the Tisza with the Danube. About two hundred ships were gathered, but only a few were equipped for battle. Most of them were transport ships and they had to work day and night to outfit them for confrontation with the Ottomans.

When this fleet was ready, Hunyadi sent his spies to inform Michael Szilágyi, the commander of the garrison in Belgrade, to be ready on the day of 14 July to attack the Ottoman fleet from behind, with the ships that were anchored at the base of the fortress. Receiving the message, Michael Szilágyi prepared about forty vessels. He manned them mainly with Serbians from the city, people who despised the Ottomans and were ready to do anything to resist them. On July 14, the fleet set sail from Slankamen toward the south. A large vessel sailed in front, powerfully armed and full of elite soldiers, chosen by Hunyadi himself. The infantry, consisting of about 15,000-16,000 soldiers, of whom many were crusaders, headed by Capistrano, concentrated on the banks of the river, in the place where the battle was going to be fought. Next to the old monk, a lesser nobleman by the name of Peter bore the flag of the crusaders. The mission of this army was to prevent the Ottomans from coming over land to aid their fleet, and also to capture the crews of the Ottoman vessels that would try to disembark and escape by fleeing.

The battle that began on the river between the two fleets lasted for five hours. Although the Ottoman had better vessels, they were defeat-

[288]Probably on July 4, considering that after this date it would have been difficult for Hunyadi to retreat along the southern bank of the Danube without being attacked by the Ottoman army concentrated around Belgrade.

ed. Three out of four of their ships were sunk, and three or four were seized by Hunyadi. Many of them retreated, having suffered serious damage. The sultan ordered that they be burned, so as to not fall into the hands of the enemy. The Danube was free again and already on the second day, July 15, new troops, weapons, and food supplies arrived in Belgrade. In fact, after this date, the encirclement of Belgrade was no longer complete. On the western side, toward Zemun, the Ottomans were not able to maintain the blockade. The naval victory on the Danube was the first key moment in the battle of Belgrade. By continuing the siege without trying to reestablish the blockade on the Danube, the sultan make a serious mistake, which probably resulted from his underestimating Hunyadi's resources. Ottoman spies seem to have been less active now than during the campaigns of 1444 and 1448.

Another mistake made by the sultan was that he focused on conquering the city and neglected the possibility of an open field battle, with a character of a maneuver, in the immediate surrounding area. This mistake resulted from the lack of information and underestimating the enemy, especially of the people's units. After breaking the blockade, detachments of crusaders began to arrive in large numbers in the camp on the left bank of the Sava River, west of the fortress. Looking out from the height of the walls at the crowd that was gathering each day, Michael Szilágyi said that he would have never thought, had he not seen it with his own eyes, that there were so many people in Hungary who would gather like the snow whirled by a blizzard.[289]

Every night, detachments left the camp to bring provisions to the city. They used the small islands between the arms of the Danube, at the mouth of the Sava. Having had his fleet destroyed, the sultan continued the siege on land more fiercely. The Ottoman cannons fired incessantly at the fortress. Often the walls would collapse and the damage was so great that eventually only a few cannons, broken in half, showed here and there, where the stone wall of the city used to be. In a letter to Ladislas V, sent immediately after the victory, John Hunyadi

[289]Nicolae Iorga, *Notes et extraits*, IV, p. 142.

wrote that the fortress could no longer be called fortress, but rather a field, as its walls were now one with the ground.

The Ottomans worked feverishly to cover the trenches around the fortress with earth, wood, and stone fragments from the walls. The defenders shot a flight of arrows at the Ottoman soldiers who were busy preparing for the general assault. They were constantly firing their cannons as well. Each day, the Ottomans launched small attacks, which were forcefully rejected. A cannonball killed Tadji Karadja, the beylerbey of Rumelia, who was in direct command of the siege. This incident demoralized the soldiers in the Rumelian army.[290]

Mehmed II decided to call for a general assault on July 21. The Ottoman army now stirred into action. All the way inside the fortress and far across the Sava, in the camp of the crusaders, the entire morning one could hear the ceaseless beat of the drums that announced the attack. John Hunyadi embarked part of his army on vessels, to be able to move it more easily to the threatened locations, and placed the other part in the immediate proximity of the fortress, in support of the garrison that had taken their posts along the walls. The strategic and tactical conception of John Hunyadi in this battle appears more complex, more flexible, in a word more modern, than that of the sultan. He anticipated varied possibilities of attack, which would bring him victory. In the late afternoon of July 21, the general assault began. The Ottoman infantry charged across the half-covered trenches, over the demolished walls, dispersed the troops that were trying to oppose it and penetrated into the city. Twice the Ottomans entered the city and each time the garrison drove them back. The third time, the janissaries advanced as far as the walls of the fortress on the steep bank of the Danube, which the cannons had not been able to destroy. They were trying to occupy the bridge which led to the fortress, to thus prevent the retreat of the troops from the city. Part of the garrison, seized by fear, abandoned their weapons and tried to escape, diving into the Danube. Even in the fortress, some jumped over the walls and out the windows directly into

[290] Guboglu-Mehmet, *op. cit.*, p. 41.

the river, swimming toward the ships that were afloat around the city. But John Hunyadi remained firm in the middle of his troops, as did the crusaders, among whom women were seen fighting as well.[291] Detachments of crusaders kept crossing the river from the camp on the Sava, coming to the aid of Capistrano, who was defending obstinately the drawn down bridge, across which the Ottomans could have entered the citadel. After fierce struggles, the janissaries destroyed this important objective.

In other area, the Ottomans had thrown up ladders, to take the last walls by assault. Boiling water and inflammable materials were thrown down upon them. Nevertheless, they began to climb the ladders. Near one of the cannons, on the parapet, was a vassal of Hunyadi who was close to him, named Titus Dugovich. He had fought at the side of his master at Varna as well. In the section he now defended, the Ottomans had reached at the height of the parapet. In front of him, a soldier carrying the flag of the Crescent prepared to place it on the wall. Titus Dugovich rushed toward him. Clenched together, the two soldiers fell off the high tower and died in the trench. The reinforcements that kept coming across the Sava allowed, toward evening, the launching of a counterattack that repelled the Ottomans completely. The city was reconquered, the janissaries ran back to the cannons where they had started a few hours earlier. The battle continued after dark, but Hunyadi gave orders to halt the pursuit, thus giving the troops time to rest.

At the break of dawn on July 22 things remained quiet. But gradually battle began again. Animated by the victory of the previous day and evening, the Christian troops could not be restrained. Without waiting for any orders, the people's detachments began to harass the Ottomans, engaging in isolated confrontations with units of Ottoman cavalry. The battle quickly gained proportion. The entire camp of crusaders crossed the Sava and rushed upon the armies from Anatolia.

---

[291]This is claimed by Tagliacozzo (see Nicolae Iorga, *Notes et extraits*, IV, p. 139), but, if the information is correct, then it is more plausible that they were inhabitants of the city or the neighboring regions.

At that time, John Hunyadi was near the ships. Seeing that the army could not be stopped from the struggle it had begun, he decided to intervene with his troops, scattered inside the fortress and throughout the city. A general attack broke out against the Ottoman camp. The cannons of the sultan were captured and turned against the Ottomans who fled. The janissaries, however, were still fighting vigorously. Mehmed II, although wounded by an arrow in his calf, stayed among them. The *aga* of the janissaries, Hassan, died protecting the sultan with his body. Mehmed repelled the troops that had penetrated into his camp and ordered that the cannons be recovered at any price. The Ottomans attacked three times, but the deadly fire they confronted vanquished them. The cannons remained in the hands of Hunyadi's army. The Ottoman army showed signs of discouragement, especially after a detachment of well-rested cavalrymen could not succeed in changing the course of the battle. The sultan and the troops around him resisted in their camp until evening. During the night of July 22 to 23, the Ottomans buried their dead according to their custom, loaded their wounded in a long row of wagons, and evacuated the camp in a hurry, heading southeast.

The victorious army entered the Ottoman camp. They found immense loot there, left behind by the retreating Ottoman army. Amidst the terrible disorder, among overturned wagons, tents, animals wandering free, wounded left behind in the rush of the retreat, one could recognize the places where the sultan and the other Muslim commanders had stayed. Heavy miasmas floated over the battlefield, on which thousands of bodies had fallen in a few days. Epidemics already swept over the army.

The letters sent by Hunyadi and Capistrano from Belgrade spread everywhere news of the great victory against the conqueror of Constantinople. Europe celebrated the victory like never before. Processions took place at the German imperial court in Venice, and in remote England, at Oxford. Pope Callixtus III praised "to the sky" the name of the illustrious voievod, as that of one of the most glorious man that had ever lived.[292] He even established a new religious holiday to celebrate the event.

The joy of the triumph made room for rumors that the papal galleys (which had not even left Italy) had reconquered Constantinople. They were waiting for the continuation of the pursuit of the runaway sultan and for news of new victories. Instead of that, unexpected and sad news came: on 11 August 1456, in his camp near Zemun, John Hunyadi had died, killed not by the enemy but by the epidemic that had spread among his army.

The whole world was deeply disturbed by the death of the one upon whom the hopes of freedom and peace of the peoples of south eastern Europe had rested. The pope, the kings, the scholars of the time, all the chroniclers recorded and grieved over his death. The Polish chronicler Długosz, who generally did not present him in a favorable light, recognized that "his death was detrimental not only to Hungary, but to the entire Christian world, because there was no one else among the Hungarian princes and noblemen to lead the struggle against the Ottomans with the same enthusiasm."[293] Even the man he had defeated, Mehmed II, was moved by his death, saying that since the beginning of time there had never been such a man in the service of a cause.

The body of the hero was brought to Transylvania and buried in the Catholic cathedral in Alba Iulia, where one can still see today the beautiful tombstone placed on his grave a few years later. He remained, even after his death, in Transylvania, from where he had been raised to the heights of glory by the devotion of his people who followed him in most of the battles that he had led with exceptional skill and bravery.

The year 1456 brought the end for two other important figures of the struggle against Ottoman expansion, comrades of John Hunyadi, more or less faithful, for a longer or shorter time. One of them was

[292]Balanyi, *op. cit.*, p. 168, note 3.

[293]Teleki, *op. cit.*, II, p. 445, note 4.

John of Capistrano, who died at the end of October; the other was George Branković, who met his end in December at more than 90 years old.

CHAPTER XIV

THE PERSONALITY OF JOHN HUNYADI

The victory at Belgrade concluded the brilliant political and military career of John Hunyadi. With the joy of the triumph in his heart, he died as he had lived: like a soldier, amidst his army, on a battlefield whose tumult had just settled. He left to the peoples, with whose destiny he had identified himself in the great battles of defense against Ottoman domination, a heritage of which the successors to the leadership of the country did not prove themselves worthy for long: freedom, a firmer will to fight for it, a spirit of solidarity, and a vast military experience.

After the battle of Belgrade, the front for the anti-Ottoman struggle became stronger. Vlad the Impaler ruled in Wallachia. A year later, Stephen the Great came to the throne of Moldavia. Hungary would resist the Ottoman onslaught for seventy more years. These seven decades were largely the result of John Hunyadi's efforts and of the continuation of his policies. After the death of his son, Matthias Corvinus, the great king of Hungary, when the feudal oligarchy again became all-powerful, resuming its practices of excessive oppression of the people, the consequences did not take long to appear: terrible internal revolts and the alienation of the masses from the cause of defending a country that represented only suffering for them. Thus weakened, Hungary and Transylvania no longer found the strength they had in the time of John Hunyadi. In 1521, Belgrade, once defended by him, fell into the hands of the Ottomans. Five years later, the terrible defeat of Mohacs put an end to the independence of Hungary and led, not long afterwards, to Ottoman suzerainty over Transylvania.

The role and historical importance of the personality of John Hunyadi do not result only from his success in halting, for more than a century, further Ottoman expansion into Europe. The outline of his personality becomes clearer only when we view his entire activity, the aims that he had, the means that he used to attain them, and especially the extent to which his goals served the cause of the economic, social, political, and cultural development of the people among whom he lived.

Ottoman conquest was a great danger for the peoples of Eastern Europe in the fifteenth century. It threatened them with the establishment of a regime of domination which would have hindered their economic and cultural progress, through the abusive politics carried on by the Ottomans in the subjugated territories. The struggle against Ottomans conquest required domestic peace and order, which were disturbed by the upper nobility. The defense of independence, the establishing of internal order, and the consolidation of royal authority were the main political goals embodied by John Hunyadi. The fulfilment of these goals represented the shield behind which the trade, commerce, the cities, and agriculture could develop.

John Hunyadi understood that, to attain these goals, he needed to attract the support of a larger section of the population. That was what determined his relations with the cities, and the partial concessions made to the peasants. The necessity to consolidate the state and to limit the power of the upper nobility coincided with the interest of the lesser nobility, to which he belonged also, to ascend to a higher political position, and to the leadership of the country.

Investigating the resources necessary for the confrontation with the Ottoman Empire, John Hunyadi took direct measures to support economic activity, with the intention of creating supplementary revenues for the state. In many treaties that he concluded, he had in view the interests of the merchants. He informed them constantly about the possibilities of commerce with Wallachia, Moldavia, Austria, and even with the Ottomans, depending on the fluctuations of foreign relations. He tried to increase the production of the salt mines, improving the situation of the miners and putting a stop to the irregularities committed by the treasurers of the salt. He encouraged trades, especially the branches tied to the maintenance and equipping of the army. He also tried to improve the cultivation of feudal estates.

This policy brought him the support of larger social elements, affording him at the same time relative independence from the upper nobility. When the latter refused to assist him, or even opposed him, Hunyadi had enough means to hire mercenary units in his army.

His methods of consolidating his power, however, bear the mark of the feudal mentality, to which he was also subjected. He strengthened his personal position, gathered immense estates,[294] took advantage of the military obligations that many lesser noblemen and *cnezi,* especially in Transylvania, owed toward him. The difference between him and other noblemen was that he put his personal power in the service of the country. Relying on the militant spirit of the people and on the use of mercenary troops, John Hunyadi was able to take the offensive against the Ottomans. By doing this, he came to the aid of the subjugated peoples in the Balkan Peninsula and was able to count on their cooperation in his military campaigns.

He tried to give this cooperation with other peoples a durable form. He fought against the parties that capitulated to the Ottomans and supported the princes or groups that favored resistance. Out of his intention to create an alliance among the peoples of southeastern Europe, in danger of being conquered by the Ottomans, arose his frequent interventions in the Romanian principalities.

Without hesitation, he addressed all of Europe, informing it of the struggle he was leading and its importance for the fate of all peoples. The Papacy, Poland, the Holy Roman Empire, the Italian cities, Ara-

[294]In the last years of his life he had come to own: 28 fortresses and castles, 87 towns and cities, about 1,000 villages, all of these with their own borders, totalling up to 7 million acres; cf. Ştefan Pascu, *op. cit.*, pp. 42-43 and note 68.

gon, France, and Burgundy were the powers that he tried constantly to awaken from their stupor and indifference. He managed to do so only to a small extent, but that was not his fault; he did not have great expectations anyway, as his confidence was in the devotion of his people and the neighboring ones. He felt that, through the way he was serving them, he would always have their understanding, eclipsed neither by passing difficulties, nor by the intrigues of the upper nobility.

Men of many nationalities fought under his flag: Romanians, Hungarians, Serbians, Bulgarians, Czechs, Poles, Germans, and even isolated elements from more remote countries like Italy, Switzerland, France, and Spain. All these men were animated not only by the instinctive consciousness of the fact that they were fighting for their own cause; some of them were also attracted by the fame of John Hunyadi, kept alive already then by legends and folklore, but perfectly justified, both through his personal example as a skillful and courageous military man, and especially through the greatness of his victories.

John Hunyadi counted himself among those true military commanders who proved their vocation through their permanent presence amidst their army. His reliance on a larger social basis and their attraction into the army were also reflected in the strong ties between him and his soldiers. He constantly concerned himself with the instruction of the army, he took care of the needs of the soldiers, he saw that they were paid on time. As severe as he was when he gave an order and oversaw its execution, he was just as gentle and friendly with his soldiers in his few moments of rest. The sources depict him with features that remind us of Caesar or Hannibal. In fact, they did not hesitate to compare him with the heroes of antiquity, even attributing him qualities borrowed from the characters of Titus Lilius.

In battle, he always occupied the most difficult spots. In the Long Campaign, during the advance, he commanded the vanguard, and during the retreat he was leading the rear guard. At Varna, he resisted with the troops around him until they could resist no more. At the Field of the Blackbirds, he was saved from the danger into which he had rushed only by the devotion of a *cneaz* from Hunedoara.

The aspiration for glory and his spirit of adventure did not lead John Hunyadi on dangerous paths. His correspondence reveals a moderate man, for whom war and victory were not an aim but a means. His great goal was always to end the war, to secure peace for his people. In view of this goal, Hunyadi, although a military man, did not support, as a unique method, war with the Ottomans. He oriented himself with calm and understanding in every situation and sometimes he supported more sincerely the conclusion of a peace or an armistice than the upper nobility, who were afraid to face the feared enemy.

The defense of freedom and independence against the invaders, the idea of solidarity among the people against aggression from a common enemy, and the wish to obtain a durable peace represent those elements in John Hunyadi's activity that remain valid throughout the centuries and preserve their actuality. The positive role that his personality played in history is not based, therefore, only on his individual qualities, but first of all on the fact that his activity, his interests, and the interests of the social strata to which he belonged, integrated themselves – under the specific circumstance of the historical moment – with the general interests. Without this wide social basis of his policies, John Hunyadi would have been a defeated general. Without his exceptional military personality, the struggle against Ottoman domination would probably not have had such resounding successes, in such a short period of time. This strong connection between his and the fate of the nations of the time raise him to the heights of simple, solemn, but all the more durable glory.

One of the first studies dedicated to John Hunyadi in Romanian historiography begins with these remarks, valid broadly for establishing of certain coordinates for our appreciation today:

> The heroism and all the military and civil virtues that characterized the brilliant life of John Corvinus won him a place of genius among the commanders and generals of all times. In the same way, his remarkable qualities as a statesman, a Christian, and a private person as-

sured his place in the most illustrious pages not only in the history of his country and nation, but also in the general history of Europe.[295]

[295]George Bariţiu, "Ioan Corvin de Hunedoara. Originea, genealogia, faptele sale imortale," in *Transilvania*, VI (1873), no. 5, p. 49.

Bibliography

Documentary Sources

Bogdan, I. *Documente privitoare la relaţiile Ţării Româneşti cu Braşovul şi cu Ţara Ungurească în sec. XV şi XVI.* Bucureşti, 1905.

Costăchescu, Mihai. *Documente moldoveneşti înainte de Ştefan cel Mare.* Vol. II. Iaşi, 1932.

Documenta Romaniae Historica, Seria A. Moldova (1384-1448). Vol. I. C. Cihodan, I. Căproşu, and L. Şimanaschi, eds. Bucureşti, 1975.

Documenta Romaniae Historica, Seria A. Moldova (1449-1486). Vol. II. Leon Şimanschi, Georgeta Ignat, and Dumitru Agache, eds. Bucureşti, 1976.

Documenta Romaniae Historica, B. Ţara Românească (1247-1500). Vol. I. P.P. Panaitescu and Damaschin Mioc, eds. Bucureşti. 1966.

Fejér, Gerogius. *Genus, incunabula et virtus Joannis Corvini de Hunyad, regni Hungariae gubernatoris.* Buda, 1844.

Hurmuzaki-Densuşianu. *Documente privitoare la istoria românilor.* Vol. I, 2. Bucureşti, 1890.

Hurmuzaki-Iorga. *Documente privitoare la istoria românilor.* Vol. XV, 1. Bucureşti, 1911.

Iorga, N. *Notes et extraits pour server à l'histoire des croisades au XV-e siècle, seria a IV-a.* Bucureşti, 1915.

Pray, Georgius. *Annales Regum Hungariae.* Parts II-III, Vienna, 1764-1766.

Teleki, József. *A Hunyadiak kora Magyarországon.* Vol. X. Pesta, 1853.

Narrative Sources

Bonfinii, Antonii, *Historia Pannonica sive Hungaricarum Rerum Decades IV et dimidia*. Köln, 1960.

Chalcocondil, Laonikos, *Expuneri istorice*. Translated by Vasile Grecu. Bucureşti, 1958.

"Cronica lui Wavrin şi românii." Ed. N. Iorga, in *Buletinul Comisiei istorice a României*, VI, 1927, pp. 57-148.

Cronici turceşti privind ţările române. Vol. I, sec XV-mijolocul sec. XVII. Edited by Mihail Guboglu and Mustafa Mehmet. Bucureşti, 1966.

Ducas. *Istoria turco-bizantină (1341-1462)*. Ed. Vasile Grecu. Bucureşti, 1958.

Minea, I. *Informaţiile româneşti ale cronicii lui Jan Długosz*. Iaşi, 1926.

Schwandtner, Ioannes Georgius. *Scriptores Rerum Hungaricarum*, vol. I-II. Tyrnavia, 1765-1766.

Sphrantzes, Georgios. *Memorii, 1407-1477*. ed. Vasile Grecu. Bucureşti, 1966.

Studies

General

Held, Joseph. *Hunyadi: Legend and Reality*. Boulder, New York, 1985.

Iorga, N. *Geschichte des Osmanischen Reiches*. Vols. I-II. Gotha, 1908-1909.

Iorga, N. *Istoria românilor*. Vol. IV. Bucureşti, 1937.

Istoria României. Vol. II. Bucureşti, 1962.

Jireček C. *Geschichte der Serben*. Vol. II. Gotha, 1918.

Magyarország története. Vol. I. Budapest, 1961.

Ostrogorski, Georg. *Geschichte des Byzantinischen Staates*. Third Ed. München, 1963.

Special

Angyal, Dávid. "Murád útja Várna felé 1444-ben," in *Hadtörténelmi Közlemények (HK)*, 1910, pp. 252-253.

Bălan, Iosif. *Iancu de Hunyad*. Caransebeş, 1897.

Balanyi, György. "Nándorfejérvár ostroma és felmentése 1456-ban," in *HK*, 1911, pp. 167-198.

Bánfi, Florio. "Hunyadi János itáliai trtózkodása," in *Erdélyi Múzeum*, XXXIX (1934), nos. 7-12, pp. 261-272.

Bariţiu, G. "Ioan Corvin de Hunedora. Originea, genealogia, faptele sale imortale," in *Transilvania*, VI (1873), nos. 5-24 and VII (1874), no. 1.

Brackob, A.K. *Mircea the Old: Father of Wallachia, Grandfather of Dracula*. Histria Books, 2018.

Brackob, A.K. *Scanderbeg: George Castriota and the Albanian Resistance to Islamic Expansion in Fifteenth Century Europe*. Histria Books, 2018.

Câmpina, Barbu T. "Dezvoltarea economiei feudale şi începuturile luptei pentru centralizarea statului în a doua jumătate a secolului al XV-lea în Moldova şi Ţara Românească," in *Lucrările sesiunii generale ştiinţifice a Academiei*, 2-12 iunie 1950. Bucureşti, 1951, pp. 1602-1638.

Dan, Mihail. "Armata şi arta militară a lui Iancu de Hunedoara (pe baza cronicilor contemporane)," in *Studii şi cercetări de istorie*, Cluj, VIII (1957), nos. 1-4, pp. 68-118.

Doberdói Bánlaki József. *A Magyar Nemzet Hadtöeténelme, part X, A Hunyadiak kora. vol. I, Hunyadi János*. Budapesta, 1936.

Elekes, Lajos. *Hunyadi*. Budapesta, 1952.

Franknói, Vilmos. "A várnai csata elözményei," in *HK*. 1889, pp. 337-388.

Guboglu, M. "Turcii osmanlîi," in *Hrisovul*, VII (1974), pp. 56-61.

Gündisch, Gustav. "Die Türken Einfälle in Siebebürgen bis zur Mite des 15-ten Jahrhunderts," in *Jahrbücher für Geschichte Osteuropas*, II (1937), no. 3, pp. 393-412.

Holub, József. "Adatok a török ellen tervezett 1455-iki hadjárathoz," in *HK*, 1911, pp. 149-153.

Huber, Alfons. "Die Kriege zweischen Ungarn und die Türken, 1440-1443," in *Archiv für Oesterreichische Geschichte*, LXVIII (1886), pp. 159-207.

Iorga, N. "Les aventures 'sarrazines' des Français de Bourgogne au XV-e siècle," in *Mélanges d'histoire générale, I, Cluj*, 1927, pp. 9-56.

Kiss, Lajos. "A régi Magyar szekérvár," in *HK*, 1895, pp. 1-42, 157-181, 339-349, 454-486.

Kropf, Lajos. "A régi Magyar szekérvár," in *HK*, 1914, pp. 297-299.

Kropf, Lajos. "Zarobotana," in *HK*, 1914, pp. 471-473.

Lupaş, Ioan. "Voievodul transilvan Ioan Huniade – 'fortissimus athlete Christi,'" in *Studii, conferinţe şi comunicări istorice*. Vol. II. Cluj, 1940.

Mályusz, Elemér. "A Magyar rendi állam Hunyadi korában," in *Századok*, an. 91, (1957), nos. 1-4, pp. 46-123 and nos. 5-6, pp. 529-602.

Minea, I. *Din trecutul stăpânirii româneşti asupra Ardealului. Pierderea Amlaşului şi a Făgăraşului*. Bucureşti, 1914.

Minea, I. *Prinicipatele române şi politica orientală a împăratului Sigismund*. Bucureşti, 1919.

Minea, I. *Vlad Dracul şi vremea sa*. Iaşi, 1928.

Miskolczi, Gyula. "Hunyadi János török-hadjóratai," in *HK*, 1913, pp. 347-369, 545-583.

Moravcsik, Gyula. "Ungarisch-byzantinische Beziehungun zur Zeit des Falles von Byzanz," in *Acta Antiqua Academiae Scientiarum Hungaricae*, 1954, tom. II, fasc. 3-4, pp. 349-360.

Mureşan, C. "Rolul lui Ioan de Hunedoara în mobilizarea maselor populare împotriva expansiunii otomane," in *Studii*, IX (1956), no. 4, pp. 55-70.

Nicolau, T. *Ioan Huniade Corvin*. Bucureşti, 1925.

Pál, Engel. *Király hatolom és arisztokrácia viszonga a Zsigmond Korban*. Budapest, 1977.

Pál, Engel. "János Hunyadi: The Decisive Years in His Career, 1440-1444," in *From Hunyadi to Rákoczi: War and Society in Medieval and Early Modern Hungary*. New York, 1982.

Pall, Francisc. "Autour de la croisade de Varna: la question de la paix de Szeged et da sa rupture (1444)," in *Bulletin de la Section Historique de l'Academie Roumaine*, tome XXII, 2, Bucureşti, 1941, pp. 144-158.

Pall, Francisc. "Byzance à la veille de sa chute et Ianco de Hunedoara," in *Byzantinoslavica*. Prague, XXX (1969).

Pall, Francisc. *Ciriaco d'Ancona e la crociata contro i Turchi*. Vălenii de Munte, 1937.

Pall, Francisc. "Iancu de Hunedoara şi confirmarea privileguiului pentru negoţul braşovenilor şi al bârsenilor cu Ţara Românească în 1443," in *Anuarul Institutului de istorie din Cluj*, IX (1966), pp. 63-84.

Pall, Francisc. "Intervenţia lui Iancu de Hunedoara în Ţara Românească şi Moldova în anii 1447-1448," in *Studii*, XVI (1963), no. 5, pp. 1049-1072.

Pall, Francisc. "Le condizioni e gli echi internazionali della lotta antiottomana del 1442-1443, condotta da Giovanni di Hunedoara," in *Revue des études sud-est européennes*, tome III, 1965, nos. 3-4, pp. 433-463.

Pall, Francisc. *Les croisades en orient au bas Moyen-Âge*. Bucureşti, 1942.

Pall, Francisc. "Les relations entre la Hongrie et Scanderbeg," in *Revue historique du Sud-Est européen*, X (1993), nr. 4-6, pp. 119-141.

Pall, Francisc. *Marino Barlezio, uno storico umanista*. Bucureşti, 1938.

Pall, Francisc. "Scanderbeg et Ianco de Hunedoara," in *Studia Albanica*, Tirana, 1, 1968.

Pall, Francisc. "Stăpânirea lui Iancu de Hunedoara asupra Chiliei şi problema ajutorării Bizanţului," in *Studii*, XVIII (1965), no. 3, pp. 619-638.

Pall, Francisc. "Ştiri noi despre expediţiile turceşti din Transilvania în 1438," in *Anuarul Institutului de istorie din Cluj*, I-II (1958-1959), pp. 9-28.

Pall, Francisc. "Un moment décisif de l'histoire du sud-est européen: la croisade de Varna (1444)," in *Balcania*, VII (1944), pp. 102-120.

Pascu, Şt. "Rolul cnezilor din Transilvania în lupta antiotomană a lui Iancu de Hunedoara," in *Studii şi cercetări de istorie*, Cluj, VIII (1957), nos. 1-4, pp. 25-67.

Popa, T. *Iancu Corvin de Hunedoara*. Hunedoara, 1928.

Prodan, D. *Iobăgia în Transilvania în secolul al XVI-lea*. Vol. I. Bucureşti, 1967.

Székely, Ottokár. "Hunyadi János elsö török hadjáratai (1441-1444)," in *HK*, 1919-1921, pp. 1-64.

Teleki, Jozsef. *A Hunyadiak kora Magyarországon*, vols. I-II. Pesta, 1852.

Thury, Josef. "A várnai csatáról," in *HK*, 1892, pp. 636-654.

Treptow, Kurt W., ed. *Dracula: Essays on the Life and Times of Vlad the Impaler*. Las Vegas, 2018.

INDEX

C

D

L

M

N

O

P

R

S

T

www.ingramcontent.com/pod-product-compliance
Lightning Source LLC
LaVergne TN
LVHW040528060926
847336LV00002B/3
* 9 7 8 1 5 9 2 1 1 0 1 2 4 *